Socialist Spaces

Socialist Spaces

Sites of Everyday Life in the Eastern Bloc

Edited by
David Crowley and Susan E. Reid

Oxford • New York

First published in 2002 by
Berg
Editorial offices:
150 Cowley Road, Oxford, OX4 1JJ, UK
838 Broadway, Third Floor, New York, NY 10003–4812, USA

Berg is an imprint of Oxford International Publishers Ltd.

Library of Congress Cataloging-in-Publication Data
Socialist spaces : sites of everyday life in the Eastern Bloc / edited
by David Crowley and Susan E. Reid.
    p. cm.
Includes bibliographical references and index.
    ISBN 1-85973-533-9 (cloth) – ISBN 1-85973-538-X (pbk.)
    1. Communism and architecture–Europe, Eastern. 2. Communism
and architecture–Soviet Union 3. Space (Architecture)–Europe,
Eastern. 4. Space (Architecture)–Soviet Union. I. Crowley, David,
1966- II. Reid, Susan Emily.
    HX520 .S65 2002
    720'.94'09171717–dc21

                                                        2002011073

British Library Cataloguing-in-Publication Data
A catalogue record for this book is available from the British Library.

ISBN 1 85973 533 9 (Cloth)
      1 85973 538 X (Paper)

Typeset by JS Typesetting Ltd, Wellingborough, Northants.
Printed in the United Kingdom by MPG Books, Cornwall.

Contents

Contents

Notes on Contributors

Paulina Bren, doctoral candidate at New York University, is currently working on a cultural history of post-Prague Spring Czechoslovakia. She has written extensively on the politics of popular and material culture and its intersections with late communism and ideology in East-Central Europe.

David Crowley teaches the history of design at the Royal College of Art, London. He is the author of various books including *National Style and Nation-state. Design in Poland from the Vernacular Revival* (MUP, 1992) and is co-editor, with Susan E. Reid, of *Style and Socialism: Modernity and Material Culture in Post-War Eastern Europe* (Berg, 2000). *Moving Warsaw*, a book on the reconstruction of the Polish capital, will be published by Reaktion Books in 2003.

Reuben Fowkes is a doctoral candidate at Essex University, and currently working on art and politics in postwar Eastern Europe. He has written widely on communist-era monumental sculpture in relation to war memorials, the cult of Stalin and the New Man and Woman of the socialist utopia.

Katerina Gerasimova received her candidate degree in sociology from the European University at St Petersburg and is an associated researcher at the European University and researcher in the Centre for Independent Social Research in St Petersburg. She is the author of 'The Soviet Communal Apartment' in J. Smith, ed., *Beyond the Limits: The Concept of Space in Russian History and Culture* (Helsinki: Studia Historica (62), 1999) and several articles on the history and sociology of housing in St Petersburg in Russian-language journals.

Astrid Ihle is currently completing her Ph.D. on 'GDR Women Photographers. 1949–1961' at the Courtauld Institute of Art in London, England. She worked as assistant to the director of the gallery EIGEN + ART in Berlin from 1995 to 1998. She was curator of *Louise Bourgeois. Drawings and Sculptures* at the Paula Böttcher Gallery, Berlin, 1999, and is curating an exhibition of photographs by Evelyn Richter at the Goethe-Institut in New York (Autumn 2002).

Stephen Lovell is a lecturer in European history at King's College London. He is the author of *The Russian Reading Revolution: Print Culture in the Soviet and Post-Soviet Eras* (2000), and of *Summerfolk: A History of the Dacha, 1710–2000* (Cornell University Press, forthcoming).

Karl D. Qualls received his Ph.D. from Georgetown University and is assistant professor of history at Dickinson College. He is the author of 'Local-Outsider Negotiations in Sevastopol's Postwar Reconstruction, 1944–53', in *Provincial Landscapes: The Local Dimensions of Soviet Power*, Donald J. Raleigh, ed. (University of Pittsburgh Press, 2001) and 'Imagining Sevastopol: History and Postwar Community Construction, 1942–1953' (*National Identities Journal*, forthcoming). He is completing work on a book entitled *Raised from Ruins: Localism, Urban Planning, and Reconstruction in Sevastopol, 1943–1953*.

Susan E. Reid is Lecturer in Russian Visual Arts in the Department of Russian and Slavonic Studies, University of Sheffield. She has published widely on Soviet art and visual culture from Stalin to the 1990s, with a special interest in the Khrushchev period. She is editor, with David Crowley, of *Style and Socialism: Modernity and Material Culture in Post-War Eastern Europe* (Berg, 2000).

Olga Sezneva, doctoral candidate in sociology at New York University, New York, is completing her dissertation on 'The Russian Life of the German Past: Memory, History and Social Transformations in Kalinin-grad, 1945–2000'. She has published widely on the politics of memory and urban history. Her research will appear in a forthcoming book edited by John Czaplicka and Blair Ruble entitled *Composing Urban History and the Constitution of Civic Identities*.

Mark Allen Svede trained in art history and architecture, and is an inde-pendent scholar specializing in Latvian visual and material culture of the modern, Soviet and contemporary periods. He is the co-author of *Art of the Baltics: The Struggle for Freedom of Artistic Expression under the Soviets, 1945–1991* (Rutgers University Press, 2002), and has made contributions to anthologies, exhibition catalogues and encyclopaedias. Other projects have included restoration of a Soviet underground film and serving as Latvian acquisitions advisor for the Dodge Collection of Nonconformist Art from the Soviet Union, Zimmerli Art Museum at Rutgers.

Socialist Spaces: Sites of Everyday Life in the Eastern Bloc[1]

David Crowley and Susan E. Reid

In 1976 the Russian artist Eric Bulatov produced the painting *Krasikov Street* depicting an unremarkable, modern Soviet street, lined with system-built housing blocks that were the hallmark of the late socialist cities of Central and Eastern Europe (Figure 1.1). The figures and traffic on this mundane stage move purposefully in a single direction into the canvas. But stepping out from a billboard towards them – and towards us, the

Figure 1.1 Eric Bulatov, *Krasikov Street*, 1977, oil on canvas, 150 x 198.5 cm. Jane Vorhees Zimmerli Art Museum, Rutgers, The State University of New Jersey, The Norton and Nancy Dodge Collection of Nonconformist Art from the Soviet Union. Photo by Jack Abraham

David Crowley and Susan E. Reid

viewers – strides the giant figure of Lenin. The street is thereby impregnated with the official ideology of state socialism, and yet the pedestrians seem oblivious to Lenin's presence. Bulatov's image is no politically orthodox treatment of the subject. Lenin, traditionally the personification of the Revolution, paradoxically closes off the horizon – according to the conventions of Socialist Realist painting, the locus of the radiant future.

'Taking to the streets' would hardly seem to be an action alien to Lenin; he was cast, often mid-stride, into the monuments and public art that punctuated the townscapes of the Eastern Bloc. Moreover, an ideal of collective movement had shaped the spectacles associated with the red-letter days of the Soviet calendar. It had even determined urban reconstruction schemes after the Second World War, with new 'civilian' parade grounds such as Plac Defilad in Warsaw or Ploshad Lenin in Sofia being accommodated at the heart of the city (Figure 1.2). On these monumental sites, marchers were arranged to animate the city and to embody the inexorable force of history. Perhaps these great new public spaces might be understood as the most self-evidently ideological spaces where the collective identities of socialism were to be forged. But what of Krasikov Street itself? Who has even heard of it? Unremarkable in its very ordinariness, how might we recognize it as a socialist space?

Historian of technology Langdon Winner, in a celebrated essay of 1980, posed the question, 'Do artefacts have politics?'[2] Asking to what extent is power served by technological systems or artefacts, he explored the example of a bridge designed by Robert Moses, the urban planner responsible for the modernization of much of New York's road network in the mid-twentieth century. This structure denied access to buses, and thereby those who could not afford to own a car, to a public beach. Through its control over space, allowing only those with private cars to go to the beach, the bridge – although not deliberately conceived as an expression of ideology – had political effects. Winner's question can clearly be understood as much as an enquiry into the political effects of space as of technology. It can also be reversed. *Socialist Spaces,* the title of this book, not only begs the question 'Do spaces have politics?' but also the converse: 'Do politics have spaces?'[3]

The historical period under consideration in this volume – from the incorporation of the countries of Central and Eastern Europe into the 'socialist space' dominated by the Soviet Union to the dissolution of the Eastern Bloc between 1989 and 1991 – offers numerous examples that suggest that in the case of postwar socialism, the answer to the first question, 'do spaces have politics?', must be affirmative. From the formation of the Bloc (and earlier in the case of the Soviet Union), the ownership and control of different orders of space, whether national territory, housing or public monuments, was socialized: that is, it was claimed by the State on behalf of the working people. The nationalization of land – and the way buildings and places were given new uses and meanings, even when the physical configuration of those spaces was little changed – indicate that space was subject to political interests. The period saw pervasive efforts to permeate not only places of work and public ceremony but also the most intimate spaces of the everyday with ideological meaning.

Figure 1.2 The opening ceremony for the Palace of Culture and Science in the name of Joseph Stalin on Plac Defilad, Warsaw, 1955. Reproduced from Jan Jacoby and Zygmunt Wdowiński, *Pałac kultury i nauki im. Józefa Stalina* (Warsaw: Sport i Turystyka, 1955).

But what of the second question? Do politics have spaces? Is there anything about the physical or aesthetic qualities of particular spaces that might render one inherently socialist, another fascist and a third democratic? What might distinguish 'socialist spaces' from any other? The question is not of mere academic interest but is one that exercised the socialist regimes of Central and Eastern Europe: how to distinguish the socialist space from earlier bourgeois or fascist configurations of the same terrain, and from that other political space, 'the West'.

Throughout the Bloc massive investment was made in the production of grand monuments and new public spaces to symbolize the new order. Parade grounds, public artworks and 'people's palaces' formed a ubiquitous environment throughout the Bloc. Official discourse about these and other spaces reproduced the shared ideological priorities and tactical operations of the socialist regimes. Marxist-Leninist ideals of progress and principles of social justice, based on an equitable redistribution of all resources through the agency of the State, were claimed to be the basis of a new spatial economy. Measured against these ideals, such 'socialist spaces' will no doubt be found wanting. To explore the political character of these spaces by reference to ideology alone would seem to be a fruitless task. Should we not, rather, consider a wider field of spatial relations, uses and discourses that goes beyond rhetoric? In expanding our frame of interest in this way, a picture of difference and change emerges that reveals space as a contested aspect of life in the Bloc. Much as authority sought to control the meanings and uses of space, the spatial practices of citizens were not contained by the party-state machine. But they were still made in relation to its priorities and tactics. If we can use the term 'socialist spaces' at all, it is only in relation to the shifting and multi-layered interaction between spatial organization, expression and use.

The essays in this book do not march shoulder-to-shoulder towards a unitary and universal definition of 'socialist space'. Our aim is to bring new perspectives to bear on the formation, uses and representations of space in Soviet-type societies. Space is an elusive and heterogeneous concept that encompasses abstract order as well as the fields of ordinary experience. As such, it provides a common ground where different disciplinary interests intersect. Coming from diverse academic traditions including art history, social history and anthropology, each of the authors in this volume examines spatial practices and symbolic meanings within specific and concrete contexts under socialism, both monumental and 'everyday'.

The political investment in the creation of highly symbolic construction projects such as the Moscow Metro or the new Socialist Realist reconstruction schemes in the satellite states during the 1940s and 1950s has been illuminated by historians of architecture and town planning, who have demonstrated how the transformation of the urban environment was invested with ideological meaning.[4] A number of authors in this volume contribute to this growing literature. In 'Accommodation and Agitation in Sevastopol: Redefining Socialist Space in the Postwar "City of Glory"', Karl Qualls explores the ways in which competing schemes for the reconstruction of the important Soviet port city might be understood as ideological cartography. Adopting the commanding bird's eye perspective enjoyed by Sevastopol's planners in the 1940s, he explores how the postwar cityscape drew on wartime propaganda to mobilize national and naval myths. Reuben Fowkes, in his essay 'The Role of Monumental Sculpture in the Construction of Socialist Space in Stalinist Hungary', shows how monumental sculpture in Budapest marked the political changes under way in Hungary in the late 1940s and early 1950s. Such sites were to be unmistakably socialist in that they were designed, in the first instance, as a measure of the triumph over fascism or, in the latter case, to demonstrate the State's commitment to 'social justice'.

As major state projects, postwar reconstruction plans and the ideological reinscription of the cityscape are perhaps most easily understood in terms of Eastern Bloc politics. Other contributors to this anthology address sites of everyday life under conditions of 'actually existing socialism'. How might the vision of a communist future, which Lenin personifies in Krasikov Street, be found in the ordinary spaces of life, whether outside on the urban street, or inside the public housing so prominent there? What claim do they have to be considered socialist spaces? Neither grand projects nor exalted spaces, the residential street and the home would hardly seem to count among the 'sacred spaces' of the socialist cosmos. Yet, it is a premise of this book that the spaces of everyday life – places of leisure, learning, consumption and domesticity – were no less important as sites for ideological intervention than the more obviously 'socialist spaces'. Investigating such spaces as a route to a better understanding of the nature and experience of this social experiment, contributors to this book call into question the absolute status of the dichotomy of the great and the ordinary sites of socialism.

The Great Spaces of Everyday Life

Everyday life has increasingly been recognized as important territory for social enquiry. It has been the object of abstract exploration by philosophers including Jürgen Habermas and Martin Heidegger, and of more concrete concern to sociologists like Erving Goffman. More recently, the social theorists Michel de Certeau and Henri Lefebvre have enjoyed attention for the way their writings challenge the dismissal of everyday life as inauthentic or impoverished existence.[5] De Certeau's suggestive *The Practice of Everyday Life* (1974) has stimulated many rhapsodic investigations into subversion and dissidence in daily life in the face of the encroachments of technocracy and bureaucracy. The everyday has also become an important theme for some of the most stimulating research on the Eastern Bloc in recent years. *Byt*, the Russian for everyday life or the daily grind, has become a central term in studies of Soviet history and culture. Svetlana Boym has incisively analysed the 'strong, almost romantic fear of banality' in Russian and Soviet culture, which had hitherto left the everyday mythologies, rituals and spaces of ordinary life beneath discussion, deemed irrelevant for the apocalyptic self-definition of Russian culture and for Soviet teleology alike. As she demonstrates, these despised and neglected 'Common Places' are in fact fundamental to an understanding of Soviet Russian culture.[6] At the same time, historians of Stalinism have turned away from the near exclusive analysis of political decision-making to study also the everyday dimensions of 'ordinary life in extraordinary times', as Sheila Fitzpatrick has put it, or of 'Stalinism as a civilization' in Stephen Kotkin's formulation.[7]

Furthermore, a number of commentators have recently remarked on the welling nostalgia in the former satellite states for the material culture of socialism in spite of the predominately negative attitude to their socialist, subaltern pasts.[8] The popularity of exhibitions in the 1990s in which interiors of Polish 'Milk Bar' workers' cafés, cinemas and homes from the 1950s and 1960s were faithfully reconstructed, or the packaging and products from the lost world of the GDR were displayed to large audiences has been a remarkable phenomenon. In a 1997 anthology of photographs and newspaper cuttings from the Kádár period in Hungary, *Befejezetlen szocializmus* (*Unfinished Socialism*), András Gerő and Iván Pető have argued that this nostalgia synthesizes memory and history. Many of the visitors to such exhibitions (and, of course, readers of their book) remember the period represented as their own everyday life while comprehending that they were also witnesses and participants in a 'great' experiment: 'History is a process in which we continue to carry with us the time we believe to have passed . . . including everything from our material surroundings to memories, distilled into life experience.'[9] As they realized, it is not only the extraordinary but also the ordinary qualities of socialism in Eastern Europe that need to be understood.[10]

No consensus surrounds the meaning of the term 'everyday life'. It has generally been used, however, to signify private life as opposed to public actions; routine matters rather than extraordinary events; and cyclical time, associated with circadian rhythms, rather than what Lefebvre calls the 'linear time' of industrial society and teleological ideologies (not least Marxism-Leninism). Rita Felski, in a recent investigation of the historiography of the term, has suggested that everyday life is a secular and democratic concept because

> it conveys the sense of a world leached of transcendence: the everyday is everyday because it is no longer connected to the miraculous, the magical or the sacred . . . Democratic because it recognises the paramount shared reality of a mundane, material embeddedness in the world . . . Everyday life does not only describe the lives of ordinary people, but recognises that every life contains an element of the ordinary.[11]

Does this characterization apply in equal measure in the so-called First World and Second World alike? Do the contours described by Felski plot the qualities of everyday life in the particular historical settings of socialist Eastern Europe and the Soviet Union? Treating everyday life as an irredeemably profane phenomenon, determined entirely by the concrete or natural – a realm of daily transience 'leached of transcendence' – is particularly problematic in regard to the Soviet Union and the People's Republics of Central and Eastern Europe. Under the ideological imperatives of socialism, phenomena that might otherwise be polarized – the utopian versus the ordinary; art versus routine; ideals versus experience – were to be synthesized. The socialist project was, after all, to make utopia real. If, for Felski, a common ordinariness is a feature of all lives, for socialist ideology the inverse was also true: every life contained an element of the *extra*-ordinary. Everyday life was not opposed to ideological life. On the contrary, it was a fundamental site of ideological intervention.[12]

The valorization of the ordinary is discussed by Katerina Clark in her seminal analysis of the mythic structure of the Socialist Realist novel. She diagnoses the 'modal schizophrenia' of this literary form: 'its proclivity for making sudden, unmotivated transitions from realistic discourse to the mythic or utopian', thereby collapsing the distance between 'what is' and 'what ought to be'. Drawing on Mircea Eliade's analysis of the dual sense of time characteristic of traditional cultures, she analyses the temporal structure of the novel in terms of a mythic 'Great Time'.[13] Events of the present, profane world become meaningful (or 'real' in Eliade's terms) only insofar as they partake of the transcendent reality by imitating a mythical archetype lodged in a historic past or an unspecified *in illo tempore*. No event of the present time could transcend its profaneness unless it could be dignified through identification with a moment either from the official heroic age or from the Glorious Future. Transposed to the Soviet context, that dignity was lent by a connection, however mythic, to the Great Time of Lenin or the radiant future of Communism.

The ontological and temporal hierarchy of present, profane time and Great Time has a corresponding spatial hierarchy based on structural equivalence or temporal projection. In Soviet discourse, ordinary spaces could become, by analogy with Clark, 'Great Spaces' through a connection with the 'grand spatial narratives' of socialism. Thus a steel foundry could figure as the 'forge of communism'; a house commune as a microcosm of the socialist order; and a children's after-school facility as a paradigm of the communist 'city of the future'.[14] At the same time, 'social justice', as conceived by Marxist ideology, demanded the 'democratization' of space. Even the 'Greatest Spaces' – whether the new 'people's palaces' of culture and education or landmark sites in Soviet history such as the Winter Palace in Leningrad – were 'everyday' in the idealized sense projected by the socialist regimes that they were to be used and possessed by all.[15]

The rhetoric of 'social justice' demanded the symbolic reordering of space in other ways too. As Fowkes shows, the destruction and erection of new monuments in the Hungarian capital after the communists had assumed power in the late 1940s might be read as a symbolic attempt to wrest the cityscape from its historic possession by the bourgeoisie. The major public spaces of Budapest, as the fastest growing European city in the nineteenth century, had been shaped first by the aristocracy and the business classes who thrived under the Habsburgs and then, in the 1920s and 1930s, by Miklós Horthy's nationalist regime. If the spaces of this city manifested their roots in a reactionary past, the dynamic and teleological force of 'progress' could at least be made visible in the narrative form of monumental public art. In the Hungarian capital, as elsewhere in the Bloc, the task for architects and planners – as also for those charged with representing space textually and visually – was to reveal the interconnections of space and time: in other words, to demonstrate that historical forces were at work throughout and on the territories of socialism.

The establishment of socialist regimes was often characterized as a radical break with the past.[16] But the urban spaces that came under their authority were not blank slates. Material traces of earlier eras inevitably remained. Urban reconstruction was as much about managing the meanings and associations of the historic city as it was about the modernization of the urban fabric. Although the strategies and techniques employed in shaping these city narratives were diverse, ranging from the demolition of troublesome symbols to their discursive assimilation, the result was invariably one of simplification. However, cities do not readily lend themselves to this kind of monologic inscription. The material past was encountered in the everyday present in the forms of buildings and streets, and allowed the possibility for people to attach a range of meanings and memories that did not fit neatly with the official account.

The ways in which traces and spaces of the past were reworked or even effaced – both physically and discursively – in a city that was drawn into the Soviet sphere at this time is the theme of Olga Sezneva's essay 'Living in the Russian Present with a German Past: The Problems of Identity in the City of Kaliningrad'. The rewriting of the political map of Europe in the 1940s subjected many places to a dramatic reversal of power and ideology – typically from fascist to socialist authority. The renaming of space was a widespread means of representing such turns of history and creating a new sense of place. Yet Königsberg's fate was shared by only a few cities, Breslau/Wrocław and Danzig/Gdańsk forming the strongest comparisons.[17] The city's annexation by the Soviet Union resulted in the exile of its German population: the same physical space was now occupied by different inhabitants as well as by a different ideology. The remaking of Königsberg as a Soviet place was conducted on two fronts: by the reconfiguration of its material space; and through new interpretations of the city's history. Sezneva stresses a disjunction between the official and popular versions of the city's history and identity. In the official version, Kaliningrad's past was reidentified with the imaginary community of the Soviet Union. In their everyday discourse, however, the Kaliningraders developed a different version, oriented towards Western Europe and drawing on Königsberg's German heritage. Ruined remains of German cathedrals became the axis for this unofficial mythology and history. Analysing visual and textual representations of these ruins, Sezneva examines the way in which official and popular histories of Kaliningrad created rival versions of place.

The relations of core and periphery are also explored by Karl Qualls in his essay on the postwar reconstruction of Sevastopol. Qualls positions local interests against those of the centre by comparing different schemes advanced by authorities in the city itself and in Moscow. Unlike Kaliningrad in Sezneva's account, where official and unofficial views are brought into conflict, Qualls's Sevastopol is the site of tensions and disputes within Soviet authority. In this Black Sea port the navy carried an authority that allowed a particularly 'local' narrative celebrating the city's long history as a naval port to shape reconstruction plans after 1945.

The struggle over the meaning of urban spaces is also the subject of Astrid Ihle's chapter, 'Wandering the Streets of Socialism: A Discussion of the Street Photography of Arno Fischer and Ursula Arnold'. She discusses the decentred representation of the socialist city, in this case Berlin and Leipzig, in the work of these two photographers. As she argues, their work represented a counter-image of the cities of postwar East Germany to the propagandistic images of heroic national reconstruction circulated in the official media. Where the latter figured the city as a sign of national progress and development, Fischer and Arnold focused on the disregarded aspects of urban life such as the mundane activities of day-to-day survival, thereby exposing the gap between the State's rhetoric and the daily experiences of ordinary East Germans. Transposing the Baudelairian concept of the *flâneur* from nineteenth-century Paris to the twentieth-century socialist city, and from a male to a female subject position, Ihle characterizes the photographers as dissenting eyes, who made the tragedy of the ruined city visible.

A shift of meaning, but of a different sort, took place even in those parts of the Bloc that had already been under socialist rule for several decades. There, the rupture was with Stalinism rather than with a capitalist past. The destalinization of an area of Moscow which in the early 1950s had become almost synonymous with the new building of Moscow State University – a late Stalinist gesture of imperial power – was effected during the Khrushchev Thaw by inserting, beneath its great tower, a new, state-of-the-art complex for the socialist upbringing of children. As Susan E. Reid discusses in her chapter, 'Khrushchev's Children's Paradise: The Pioneer Palace, Moscow, 1958–1962', the building of the Pioneer Palace reoriented the associations of its locality, the Lenin Hills, in directions more congenial to the post-Stalinist regime. But rather than denying its presence or competing with it on its own terms, the Pioneer Palace assimilated Moscow University into an image of modernity, rejuvenation, social progress and people-oriented values that accorded with the self-image the Khrushchev regime sought to project.

Utopia

The Pioneer Palace was in many ways heir to a long tradition of utopian thought about the power of a harmonious, purposefully designed environment to bring about a perfect social order. Utopia, an ideal of impossible perfection, is by definition a non-place – a fictional island enjoying perfect government. For this reason utopianism was consistently denied by socialist regimes which claimed to be constructing a perfect order in real, existing space; the ideal socialist society was not a utopia because it was being built in the present on the basis of objective laws of development. However, it was no secret that, just a year after the Bolshevik Revolution, Lenin was inspired to launch his Plan for Monumental Propaganda by the seventeenth-century philosopher Tommaso Campanella's vision of a 'City of the Sun', a city whose built structure determined the ideal organization of society, reinforced by edifying public art.[18] In the 1920s, radical efforts to effect a total cultural revolution were premised on the principle of environmental determinism, which was rooted in late nineteenth-century design discourse but given new authority by the Marxist premise that matter determines consciousness. To change how a person thought and behaved one must change his or her material surroundings. Thus the architectural form of the city and planning of urban space were vested with a social-transformative role in the lives of its residents. The configuration of cities was 'the strongest factor for organizing the psyche of the masses'.[19] The environmental determinism of the revolutionary avant-garde of the 1920s and first five-year plan was reinvigorated during the 1950s and 1960s. At a time of great political upheaval, it was recognized that if monuments and monumental space influence people's mentality, the monuments of the *ancien régime* – whether Stalinist or monarchist – could not be left in peace but must be either reconfigured or torn down and replaced.

Domestic space was a particularly important site for ideological intervention, both at the level of design and production, and at the level of representations and efforts to shape popular taste. As Stephen Kotkin has noted with reference to the 1930s, the 'configuration of housing was a political determinant of consciousness and behaviour, including a person's political reliability'.[20] The realization that living space could be ordered and used for political ends became particularly important with the Khrushchev regime's intense house-building programme. While taking measures to provide one-family flats for all, it also made the home and spaces of leisure – in addition to those of labour and political ritual – crucial sites for ideological intervention. The official faith in the capacity of the material environment to shape mentality was to some extent internalized and reproduced by ordinary people such as this young Soviet respondent to a questionnaire on 'Your Ideas about the Young Family' in 1962:

> A separate, isolated apartment which opens onto a stair landing encourages an individualistic, bourgeois attitude in families – 'my house!' But soon it will

be possible to walk out of an apartment straight into a pleasant throughway with flowers and paths leading to the house café, the library, the movie hall, children's playrooms. This new kind of housing will have an effect on the family spirit. The woman will no longer resist the idea of service installations and apartment house kitchens, saying: 'I can do it faster myself at home!' I know the time will come when a husband and wife moving into a new apartment will take along only a couple of suitcases of personal clothing, favorite books and toothbrushes.[21]

Public and Private

The challenge that socialist ideology apparently posed to privacy has long fixated Western observers. As Walter Benjamin claimed, on visiting the Soviet Union in 1928, 'Bolshevism has abolished private life.'[22] Benjamin had in mind the young socialist State's tightening grip on formal and informal cultural institutions, such as the café, the press and voluntary societies. The interests of the State appeared to have consumed private, domestic spaces. Benjamin describes how nineteenth-century apartments, once privately owned by the Russian bourgeoisie, had become common property and were now over-populated by numerous families and their meagre possessions. 'Through the hall door one steps into a little town', he wrote. This characteristically surreal metaphor, reversing inside and outside, significantly also convolutes what are conventionally the spaces of public and private.

During the Cold War period, the absence of privacy was the stock-in-trade of Western indictments of Eastern European societies. Efforts by the Party and its agents to infiltrate the spaces, and influence the practices, of everyday life were identified as evidence of the 'totalitarian' character of these societies. As one Soviet agitational brochure of 1959 proclaimed in its title, 'Everyday Life is Not a Private Matter'.[23] Thus Erich Goldhagen wrote in *Problems of Communism* in 1960 about 'the discipline of leisure' in the Soviet Union: 'In the past few years the Party has evinced a growing concern with the uses to which Soviet citizens put the leisure gained by technological advances. For it is, indeed, endemic to a totalitarian regime that it insists on integrating *res privata* into *res publica*.'[24]

The limitations that the totalitarian paradigm placed on historical understanding of Soviet-type societies are well established and need not be rehearsed here. But notwithstanding the Cold War framework within which Goldhagen approached the issue, the efforts of states to absorb the private into the public realm remains a valid and necessary object of research.[25] What is important in this context is that scholars have paid increasing attention to the degree of *negotiation* that went on between State and people in the ascription of meanings to particular spaces, as well as to the resilience of counter-hegemonic practices, representations and memories. This book contributes to this important line of historical investigation and analysis.

The contributing authors attach varying meanings to private and public spatial practices in different settings. The identification of the home or dwelling with the realm of privacy is a relatively recent Western construction. Historically and geographically specific, it cannot be taken for granted in the context of socialism. Katerina Gerasimova and David Crowley both examine the limits of 'privacy' within public housing. In her chapter 'Public Privacy in the Soviet Communal Apartment', Gerasimova takes an ethnographic approach to public and private spaces in communal apartments in St Petersburg in the immediate aftermath of the collapse of the Soviet Union. She analyses the spatial practices of inhabitants of communal apartments, as well as the ways in which they describe this particular form of 'communalism'. Forced into collective patterns of life and mutual dependency that were shaped by the space of the communal apartment, the inhabitants exercise mutual discipline upon one another. In their eyes, privacy is associated with an escape from this confining form of 'home'. By contrast, Crowley's chapter 'Warsaw Interiors: The Public Life of Private Spaces, 1949–65' examines public discourses about private life in Poland in the 1950s. The difference in the experience and attitudes to socialism in Poland and the Soviet Union is significant here. In this essay, his characterization of the public/private dichotomy extends not only to spaces and spatial practices but also to the public representations of 'private' experience. Contrasting the years before and after the political upheaval of the Thaw, Crowley stresses that the State reached a kind of accommodation with people's demands for the spaces and material required to produce privacy.

To what extent should 'private' space be seen either as a 'gift' bestowed by the State in return for loyalty or acquiescence, or as an illicit haul? This issue is explored by Paulina Bren and Stephen Lovell in their contributions dealing with the weekend home in the Czech and Russian countryside respectively. The intense attachment felt by many city-dwelling Eastern Europeans towards their often small and primitive holiday homes in the mountains and forests has shaped their interconnected sense of self-identity and place in ways that did not accord with the conventional socialist representations of the countryside. In 'Weekend Getaways: the *Chata*, the *Tramp* and the Politics of Private Life in Post-1968 Czechoslovakia', Bren contrasts two interrelated forms of weekend escape from the city, the occupation of the *chata*, a home that had to be constructed within the resources and regulations of Czechoslovakia, and the practice of '*tramping*', an unregulated and unsanctioned hiking in the countryside. Bren argues that widespread *chata* ownership was tolerated and even encouraged by the Czechoslovak communist regime – in spite of the drain that it made on labour and resources – in a deliberate effort to defuse unregulated *tramping*. But if the politics of 'normalization' in Czechoslovakia produced encouraging conditions for *chata* ownership, such retreats were viewed with equivocation at other times and in other parts of the Bloc. In the Soviet Union in the early 1960s, Nikita Khrushchev campaigned against *dacha* ownership. The status of a building built with one's own hands (or by privately sub-contracting labour) and dedicated to leisure, as Lovell shows in his essay 'Soviet Exurbia: Dachas in Postwar Russia', was at best anomalous in a society allegedly advancing towards collectivism. If the communal apartment, in Gerasimova's analysis, was the space of 'public privacy' – however paradoxical that formulation might seem – *dacha* settlements were characterized, according to Lovell, by 'private publicness', that is by forms of communality and sociability which – though tied to an official system of organization – allowed a degree of agency and autonomy on the part of 'dacha folk'.

The conclusions drawn by our contributors cannot be aggregated into a picture of a monolithic socialist space, the Eastern Bloc. Rather, they collectively raise questions about the contrasting experiences of socialism in the satellite states and the Soviet Union, and of competing patterns for socialist space between the centre and localities. If the housing block – the building type most associated with the modernization of the urban landscape from the early 1960s – was made to almost indistinguishable blueprints throughout the Bloc, utilizing similar prefabrication systems, does it follow that the conceptions of domestic or 'private' life it was to accommodate were held in common too?[26] We should be wary of overstressing a direct relationship of ideology – whether in terms of resistance or of determination – to the production and occupation of the sites of everyday life: longer historical processes were also at work, as Richard Stites has pointed out: 'not all the peculiarities of Russian spatial . . . culture are attributable solely to Soviet socialism.'[27] The material heritage of buildings and streets that had been fashioned in very different historical circumstances, together with established ways of living – what the sociologist Pierre Bourdieu would call 'habitus' – meant that many significant spatial practices such as those of 'home-making' in the Soviet Union and the People's Republics cannot be described adequately in terms of either accommodation with or resistance to dogma.[28] As scholars working on the modernization of the home in Eastern Europe have noted, apparently new patterns of domestic 'occupation' sometimes reproduced older, established ways of living. Thus the spatial and social arrangements of communal apartments in the Soviet Union might reproduce the spatial and gender relations of the one-room peasant *izba*.[29] The discourse of the new apartment was, on one level, a campaign to inculcate modern habits of living in a recently urbanized people and, as such, was a response to the specificity of Russia's demography.

If the traditional peasant habitus pervaded urban life in the Russian socialist city, to what extent did the experience of socialism, over seventy years in the Soviet Union and forty years in the Eastern Bloc, succeed in creating new kinds of subjects and shaping new consciousness? Space, as a number of contributors to this volume note, was a *socializing* project that undertook the formation of a new kind of person or moral subject. New ways of organizing the home, the workplace or the street would, it was claimed, produce new social relations that would, in turn, produce a new consciousness. What indications do we have that that the actions and behaviours of individuals were shaped by the spaces in which they lived and through which they passed every day? Perhaps most problematically, how can we calibrate the effects of socialist spaces?

It will come as no surprise that the research presented in this volume finds little evidence that the spatial project of socialism succeeded in making utopia reality. Authority's investment in 'environmental determinism' appears to have produced limited social returns. On the contrary, if socialist spaces had any effect in shaping new social relations, then they must surely be held responsible for the failures of the system as much as for its achievements. Gerasimova, in her essay on the communal apartment, explores the tactics used by tenants to minimize the social tensions that accompanied the conditions of 'public privacy' forced on them by the shared occupancy of pre-revolutionary apartments. Far from altruistic communalism, the attitude of some tenants to their near neighbours is described as 'depersonalized'. Tactics of indifference and exclusion turned neighbours into 'mere elements of the setting' or, in other words, people into things.

If the effectiveness of 'real existing socialist' spaces in creating socialist subjects is in doubt, they were not necessarily anti-social. The queue was an institution of life under socialism and a spatial manifestation of the 'economy of shortage' that characterized all Eastern Bloc states. Albeit much hated and ridiculed, the queue outside the shop produced forms of sociality that might be coded to demonstrate the existence of values and a close-knit solidarity in spite of the alienating effects of socialism.[30] In

Poland, after the repression of the Solidarity trade union in the early 1980s, the control over the flow of goods into the shops was widely understood as oscillating between displays of relative largesse and punishment by ordeal. Consequently, the queue became a place to demonstrate resistance. Maintaining and even exaggerating polite social conventions in the queue was a signal of 'Polish gentility' and a silent rebuke to 'Russian philistinism'. Neither anti-social space nor a socialist one, the queue and the forms of sociality it embodied were a real product of 'real existing socialism', albeit an unintended one. As these two examples suggest, much more analysis needs to be made of the movements, intentions and actions of agents within the spaces of socialist societies if we are to understand the complex relations of people to authority.

Spatial Practices

Dissent in Soviet-type societies is often identified with 'the underground', a term that expresses an ideological and social position through spatial metaphor. Not only does this label mystify the identities of those who acted against authority, but it also suggests a murky habitat of secret networks, shadows and prisons. Dissent did have its sites, of course, but they were often far more ordinary than the romanticized image of the underground would allow: kitchen tables, café corners and, as Bren shows, the countryside. Unregulated exchanges took place in the shadow of the monuments of official culture. Pushkin Square in Moscow was, for instance, a meeting place for subcultural groups in the 1980s. Young people would display their disregard for the socialist moral economy and official valorization of labour by spending hours 'hanging out', while others would trade currency illegally in the very places most charged with producing a socialist mentality.

While the leading voices of opposition may have vented their objection to state possession of space, figures like Andrei Sakharov or Mircea Dinescu rarely employed tactics of what might be called spatial dissent (though they were often physically marginalized by expulsion from the metropolitan centre as a punishment for articulating their views). In their commitment to charters and 'samizdat' publications, their dissent tended to be literary rather than embodied. However, numerous, less textual but none the less articulate 'incursions' into the public spaces of the Bloc occurred. These events used space to articulate suppressed views or challenge the legitimacy of communist authority. Jan Kubik, in his 1994 study *The Power of Symbols Against the Symbols of Power*, has investigated a series of public spectacles and monuments associated with Solidarity in Poland in the early 1980s.[31] He charts how, despite prohibition, opponents of the regime ritualistically occupied cities like Craców and Poznań. Symbolic demonstrations of this kind drew on a commonly understood but repressed 'map' of meanings constituted by the historic fabric of the city. Not only was the body politic manifest in the hundreds of ordinary people who took part in these spectacles, but a set of spatio-historic associations was activated. In the same period, a group of young Poles known as *Pomoranczowa Alternatywa* (Orange Alternative) produced different forms of spatial dissent. In Situationist manner, they performed events from the history of the Bloc according to the official record.[32] In 1987 hundreds of young men and women re-enacted the events of the October Revolution in Wrocław to commemorate the seventieth anniversary of the event. Cardboard models of the battleships Potemkin and Aurora sailed through the city streets while the crowd, dressed in red, shouted 'revolution', and a 'Komissar's Revolutionary Council' met in a pizza parlour. The Winter Palace was the local department store. Many of the participants were arrested, most singing the 'Internationale' as they were taken away. The city was not simply a convenient setting for a political carnival; *Pomoranczowa Alternatywa* ridiculed the regime's continued rhetorical evocation of 'the revolutionary spirit' at a time when Poland seemed to have succumbed to consumerism. If Bulatov discovered Lenin on Krasikov Street, these young Poles found him in a pizza parlour.

Mark Svede, in the final chapter of this volume, 'Curtains: Décor for the End of Empire', reflects on spatial tactics that lie somewhere between the poles of spectacular irony and the sombre articulation of suppressed values. Exploring the history of the competition for the ill-fated Soviet Pavilion at Expo92 in Seville, he locates the winning entry by young Latvian architects within an indigenous, anti-colonialist tradition of 'architectural expression of political dissent' and a 'facility for compromising monuments'. Riga's main statue of Lenin had been employed as a prop in a popular theatricalization of the city; photographers – often ordinary Latvian tourists – aligned their cameras to make the leader of the Revolution hail the Orthodox cathedral behind or, later, the rehabilitated Latvian flag. Similarly, the *Freedom Monument*, which had been erected during the first period of Latvian independence in 1935, became a magnet for dissent during the 1980s. These Latvians produced unorthodox meanings for the city through their negotiations and use of space. Theirs was a kind of interpretative spatial practice in that they did not simply occupy space but, in a phenomenological sense, invested it with memory and imagination, conjuring up and exorcizing its historic ghosts.

Svede's analysis focuses on the Soviet pavilion for Seville, a building commissioned by major competition launched by major state bodies including the State Architectural Commission of the USSR in 1988. Most accounts of architecture locate the interests of architects and planners within the sphere of authority; indeed an international exhibition pavilion, patronized by the State, would seem necessarily to embody the close, intentional relations of architecture and political ideology. Not only were architects tied to socialist states by the latter's monopoly over resources, but architecture is intrinsically constructive and affirmative. Indeed, what could be more affirmative than an exhibition pavilion, charged in this instance with representing the banal credo 'Humanity discovers the world and so achieves happiness'? Yet, as Svede's attentive reading of the Latvian-designed Soviet pavilion shows, it was loaded with irony. His discussion raises the provocative potential of architecture to be the kind of critical practice that postmodern critics have repeatedly demanded in the West since the 1970s.[33]

The essays commissioned for this book open up a new dimension to the exploration of the complex and divergent experiences of socialism in Eastern and Central Europe by exploring the socio-spatial economy and its discursive formations. For, as Doreen Massey has claimed, 'It is not just that the spatial is socially constructed; the social is spatially constructed too'.[34] These essays together show that – whether at the most domestic, 'private' level of the home or at the most extended level of the nation – space played a fundamental role in the shaping of everyday sociality, large social formations, and indeed of socialism itself in the Eastern Bloc.

Notes

1. The concept of this book emerged out of a symposium organized by the editors, 'Socialist Artefacts, Places and Identities'. This event was hosted by the Victoria and Albert Museum, London, in November 1998 with sponsorship from the British Academy.
2. Langdon Winner, 'Do Artefacts Have Politics?', *Daedalus*, 109, no. 1 (Winter 1980), reprinted in Donald McKenzie and Judy Wajcman, eds, *The Social Shaping of Technology* (London: Open University Press, 1985).

3. Raymond Stokes has explored these questions in relation to 'socialist technology'. See his 'In Search of the Socialist Artefact: Technology and Ideology in East Germany, 1945–1962', *German History,* 15, no. 2 (1997), pp. 221–39.

4. For recent writing on the Moscow Metro see *Studies in the Decorative Arts,* 7, no. 2 (Spring-Summer 2000), a theme issue edited by Karen Kettering. For Socialist Realism, see A. Åman, *Architecture and Ideology in Eastern Europe during the Stalin Era. An Aspect of the Cold War* (Cambridge, MA: MIT Press, 1992); Orszagos Műemlékvédelmi Hivatal Magyar Építészeti Múzeum, *Építészet és Tervezés Magyarországon 1945–1959* (Budapest: 1996); Radomíra Sedláková, ed., *Sorela. Česká Architektura Padesátych Let* (Prague: Národní Galerie, exh. cat., 1994).

5. Henri Lefebvre, *Everyday Life in the Modern World* (New York: Transaction, 1984); Michel de Certeau, *The Practice of Everyday Life* (Berkeley and Los Angeles: California University Press, 1988).

6. Svetlana Boym, *Common Places: Mythologies of Everyday Life in Russia* (Cambridge, MA: Harvard University Press, 1994); Irina Gutkin, *The Cultural Origins of the Socialist Realist Aesthetic, 1890–1934* (Evanston, IL: North Western University Press, 1999); N. B. Lebina, *Povsednevnaia zhizn' sovetskogo goroda: normy i anomalii, 1920–1930 gody* (St Petersburg: Letnii sad, 1999).

7. Sheila Fitzpatrick, *Everyday Stalinism: Ordinary Life in Extraordinary Times. Soviet Russia in the 1930s* (Oxford: Oxford University Press, 1999); Stephen Kotkin, *Magnetic Mountain. Stalinism as a Civilization* (Chicago: University of Chicago Press, 1995); Konrad H. Jarausch, ed., *Dictatorship as Experience: Towards a Socio-cultural History of the GDR* (New York and Oxford: Berghahn Books, 1999).

8. Paul Betts, 'The Twilight of the Idols: East German Memory and Material Culture', *Journal of Modern History,* 72 (September 2000), pp. 731–65; András Gerő and Iván Pető, *Befejezetlen szocializmus* (Budapest: Te-Art Rt, 1997), published in English as *Unfinished Socialism: Pictures from the Kádár Era* (Budapest: CEU Press, 2000); David Crowley, 'A Strange Nostalgia', *The Art Book,* 8, no. 2 (March 2001), pp. 9–11; Svetlana Boym, *The Future of Nostalgia* (New York: Basic Books, 2001); Vieda Skultans, *The Testimony of Lives: Narrative and Memory in Post-Soviet Latvia* (London: Routledge, 1998); Alon Confino and Peter Fritzsche, eds, *The Work of Memory: New Directions in the Study of German Society and Culture* (Urbana, University of Illinois Press, 2002).

9. Gerő and Pető, *Unfinished Socialism,* p. 5.

10. For a related discussion of history and memory in the People's Republic of Poland see Tomasz Szarota, 'Zycie codzienne w Peerelu – propozycja badawca', *Studia i Materiały*, I (1995), pp. 201–15.
11. Rita Felski, 'The Invention of Everyday Life', *New Formations* (Winter 1999–2000), p. 16.
12. See, for instance, Deborah Ann Field, 'Communist Morality and the Meanings of Private Life in Post-Stalinist Russia, 1953–1964' (Ph.D. dissertation, University of Michigan, 1996); Victor Buchli, *An Archaeology of Socialism* (Oxford and New York: Berg, 1999); Victor Buchli, 'Khrushchev, Modernism and the Fight against *Petit-bourgeois* Consciousness in the Soviet Home', *Journal of Design History,* 10, no. 2 (1997), pp. 161–75; Karen Kettering, '"Ever More Cosy and Comfortable": Stalinism and the Soviet Domestic Interior, 1928–1938', *Journal of Design History,* 10, no. 2 (1997), pp. 119–38; Susan E. Reid, 'Destalinisation and Taste, 1953–1963', *Journal of Design History,* 10, no. 2 (1997), pp. 161–75; Olga Matich, 'Remaking the Bed', in J. Bowlt and O. Matich, eds, *Laboratory of Dreams. The Russian Avant-Garde and Cultural Experiment* (Stanford, CA: Stanford University Press, 1999), pp. 59–78.
13. Katerina Clark, *The Soviet Novel. History as Ritual* (Chicago: University of Chicago Press, 1981, 1985), pp. 38–41; Mircea Eliade, *The Myth of the Eternal Return*, ed., Willard R. Trask (Pantheon Books, 1954 (second printing, 1965)).
14. Eliade wrote 'The world that surrounds us, in which the presence and work of man are felt, has "an extraterrestrial archetype", be it conceived as a plan, as a form, or purely and simply as a "double" existing on a high cosmic level. Reality is conferred on objects, buildings, spaces through repetition of a celestial archetype.' Eliade, *Myth of the Eternal Return*, p. 8.
15. Anne White, *Destalinization and the House of Culture. Declining State Control Over Leisure in the USSR, Poland and Hungary, 1953–1989* (London and New York: Routledge, 1990).
16. Warsaw presents the example where, perhaps, the greatest ideological investment in the image of the city's complete destruction during the war was made. See Jerzy S. Majewski and Tomasz Markiewicz, *Warszawa Nie Obdudowana* (Warsaw: DIG, 1998).
17. See Carl Tighe, *Gdańsk. National Identity in the Polish-German Borderlands* (London: Pluto Press, 1990); Norman Davies and Roger Moorhouse, *Microcosm. Portrait of A Central European City* (London: Jonathan Cape, 2002). Erica Carter, James Donald and Judith Squires, *Space and Place. Theories of Identity and Location* (London: Lawrence and Wishart, 1993), p. X.

18. Tommaso Campanella (1568–1639), *The City of the Sun: A Poetical Dialogue*, trans. D. Donno (Berkeley: University of California Press, 1981). Khrushchev acknowledged the contribution of the utopian socialist tradition in his report to the Twenty-Second Party Congress in 1961. In this, he made reference to Saint-Simon, Fourier, Owen, Campanella and More, although he added the caveat that 'only Marx, Engels and Lenin created a theory of scientific communism and pointed out the true paths toward the establishment of a new society'. Khrushchev, cited by Jerome M. Gilison, *The Soviet Image of Utopia* (Baltimore and London: Johns Hopkins University Press, 1975). Campanella's *Città del Sole* was republished in Russian translation in 1947. It was invoked favourably in discussions promoting the synthesis of architecture and monumental art in the context not only of the Moscow Pioneer Palace but also of new projects for a Palace of Soviets. E. N. Sil'versan, *Dvorets Sovetov: materialy konkursa, 1957–1959 gg.* (Moscow, 1961), p. 33.

19. Stephen Bittner, 'Green Cities and Orderly Streets. Space and Culture in Moscow, 1928–1933', *Journal of Urban History,* 25, no. 1 (November 1998), p. 24.

20. Stephen Kotkin, 'Shelter and Subjectivity in the Stalin Period: a case study of Magnitogorsk', in William Craft Brumfield and Blair Ruble, eds, *Russian Housing in the Modern Age. Design and Social History* (Cambridge: Cambridge University Press / Woodrow Wilson Center Press, 1993), p. 174.

21. A response to the survey 'Your Ideas About the Young Family', conducted by the Komsomol newspaper *Komsomol'skaia pravda.* Translated in *The Soviet Review*, 3, no. 8 (August 1962), p. 32.

22. Walter Benjamin, 'Moscow' (1927), in *One Way Street* (London: Verso, 1979), pp. 187–8.

23. O. Kuprin, *Byt – ne chastnoe delo* (Moscow: Gospolitzdat, 1959).

24. Erich Goldhagen, 'The Glorious Future – Realities and Chimeras', *Problems of Communism,* 9, no. 6 (1960), p. 7.

25. See O. Kharkhordin, 'Reveal and Dissimulate: A Genealogy of Private Life in Soviet Russia', in J. Weintraub and Krishan Kumar, *Public and Private in Thought and Practice* (Chicago: University of Chicago Press, 1996), pp. 333–63.

26. See A. Ludwig and M. Strumpfe, *Tempolinsen und P2 Alltagskultur der DDR. Begleitbuch zur Ausstellung* (Berlin: be.bra Verlag, 1995).

27. R. Stites, 'Crowded on the Edge of Vastness', in J. Smith, ed., *Beyond the Limits: The Concept of Space in Russian History and Culture* (Helsinki: Studia Historica 62, 1999), p. 259.

28. Pierre Bourdieu, *Outline of a Theory of Practice* (Cambridge: Cambridge University Press, 1997), pp. 79–87.
29. Buchli, *Archaeology of Socialism*, p. 156; Boym, *Common Places*, p. 151.
30. On the social institutions connected to the queue, see Janina Wedel, *The Private Poland. An Anthropologist's Look at Everyday Life* (New York: Facts on File Publications, 1986).
31. Jan Kubik, *The Power of Symbols Against the Symbols of Power* (Boulder: Penn State Press, 1994).
32. B. Misztal, 'Between the State and Solidarity: one movement, two interpretations – the Orange Alternative Movement in Poland', *The British Journal of Sociology*, 43, no. 1 (March 1992).
33. See, for instance, Frederic Jameson, 'Is Space Political?', in Cynthia Davidson, ed., *Anyplace* (Cambridge, MA: MIT Press, 1995), pp. 192–205. See also Andrei Bokov, 'Enriching our Fantasy', in Catherine Cooke, ed., *The Uses of Tradition in Russian and Soviet Architecture* (London: Architectural Design, 57, no. 7/8, 1987), pp. 39–46.
34. Doreen Massey, 'Introduction: Geography Matters', in Doreen Massey and John Allen, eds, *Geography Matters! A Reader* (Cambridge: Cambridge University Press, 1984), p. 6.

–2–

Accommodation and Agitation in Sevastopol: Redefining Socialist Space in the Postwar 'City of Glory'

Karl D. Qualls

In late 1949 city officials stretched a banner that read 'SEVASTOPOLIANS! What have you done for the restoration of your *hometown*'[1] across one of the most heavily travelled streets in the Crimean port city of Sevastopol. It spoke volumes about the city and its transformation during the five years after liberation from a two-year Nazi occupation. To the social, psychological and physical damage caused by revolution, civil war, collectivization, industrialization and purges, war scars added one more trauma. When, after the war, the regime asked how it could repair the damage, it found the answer in urban reconstruction.

The process of replanning and rebuilding cities after the devastation of the Second World War was one of many ways by which the Soviet party-state attempted to repair its image in the eyes of the population after nearly thirty years of disorientation. The creation of socialist spaces was part of a larger project of creating a new system and a new society, but the process and rationale are still poorly understood. Throughout the 1920s and 1930s, not only in regard to the well-known 1935 General Plan for the reconstruction of Moscow, but also to the revitalization of other cities, architects and ideologues debated the future face of Soviet urban space. Many planners wanted a socialist space that met the population's needs through communal living, eating, childcare, laundry and more. The counter-view sought monumental architecture that would serve as symbols of power and representations of the Soviet state and its institutions, with the names and statues of Marx, Engels and other socialist luminaries prominent throughout. What transpired was a combination of pre-revolutionary and NEP-era utopian-idealist schemes for the new city all bundled up in the latest verbiage about the socialist system's concern for the population's wellbeing. Much as steel had become the trademark of progress in the 1930s, in the postwar decade officials used reconstructed buildings and revitalized cities as symbols of progress and economic strength. New buildings rising from and above the ruins offered more than space for housing, production, convalescence and education. Each new building represented progress, healing and recovery. The city's new planners, moreover, diverted huge sums of money to massive and ornate structures that symbolized the regime's public pronouncements of concern for the population. Theatres, cinemas, hospitals and hotels, built in a neoclassical style, became the centrepieces of the city. This feat of rebuilding, often compared to the valour and sacrifice attending military victory, became one focus of persuasion in Stalin's last decade. Each new building was hailed as another 'victory' (rarely abandoning military terminology) for Soviet city building and for society in general.[2] The delayed Pyrrhic victory over Nazi Germany left numerous cities ravaged; the 'victory' of construction sought to heal those wounds.

The model settled on by the mid-1930s was carried out on a massive scale after the Second World War, but the vast destruction allowed for further negotiation among residents, architects and institutions of power on how cities would be raised from their ruins. With numerous military and industrial cities almost completely destroyed, the regime was willing to bend its stated policies if this would ensure rapid reconstruction and a mollified population. Five years after Sevastopol's liberation from German occupation and the beginning of reconstruction in the war-ravaged city, urban planners began to use the appeal of particular geographic places as a tool to motivate greater effort for construction of a new socialist space. However, this had not always been the case. Local citizens and officials opposed the projected future face of the city – emanating from Moscow – that sought to marginalize local history and tradition while centring Soviet institutions and the history of socialism and the USSR in the heart of the city. Local opposition initiated a connection with the hometown, its tradition and heritage by preserving and resurrecting pre-revolutionary names and buildings and placing the seats of Soviet institutions in their shadows. Maintaining schools, hospitals, housing and more remained consistent in all plans, but the socialist space was redefined from one that excluded much of the urban biography in favour of honouring the Soviet and socialist past to one that interwove Soviet history with a longer local history. Although the regime had intended the plans designed in Moscow by award-winning architects to become the blueprint for the reconstruction of other provincial cities that had suffered so much devastation during the Second World War, the idealistic plans conflicted with local desires to rebuild and remember a more familiar city. This process of negotiation was long and arduous, but eventually, in Sevastopol at least, local interests won out over central dictates. Socialist space became the buildings of Party and government and the occasional invocation of Lenin surrounded and intersected by sites of and monuments to pre-revolutionary lore. 'Soviet' and 'socialist' were at harmony with a selectively created and remembered past.

Accommodation and Agitation

Soviet social and political policy has sometimes been described as 'bread and circus', a duality whereby the population is both appeased and entertained. 'Accommodation and agitation' seems, however, to be more reflective of a broader set of policies.[3] Accommodation represents a series of policies satisfying the basic needs and wants of a population, keeping it content and maintaining the illusion of socialism's superior humanity. The cradle-to-grave system of social welfare and services provided benefits to single mothers and their children, down-on-their-luck workers, Stakhanovites and shock-workers, widows and orphans. Agitation means a simple and popularized propagation of political, social and/or cultural messages that seeks not just to convince, but also to motivate further action.

In postwar urban reconstruction, these methods took on various forms. Accommodation was an attempt to meet the immediate needs of a city and its residents, but also to incorporate, and thus validate, 'local' practice and tradition. Accommodating the population's psychological needs was as important as meeting its physical demands. Agitation, on the other hand, included the discourse and practices of moulding the myths of a glorious past and the power of the Soviet present with the future promise of the great Soviet experiment. Agitation in the context of postwar urban reconstruction created an alternative reality, a mythology based on tradition and ideological aspirations for the future. Hoping to encourage further effort for reconstruction, the architects and officials who redesigned Sevastopol after the Second World War created an aesthetic matrix of monuments, buildings, squares and streets honouring the heroes of the 'two defences' of the Crimean War and Great Patriotic War. Using the awe-inspiring architectural forms of the city's ancient Greek heritage, designers combined images of patriotic heroes with the legendary martyrs of two revolutions and a civil war. This form of agitation through incorporating an existing set of myths was also a method of accommodating residents' desire to live in a city that was familiar to them, not one radically changed.

Accommodation and agitation were not mutually exclusive; often they overlapped. For example, as with carefully designed buildings, architects paid close attention to the design of parks. In their purest form, green areas in cities provided space for recreation, relaxation and communing with nature and fellow citizens amidst the asphalt and concrete. Parks also occupied a central place in health maintenance (*zdravookhranenie*) plans. They provided fresh air and exercise to urban dwellers who could not escape to dachas. Moreover, parks served an important agitational purpose. Not only did they project the image of a state concerned with the health and welfare of its citizens, but also the addition of historical monuments linked those who strolled in the present with the heroic defenders of the Motherland who had lost their lives on battlefields past. When parks and monuments were preserved or rebuilt they only furthered the local population's identification with a familiar urban biography.

As architects proposed additional spaces for recreation, leisure and entertainment, the glorious past and future of Sevastopol was seen to rise from the ashes. Agitation was meant for mass consumption as a tool for aesthetic persuasion that utilized easily understood symbols of power and strength and was devoid of abstract (and unintelligible to most) political theory more common in written propaganda, which was meant primarily to persuade rather than encourage action.[4] Monuments, memorials and historical architecture supplied the regime with omnipresent symbols of Soviet power and a history of heroic actions around which the population could rally. Moreover, the style and monumental scale of construction represented the power, stability and economic viability of a country and system devastated by war. Accommodation in city services and housing planned to improve the standard of living of the population, thereby avoiding urban unrest and, more importantly, proving that Marxism-Leninism-Stalinism could provide the best possible life for people. The Revolution's true believers had not yet seen the fulfilment of the social-(ist) contract: if the State provides for the population's welfare, the latter will work and sacrifice for the creation of the communist society.

For both agitation and accommodation, the city centre was most important because it was the locus of city services and the party/state institutions, it was the most visible and travelled region of the city and it contained numerous historical sites. If one lived in the city centre or travelled there to work or to conduct business with the authorities, one was brought into contact with the first stage of postwar reconstruction. Planners looked first to the urban core both because the concentrated construction was more economical and efficient, but also because restoring the institutions of power, essential city services (e.g. water systems, hospitals, schools) and leisure activities (e.g. parks, theatres, museums) restored a sense of normalcy to a bomb-ravaged city and more quickly showed that through Soviet power a city could rise from its own ashes.

Sevastopol Before Reconstruction

Since the fifth century BCE the region surrounding present-day Sevastopol has served as a trading port for Greeks, Tatars, East Slavs and others. In 1783, Catherine established the city of Sevastopol, on the site of the ancient Greek city of Chersoneses (Khersones), as a Russian trading port and naval outpost against the Turks. But before the Second World War, Russians, Turks and Europeans remembered Sevastopol as the bloody battleground of the Crimean War. The costly war of attrition against disease, as much as enemy fire, became the focal point of the city's identity. In the last decade of the nineteenth century, naval, municipal and imperial officials commissioned statues and monuments to the 'great defence' of Sevastopol. Although Russia suffered great losses, the Crimean War demonstrated the power of a strong fortress and population. Thus, Sevastopol's heroic image served as the foundation on which the Soviets later built the myth of Red Sevastopol.

As the Crimean defence was being immortalized in stone and marble, revolutionaries arose in Sevastopol. Beginning with the mutinies in the Black Sea Fleet in 1905 and 1917 and then the 1919 insurrection against General Petr Wrangel and his men, Sevastopol gained its reputation as a bastion of the Revolution and defender of Soviet power. Operation Barbarossa in 1941 became yet another touchstone for fortress Sevastopol. Like the sailors who had established Soviet power in the city, their successors had to defend both Sevastopol and the nation from German invaders. After the lightning-quick and highly destructive Nazi offensive against the home of the Black Sea Fleet in November and December 1941, mythmakers in the Soviet press began to link the heroic mid-nineteenth-century defence of the city with the battle at hand.[5] All the themes of the Crimean War – heroism, self-sacrifice, disease and homelessness – were resurrected in the 1940s.

The scale of damage resulting from 250 days of siege and a two-year occupation in Sevastopol is simply unimaginable. Of 110,000 Sevastopolians, only 3,000 remained until liberation and 24,600 had been carried off to Germany as captive labour.[6] Residents returning from evacuation soon found that their homes had fared little better than the city at large. Only 1,023 of 6,402 residential buildings were habitable and only seven half-destroyed buildings remained in the city centre. The long German siege and the Red Army's return to the city two years later took its toll on Sevastopol's infrastructure as well. German forces destroyed the city's water system, shelling wreaked havoc on sewers, retreating forces cut phone and telegraph lines, special battalions destroyed railroad tracks and tunnels and Nazi rail cars hauled industrial equipment – including some of the city's electric generators – back to Germany. All told, Soviet officials claimed a loss of 25 billion roubles.[7] So thorough was Nazi destruction, however, that little remained in the city to meet even the most basic human needs. Water and sewer systems, electrical stations, flour mills, breweries and food processing industries were ruined and human faeces floated in one of the city's central bays.

Spatial Organization

On and around the central hill of Sevastopol one finds remarkable examples of the process of accommodation and agitation in the postwar design of a city with several loci of identification (Figure 2.1). Vladimir Cathedral, although damaged by war, remained the visual centrepiece at the highest point on the central hill. Nearby, a complex of naval administrative buildings pointed to the city's military identity. On the ring road surrounding the hill, the offices of the Party and of government stood near centres of entertainment such as theatres. Throughout the city were monuments and statues to admirals and heroes of socialism. The new socialist space in postwar Sevastopol was dominated by various symbols

Figure 2.1 Central hill taken from Artillery Bay. Note the statue of Lenin with arm outstretched with Vladimir Cathedral to the right and a large naval complex to the left. © Karl D. Qualls, 1997. All rights reserved

and reminders of the presence of the Soviet state, like Lenin Street. Others, like the statues honouring pre-revolutionary admirals, fitted well with the re-emergence of Russian nationalism during the war and maintained the city's tradition. Despite being heavily damaged, or decapitated in the case of Totleben, these symbols of Sevastopol's heroic past were restored to their previous condition. However, another set of structures, specifically the churches that still stand so prominently throughout the urban core, were completely at odds with state atheism, even though the regime retreated from its hard line during the war. None of the places of worship in the city centre, although heavily damaged by war, were completely demolished before reconstruction because the lack of time and materials necessitated the use of all building space. They also had stood as part of the city's heritage and identity before the arrival of Soviet power. Looking at how and why some of these structures were built or restored, it becomes clear that several groups were engaged in protracted conflict and negotiation to design Sevastopol's postwar socialist space.

Sevastopolians received their first indication that their city was to be reborn on 9 August 1944. Boris Rubanenko, deputy chair of the Committee on Architectural Affairs (KA), sent a brief note to one Sud'bin of the navy's Central Planning Bureau informing him that a closed competition for the city plan of postwar Sevastopol must be completed by 15 November.[8] The KA directed two prominent Moscow architects to compete for the honour of designing Sevastopol's new face. Moisei Ginzburg (1892–1946), once the leading theorist of Constructivism and designer of Crimea's southern shore in the 1920s, represented the Academy of Architecture. Grigorii Barkhin (1880–1969), professor of architectural planning and adviser to graduate students at the Moscow Architecture Institute, spoke for the navy. Despite years of experience and intimate knowledge of the city, Georgii Lomagin, Sevastopol's prewar municipal architect, was not included in the competition. In all prominent Soviet cities like Sevastopol, only the best practitioners from Moscow received commissions for planning competitions. These were men who had survived the relatively bloodless purge of the architectural community in the 1930s and therefore could be trusted to follow the official line.[9] Lomagin's exclusion from the competition showed that the regime initially believed that such an important task could not be left to local officials. This soon changed as retaining local tradition took precedence.

Ginzburg's plan for Sevastopol's new face echoed one of the prominent practices in postwar Soviet architecture – the creation of outdoor museums. When the Council of People's Commissars (Sovnarkom) created the KA on 8 April 1943, it invested the new organization with the 'architectural and planning work for the restoration of cities and other populated areas of the city type destroyed by the German invaders'.[10] As a sign of the importance of non-war-directed construction and preservation, of all the structures mentioned in the decree, Sovnarkom elaborated only on the rubric of architectural structures: 'triumphal arches, obelisks, columns and others'. The emphasis on memorial and monumental architecture underscored the regime's desire to recreate a mythology for the cities under construction while continuing to strengthen political and economic power. For older cities like Novgorod, Pskov and Smolensk, this meant preserving the architectural heritage.[11] Ginzburg's variant for the relatively young Sevastopol created a city of monuments to war and revolutionary heroes. He proposed a four-point programme:

> 1. Maximal utilization and opening of Sevastopol's landscape peculiarities. 2. Maximal utilization of material valuables preserved in Sevastopol. 3. Rational solution for all vital functions of the city as an organism. 4. Opening of the city's artistic form as a hero-city, as a city of Russian glory.[12]

Of this limited programme, Ginzburg developed only the last point. Rather than highlight the benefits for the city's inhabitants, Ginzburg proposed a plan of architectural symbolism; agitation was more important than accommodation. His plans were rejected, for the most part, because he provided little detail beyond ensemble sketches of his plans and he failed to include any analysis of space needs for housing, recreation, municipal services and more, and proposed no budget.

The main thrust of Ginzburg's effort was to memorialize the war, highlight naval interests and glorify Stalin. At the site of the Crimean War Panorama, he wanted to add a war museum, thus creating a square of the 'two defences'. For added effect, he proposed an 'Obelisk of Victory' nearby. At 80m high it was to be the termination point for a line of statues beginning at Count's Pier, ascending the central hill to a 'monumental sculpture of Stalin dominating over this part of the city',[13] and on to the Square of the Two Defences. The creation of this new pantheon of victors was accompanied by the preservation and restoration of monuments to heroes past. On the central hill, near Stalin's likeness, Ginzburg planned an ensemble for the naval command as well as for the Party and government offices. In his presentation, he made sure to note that Stalin's statue and the Obelisk of Victory could be seen from the shore and nearly every part of the city. Armed with research on monuments from around the world, Ginzburg sought to satisfy the population's psychological need to remember and the regime's desire for a new pantheon of heroes. Atop the central hill, all important symbols of socialism and heroism would meet in one great outdoor display of power. Ginzburg sought to accommodate Moscow's need to project its power rather than local physical needs or desires to maintain tradition.

Barkhin's design for the city centre, however, proposed a new spatial organization that greatly differed both from Ginzburg and the city's past, and Barkhin included much more detail than his opponent. In his July 1945 revision, Barkhin explained his use of the artistic device of triangulation. He used three monuments to the Crimean War as the points of intersection. The segments drawn from Historical Boulevard in the Central Region to Malakhov Kurgan in the Shipside Region to the Fraternal Cemetery in the Northern Region created the boundaries of the triangle. The focus, at the triangle's centre, was Sevastopol's central hill. The former Cathedral of St Vladimir occupied centre stage (Figure 2.2). The navy's most important buildings surrounded what was once known as

Figure 2.2 Lenin statue with Vladimir Cathedral in the background. 1997. © Karl D. Qualls, 1997. All rights reserved

Vladimir Square, and damage to the enormous naval library and other buildings left architects free to replan the city's centrepiece. Bounding the central hill was a ring road composed of three streets and four squares that housed all the government, party and military headquarters in addition to the main leisure facilities for residents. Barkhin, like Ginzburg, also located most major symbols in the city centre. Utilizing one of the oldest concepts in urban design, Barkhin and the experts who reviewed his plans and provided advice on corrections sought to place the most important buildings and monuments where they could be seen from many places (on hills and squares and at the junctions of important streets). Various plans placed statues of Lenin or Stalin or a war museum at the peak of the central hill, on the square of Vladimir Cathedral. Naval clubs, libraries, party and government buildings and the naval staff were all to be located at the intersections of the city's three main streets around the central hill. Barkhin's design sought to marginalize the Crimean War to the vertices of his triangle, which surrounded his centrepiece: the Soviet institutions. This would clearly have been a Soviet space with pre-revolutionary images pushed to the background.

Contested Spaces: Shaping the Cityscape

Contestation was not limited, however, to the two architects appointed by Moscow. In the years following the Barkhin and Ginzburg plans, local officials and residents intervened at nearly every stage to protect and project their image of the new Sevastopol. The 'dialogue' that emerged between Moscow and Sevastopol significantly altered the initial postwar plans and created a renewed Sevastopol that, while still Soviet, focused primarily on the city's pre-revolutionary Russian and local heritage, often at the expense of Soviet images.

Given the prohibitions on religion and the consensus behind a need for agitational space, how can we account for the dispute that arose after Barkhin suggested that all the buildings on the central hill, including Vladimir Cathedral, be razed?[14] A local review committee composed of naval and civilian representatives that included architects, engineers, a physician, the head of the city planning bureau, air defence and fire control met at the end of 1945 and argued vehemently against Barkhin's plan.[15] Asserting that the cathedral was central to Sevastopol's heritage and aesthetic uniqueness, the committee argued that it should be restored and not pulled down and that Barkhin's planned ensemble would over-shadow the Parthenon-like Peter and Paul Cathedral adjacent to proposed

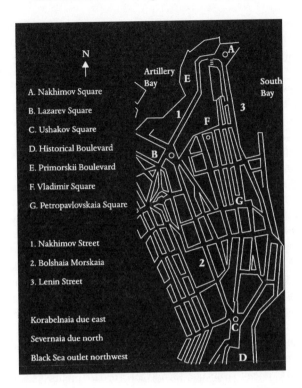

Figure 2.3 Map of Sevastopol's city centre.

construction.[16] Only after this local input was a plan to preserve the cathedral articulated. Barkhin altered his position and criticized a similar plan to rebuild the central hill, saying that Vladimir Cathedral was a 'monumental memorial of the first defence of Sevastopol in which the four hero admirals were interred'. He labelled the competing, but equally destructive plan, as 'vandalism and an unpardonable attitude toward the historical past of the Russian people'.[17] What is most telling is that despite the fact that over one third of the committee membership came from the navy, it rejected plans to enlarge a naval complex at the expense of Vladimir Cathedral.[18] Local naval and civilian officials were able to alter the plan of the Moscow architect selected to redesign Sevastopol and promote a mutually shared image of Sevastopol as a long-time naval bastion. It appears that image and tradition were more important to the navy than expanding its own administrative facilities, and in the closing days of the war the navy held considerable power of persuasion.

Although there are numerous reasons why the committee might have chosen to restore the cathedral, its historical significance is most instructive. Municipal and naval authorities, as Barkhin noted in his retraction, sought to direct the local community toward a particular history that highlighted heroism, sacrifice and defence of the city and country. The 'four hero admirals' that Barkhin noted included E. I. Totleben, V. I. Istomin, V. A. Kornilov and P. S. Nakhimov, who were central to Sevastopol's founding as a naval city and its defence against invaders of superior power. This mythology resonated with a population that had just emerged from war against the mighty Nazi forces. Rather than destroy a religious building as Moscow's architect had desired, local officials argued for and won the preservation of a monument to the city's heritage. Accommodating the local population's desire to retain its history was well within the bounds of postwar socialist space because defence of the Motherland and a renewed sense of Russian history had become more important than Marxism during the war, and the nineteenth-century admirals represented the city's heroic fighting spirit.[19] 'Soviet' space could be many things to many people, and creating tradition was a complicated process of contestation and negotiation that resulted in a selective 'writing' of the city's past.

Sevastopol's history before the Second World War was rich and heroic, but new policy dictates forbade recognition of its Tatar and Jewish heritage. With Crimean Tatars banished to Siberia and Central Asia, municipal officials set about removing all visual reminders of their earlier presence.[20] In addition to the Tatar people, the most prominent visual representation of their culture was the beautiful, turn-of-the-century mosque near the central ring road. Like nearly all buildings in the city centre, the mosque fell prey to artillery and bombs; yet, in this case, the exterior structure remained intact. Photographs from 1944 and 1946 show that the central dome and minaret still towered over nearby buildings much as they had done before the war.[21] Numerous organizations asked municipal officials for the authority to rebuild the structure, but no one wanted to reopen it as a mosque. The city and *oblast'* (province) governments, as well as the Council on Religious Cults, approved initial plans for the mosque's resurrection as a cinema/club for the Sevastopolstroi construction trust.[22] Yet, when the better-connected navy heard that the building was under consideration, it submitted its petition to renovate the building as the city's new naval archive.[23] But not even these organs could spare labour and materials to start anew. Gorispolkom (the Municipal Executive Committee) approved the navy's request,[24] but chief city architect Iurii Trautman warned the navy not to waste money trying to 'cleanse' the building of the last vestiges of its former owners. He limited them to three points: 'Remove all quotations both Arabic and Russian . . . remove emblems of half-moons, tear down the minaret.'[25] After the restoration, little remained of the Tatar shell. The new naval archive was a testament to the postwar rewriting of history. The façades were 'erased' and quotations from the Koran, dissonant with the building's new image, were expunged.[26] The archive came to represent the navy, the city's most powerful institution. At the same time it 'nationalized' and unified the city and simplified its past by removing the vestiges of a non-Slavic group and its faith. Whereas the navy was central to preserving a Russian Orthodox cathedral instead of expanding its purview on the central hill, it had no qualms about significantly changing a mosque to suit its needs.

Many other religious buildings were transformed into clubs, cultural centres and museums. The Karaimskaia *kenasa*, a Jewish prayer hall along the city's main ring road and in the shadow of Vladimir Cathedral, also suffered from the rewriting of history with urban space. Although the Karaite Jewish building survived 1941 with little damage, by liberation in 1944 only three heavily shell-pocked walls remained standing.[27] The roof's destruction obliterated the interior and allowed further damage from the elements. The demand for usable space in the city centre forced the kenasa's resurrection as the Spartak sports club. The façade, lacking any noticeable religious symbols, was rebuilt and restored to its original condition during the 1950s. Like the Tatars, although for different reasons, Jews were excluded from the postwar histories of the war. The chief architectural symbol of Judaism was co-opted, this time for leisure space, and named after one of history's first revolutionaries: Spartacus.

In many ways, the restoration of religious buildings helped to define the new socialist space as atheist, primarily Russian and military. Vladimir Cathedral accommodated the need for tradition and symbols of heroism, the mosque became one of many emblems of naval power in the city, and the kenasa provided a place for recreation for the city's inhabitants. All three structures, however, rewrote the past and highlighted the city's heroic and Russian heritage, which was wholly consistent with the contemporaneous martial and national character of the Soviet Union. Because the city was predominately Slavic after the war, the removal of the last vestiges of Tatars and Jews – whom the regime and press chided respectively as Nazi collaborators and non-participants in the war – further enhanced the dominant population's view that Sevastopol was a locale of Russian glory and therefore first among equals in the USSR.

Beyond religious buildings, symbols of institutional authority and power abounded in postwar Sevastopol. Plans from both Moscow and municipal architects placed the city's party and government headquarters in the city centre, usually on one of the chief squares that functioned as intersections for major streets. This gave the regime a physical presence in the very heart of the city. In addition to these grandiose building projects, all planners realized that urban space allowed for a more agitational use of naming and labelling. The streets and squares of Sevastopol's urban core became a battleground for competing visions of the city's identity as central planners looked to highlight the regime and locals clamoured for greater recognition of the city's history.

The 1944 decree on municipal architects stated that they held sole 'responsibility for planning, construction and architectural organization of the city', but many groups consistently infringed on this power.[28] The first infringement was the appointment of Moscow-based architects like Barkhin to create general plans. In Sevastopol, the navy also had great power to influence the development of various planning details, and even the general population raised objections to various projects emanating from Moscow or the chief municipal architect in Sevastopol. For example, in 1945 Vice-Admiral F. S. Oktiabrskii, commander-in-charge of Sevastopol's defence, recommended 'the naming of squares and main streets of Sevastopol take into account the historical events and names of the organizers and heroes of the two defences of Sevastopol'.[29] This emboldened local planners to attack Moscow's version of Sevastopol's heritage as first and foremost a Soviet socialist city.

Barkhin clearly wanted to define the new space as Soviet and socialist and he marked it as such on new city maps. The principal streets ringing the central hill took names familiar to any Soviet citizen: Lenin, Marx and Frunze. Likewise, most of the main squares along the ring road evoked Soviet socialism: Commune, Revolution and Parade. Lenin connected Parade and Commune and then Marx led from there to Revolution, which emptied into Frunze and back to the Square of Parades. The author of the Soviet Union's ruling ideology, the father of the Soviet state and the man who established Soviet power in Crimea were all connected by squares marking significant moments in the history of socialism. The Square of Parades is the obvious exception to this formula, but Barkhin had planned to use its prewar name, Third International, before naming it after its function. The city centre, which housed all the institutions of power and most of the leisure activities and city services (not to mention a significant proportion of housing) was thus prescribed by a history of socialism in street signs. One could not escape this lesson either; while walking the streets or giving directions to someone, the symbols of socialism's past were invoked.

Local planners, led by Iurii Trautman, wanted to design a socialist space that was more than merely another city dominated by symbols of Soviet power, but rather a city that took into account the residents' material needs and desire to 'remember' a familiar and glorified pre-revolutionary history. Trautman was neither bold nor stupid enough to try to change the name of Lenin Street or have it revert to its pre-revolutionary Catherine Street. However, the names of most other main streets and squares were transformed (Figure 2.3). Marx and Frunze reverted to their pre-1917 Big Naval and Nakhimov streets. The Square of Parades was also renamed after Nakhimov (although Lenin was toyed with for a while), and Nakhimov's statue replaced the rubble of Lenin's. Commune Square was renamed after Admiral Ushakov and Revolution Square eventually took the name of the founder of the Black Sea Fleet, Lazarev. In the post-Barkhin plans, Sevastopol's centre was marked by its naval heritage with Lenin as the sole exception. The naming of socialist space did not have to invoke socialism and its founders directly; rather, the ideal Soviet city was based on its willingness to sacrifice for and participate in the protection of the Motherland.[30] Local officials marked the new socialist space with the names that they thought best exemplified Sevastopol, not just Soviet Sevastopol. Moscow was likely to have acquiesced because reviving the city's pre-revolutionary past did not preclude Sevastopol from being 'Soviet'; rather, a greater focus on a century of military valour strengthened Sevastopol's principal role within the USSR and allowed the population to feel part of something familiar.

Primorskii Boulevard, which, from the late nineteenth century to the present has been the most attractive and appealing leisure space in Sevastopol, also marked the naval heritage of the city. Initially restricted to the city's elite, after the Revolution it became a space for the masses as well. Strolling, fishing and summer theatres were just some of the entertainments available in the lush green area on the bay within view of the opening to the sea. For this reason, Barkhin's initial plans to expand the nearby Square of Parades at the expense of Primorskii drew the ire and consternation of locals. Whether out of a genuine desire to glorify Stalin, or as a strategy to get his plan approved, Barkhin used the parks and squares of the city for blatant agitational purposes. On the Square of Parades, Barkhin unleashed all his talent for symbolic architecture. This square, on a small peninsula where the oldest street of the city met its first wharf and Primorskii Boulevard, Barkhin designed a complex of naval buildings and a military museum with three sides of the square open to the bays. Over the entire square and in front of the 'Forum' garden park with memorials to the heroes, Barkhin proposed an enormous statue of

Stalin – 'the great organizer and inspiration for victory'.[31] But even Stalin was to be no match for the 110m Tower of War with its four triumphal arches adorned with heroic sculptures. In order to illustrate the effect of his plan, Barkhin included a description of a parade route that began on Karl Marx Street, continued along Frunze Street, flowed into the square and past monuments and the memorial to Stalin and finally emerged onto Lenin Street to South Bay or down the incline to Count's Pier to the water. For Barkhin's opponents, the current square already satisfied the city's parade needs and as a centre for demonstrations. For them, it was more important to preserve the city's traditional place of leisure than it was to eliminate green space for gaudy monuments.

In 1950, the head of Sevastopol's new government, Sergei Sosnitskii, submitted a modest request to Moscow that the planning for Primorskii Boulevard, one of the oldest places in the city, not be changed because the 'citizens of Sevastopol are very accustomed to the present layout, they will love [it] and be thankful if it remains in the present condition'.[32] When Viacheslav Shkvarikov, chairman of the Russian Federation's Administration on Architectural Affairs, suggested that more advisers from Moscow take part, the city's chief planner, Tamara Aleshina, argued that the 'boulevard must preserve its historically complex arrangement'. That included replanting chestnut trees destroyed during the war.[33] Local officials had grown weary of Moscow not recognizing the need for accommodating the population. Primorskii remained relatively untouched and Sevastopol's leaders got their wish, although, as Sosnitskii's remarks made clear, local officials knew that Moscow could decide all things. However, it appears that appeals such as this from the periphery to the centre showed officials in Moscow that local morale – essential in a military city – would be much higher if the city's heritage and traditions were preserved right down to the last chestnut tree.

In addition to places for strolling, an important locus for cultured leisure was the theatre. During Sevastopol's reconstruction, the planning of the new Lunacharsky Drama Theatre, replacing the old one that had been bombed to rubble, became the battleground for public and private contestation of space. In November 1948, chief municipal architect Iurii Trautman released his plans to complete the reconstruction of Sevastopol in 'three to four years', per Stalin's decree.[34] Part of this plan included the placement of the new, ornate theatre opposite Vladimir Cathedral. Trautman was following the recommendations that the Committee on Architectural Affairs in Moscow had given Barkhin.[35] Renowned Moscow architect I. V. Zholtovskii's proposed theatre, despite the over 17 million rouble price tag which ballooned to 21.1 million roubles before the plan was scrapped and handed to Trautman, had been approved by a group of experts that preferred a site on the central hill where the theatre could be seen from anywhere in the city. The variant plan had placed it along the ring road below. [36]

When Trautman made the plans public nearly two years later, the local population was furious at not being consulted properly and at what it perceived as the destruction of tradition. The local population countered, noting that the theatre would only accommodate the needs of the population if it was accessible. Both the theatre administration and audience were enlisted to level criticism against the planned location. [37] The published letters echoed much of the sentiment of the unpublished: building must take place near a central square with trolleybus stops so as to eliminate the dangerous winter climb up stairs to the hilltop. Unpublished letters from the workers and administrators at the State Khersones Museum wanted the theatre placed near its prewar location on Primorskii Boulevard. Moreover, the unpublished letters provided sketches of a new façade that represented a style closer to south shore Crimean traditions. [38] The amount of detail in the unpublished letters surely excluded them from the chief municipal newspaper *Slava Sevastopolia* because they countered the new policy of centralism that began to re-emerge in 1948. Moreover, the drawings challenged prevailing aesthetic trends, taking localism too much to heart. [39] However, local input carried the day as Trautman's theatre was placed back on the perimeter of Primorskii Boulevard between the ornate Corinthian façades of Trautman's new Sevastopol Hotel and the House of Pioneers (the prewar Sechenov Institute of Physical Therapy) in nearly the exact same spot that, two years earlier, the Committee on Architectural Affairs had rejected in favour of the central hill. The theatre was now bounded by the main ring road along the bus route, the waterfront of Artillery Bay and residents' favourite park, thus accommodating both the need for leisure and tradition.

Conclusions

Defining socialist space in the reconstruction of Sevastopol after the Second World War was not easy and it strayed in many ways from more accessible definitions of 'socialist'. There was no discussion of class, the means of production, the evils of capitalism or social justice. The socialist space in postwar Sevastopol was in step with Russian and local traditions and history that could be incorporated into a larger and newly defined type of Soviet socialism. Glorification of Russia and Russians replaced the ethnic heterogeneity of internationalism as Tatar and Jewish heritage was erased from the city map. The new socialist space was marked as often by heroes who had defended the Russian Empire from France and Great Britain, as by those who had fought against Hitler's forces, and frequently they were placed in graves next to each other as sites of mourning and remembrance for the ritualised visits of schoolchildren. Heroism and a willingness to sacrifice for the defence of the Motherland was the trait most prized, whether before or after the Revolution. The new space accommodated the need to remember and be recognized as a unique part of something larger. Acquiescing to local needs for a familiar space created less dissension than Moscow's reconceptualization of the space would perhaps have done in a vitally important part of the USSR's Cold War machine. Likewise, the renewed Sevastopol contained the services necessary for the population. In addition to places of leisure and recreation discussed here, hospitals, schools, water facilities and more were all restored over the first postwar decade. In the end, the regime, through consultation with local officials and residents, arrived at a new definition of socialist space that recognized the material needs of the population, respected its tradition and still maintained the veneer of authority by reserving the right to approve all plans. The new socialist space as it emerged in Sevastopol after the Second World War was one steeped in its own history of heroic defence of the Russian/Soviet Motherland, which respected the city's traditions and needs. Power was diffuse in the Soviet system and in cases where one industry (or in this case the navy) dominated, that fiefdom could often alter policy. It is not coincidental that the Sevastopol that emerged after the Second World War was more centred on it naval heritage; naval officials were an integral part in the redesign process and the most prominent institution in the city. Although other local studies like this have not yet been written, some scant material in Moscow's central archives shows that Sevastopol was not alone in proposing an urban biography quite different from that envisaged by appointed architects from the centre. Further local studies may well bring this to light. Throughout four turbulent decades of dramatic destruction and change, the Soviet regime simply could not operate as a monolith, and reconstruction was no exception. After the unprecedented freedoms of wartime, during which the military gained significant prominence, the regime chose to accommodate the needs of local residents and institutions rather than waging a costly internal battle as the Cold War emerged.

In the end, Sevastopol's planners had reached a compromise. Soviet institutions such as the Party, government, NKVD, and navy had prominent headquarters in the city centre; however, the dominant theme that emerged in the postwar decade was reverence for the city's Russian Imperial history. No longer did the urban space remind residents of the city's heterogeneous ethnic and religious heritage. Moreover, although in 1957 a statue of Lenin again stood in the city, this time high on the central hill, it was the only monument to Soviet power in the city centre and was surrounded by reminders of another past. Vladimir Cathedral and the crypts of the four admirals remained directly opposite his statue on the central hill, and on the square below a statue to Admiral Nakhimov was erected where Lenin's statue had stood before the war.

Notes

My thanks to the Kennan Institute for Advanced Russian Studies, the American Council of Teachers of Russian and the Center for the Study of Russia and the Soviet Union for their financial and administrative support of this project.

1. *Slava Sevastopolia* (hereafter *Slava*), 4 November 1949, p. 1. The translation of *rodnoi gorod* as 'hometown' masks a more intimate relation. *Rodnoi* implies a deep, personal and affectionate relationship. Moreover, it is the only word on the banner written in script and not block letters, thus drawing attention to its significance.
2. The non-martial use of military terminology was not an invention of the postwar years. After the civil war and especially during the 1930s, every campaign for production, whether industrial or agricultural, was couched in similar terms. See Hiroaki Kuromiya, *Stalin's Industrial Revolution: Politics and Workers, 1928–1932* (Cambridge: Cambridge University Press, 1988); Lewis H. Siegelbaum, *Stakhanovism and the Politics of Productivity in the USSR, 1935-1941* (Cambridge: Cambridge University Press, 1988); Sheila Fitzpatrick, *Stalin's Peasants: Resistance and Survival in the Russian Village After Collectivization* (New York: Oxford University Press, 1994); Lynne Viola, *The Best Sons of the Fatherland: Workers in the Vanguard of Soviet Collectivization* (New York: Oxford University Press, 1987).
3. Stephen Kotkin, in his detailed history of the construction of Magnitogorsk, defined 'bread' as 'state supply', and 'circus' as 'the entire panoply of political propaganda and organized amusement'. These

definitions, however, are less than adequate when explaining the construction of socialist spaces because too much focus is placed on economics and entertainment. Stephen Kotkin, *Magnetic Mountain: Stalinism as a Civilization* (Berkeley: University of California Press, 1995), pp. 238–79; quote p. 276. See Vera Sandomirsky Dunham, *In Stalin's Time: Middleclass Values in Soviet Fiction*, enlarged and updated edn (Durham: Duke University Press, 1990) for a similar process that she calls the 'big deal'.

4. Timothy Dunmore described agitation as 'political education of the masses through such media as radio, daily newspapers and books'. See his *Soviet Politics, 1945–1953* (New York: St Martin's, 1984), p. 104. Architecture, although he does not include it as an agitational medium, is meant for mass consumption and does not rely on abstract theory (a principal tool of propaganda) as a persuasive force. For a further discussion see Peter Kenez, *The Birth of the Propaganda State: Soviet Methods of Mass Mobilization, 1917–1929* (Cambridge: Cambridge University Press, 1985).

5. The most accessible source of press material on the battles for Sevastopol remains the collection of articles translated for foreign consumption: *The Heroic Defence of Sevastopol* (Moscow: Foreign Languages Publishing House, 1942); *Sevastopol: November, 1941– July, 1942: Articles, Stories and Eye-witness Accounts by Soviet War Correspondents* (London: Hutchison, 1943). These are adequate translations of the original articles that appeared in *Pravda, Krasnaia zvezda* and other newspapers.

6. Gosudarstvennyi arkhiv goroda Sevastopolia, hereafter GAGS f. R-79, op. 2, d. 20, ll. 12–14 and *Sevastopoliu 200 let, 1783–1983: Sbornik dokumentov i materialov* (Kiev: Naukova dumka, 1983), pp. 259–66.

7. *Istoriia goroda-geroiia Sevastopolia, 1917–1957* (Kiev: Akademiia nauk Ukrainskoi SSR, 1953), pp. 289–90; GAGS f. R-359, op. 1, d. 7, l. 23; GAGS f. R-359, op. 1, d. 10, l. 18.

8. Rossiiskii gosudarstvennyi arkhiv ekonomiki, hereafter RGAE, f. 9432, op. 1, d. 243, l. 1.

9. A short list of architects and their cities would include: Georgii Gol'ts (Smolensk), Boris Iofan (Novorossisk), Aleksei Shchusev (Istra), Lev Rudnev (Voronezh) and V. N. Semenov (Rostov on Don). For more on the purges see Hugh Hudson, *Blueprints and Blood: The Stalinization of Soviet Architecture, 1917–1937* (Princeton: Princeton University Press, 1994). On a similar purge starting in 1948 see K. Alabian, 'Arkhitekturnaia praktika v svete reshenii TsK VKP(b) o literature i iskusstve', *Arkhitektura i stroitel'stvo* (henceforth *AiS*) 14 (1947),

pp. 1–4; G. A. Simonov, 'Vazhneishie zadachi sovetskikh arkhitektorov', *AiS*, 3 (March 1948), pp. 1–4; 'Na sobranii aktiva moskovskikh
arkhitektorov', *AiS*, 4 (April 1948), pp. 13–16; 'O lozhnoi kontseptsii
knigi "Gradostroitel'stvo"', *AiS*, 4 (April 1948), back cover; 'Za
marksistskuiu nauku ob arkhitekture', *AiS*, 9 (September 1948),
pp. 1–3. A brief overview can be found in Karl D. Qualls, 'Raised
from Ruins: Restoring Popular Allegiance Through City Planning
in Sevastopol, 1944–1953' (Ph. D. dissertation, Georgetown University, 1998), ch. 6. Peter Blake, 'The Soviet Architectural Purge',
Architectural Record 106 (September 1949), pp. 127–9, provides a
limited evaluation of this bloodless purge.

10. RGAE f. 9432, op. 1, d. 3, l. 54.
11. V. A. Lavrov, 'Istoricheskie pamiatniki v plane vosstanavlivaemykh
    gorodov', *PSG* 1 (1947), pp. 10–17; N. Voronin, 'The Destruction of
    Old Russian Cities', *VOKS Bulletin* 4 (1943), pp. 14–21; V. A. Lavrov,
    'Vosstanovlenie velikogo Novgoroda', *Arkhitektura SSSR* (henceforth
    AS) 9 (1945), pp. 9–15; G. Gol'ts, 'Smolensk: k proekty vosstanov-
    leniia goroda', *AS* 10 (1945), pp. 3–6; V. A. Lavrov, 'Puti vosstanov-
    leniia Pskova', *AS* 13 (1946), pp. 3–7.
12. RGAE f. 9432, op. 1, d. 243, ll. 9–11ob.
13. RGAE f. 9432, op. 1, d. 243, ll. 11.
14. G. Barkhin, 'Proekt budushchego: pochetnoe zadanie', *Slava* (18
    May 1945), p. 1; GAGS f. R-79, op. 2, d. 30-a.
15. For a further discussion of the dynamics between 'local' and central
    officials see Karl Qualls, 'Local-Outsider Negotiations in Sevast-
    opol's Postwar Reconstruction, 1944–53', in Donald J. Raleigh, ed.,
    Provincial Landscapes: The Local Dimensions of Soviet Power
    (Pittsburgh, PA: University of Pittsburgh Press, 2001).
16. *Gosudarstvennyi arkhiv Rossiiskoi Federatsii*, hereafter GA RF, f. A-
    150, op. 2, d. 52, ll. 1–10; GA RF f. A-150, op. 2, d. 52, ll. 1–10.
17. RGAE f. 9432, op. 1, d. 241, ll. 15–25; quote l. 21.
18. GA RF f. A-150, op. 2, d. 52, ll. 32–35. This document also shows
    that the City Architectural Commission met on 15 May 1945 to
    discuss the general plan with municipal and naval organizations after
    the 16 April city-wide viewing. On 13 October the Architectural
    Council of Crimea and City Architectural Commission met to discuss
    the plan further. Two days later the commander of the Black Sea
    Fleet called an interdepartmental commission together to discuss the
    plan with Barkhin and the city commission.
19. Many of these admirals and others had been 'created' heroes in the
    late nineteenth century, despite less than valorous activity during the

Crimean War. See Serhii Plokhy, 'The City of Glory: Sevastopol in Russian Historical Mythology', *Journal of Contemporary History* 35 (2000), pp. 369–83.

20. See Alexander Nekrich, *The Punished Peoples: The Deportation and Fate of Soviet Minorities at the End of the Second World War*, trans. George Saunders (New York: Norton, 1978); Robert Conquest, *The Nation Killers: The Soviet Deportation of Nationalities* (London: Macmillan, 1970); V. N. Zemskov, 'Spetsposelentsy (po dokument-atsii NKVD-MVD SSSR)', *Sotsiologicheskie issledovaniia* 11 (1990), p. 9.

21. GAGS photos 6411 (1939), 1-11807a and 1-12028 (1944), 3424 and 3332 (1946) and 12483 (1914).

22. GAGS f. R-79, op. 2, d. 56 (Gorispolkom Protocol 35/44); GAGS f. R-79, op. 1, d. 51, l. 20 (*oblast*'s decision); GAGS f. R-79, op. 2, d. 63, l. 11 (Council approval). The *oblast*'s decision noted that 70–75 per cent of the building had been damaged, but since 'at the present time Sevastopol has no believers of the Muslim creed' there was no reason to preserve the building as a mosque.

23. Throughout 1946 various administrations exchanged letters, petitions and evaluations. Sevastopol's leaders mediated the debate, made rulings and overturned themselves. GAGS f. R-308, op. 1, d. 24, l. 23; GAGS f. R-308, op. 1, d. 20, l. 85; GAGS f. R-308, op. 1, d. 31, ll. 187–188ob; and GAGS f. R-308, op. 2, d. 5.

24. GAGS f. R-79, op. 2, d. 57.

25. GAGS f. R-79, op. 2, d. 131, l. 88.

26. GAGS photo 3394 (1951) of the nearly completed archive.

27. GAGS photos 5221 (1941) and 5222 (1944).

28. For the full text of Sovnarkom resolution 1384 and appended instruc-tions see GAGS f. R-308, op. 1, d. 1, ll. 7–10 and RGAE f. 9432, op. 1, d. 6 from 13 October 1944.

29. GA RF f. A-259, op. 5, d. 279, ll. 16–18.

30. Amir Weiner, likewise, argues that one's role in the war, not class or ethnicity, became the marker of status for the postwar generation. This seems equally true when discussing the hierarchy of cities in the national myth and the presentation of cities in urban planning. See Weiner's 'The Making of a Dominant Myth: The Second World War and the Construction of Political Identities within the Soviet Polity', *Russian Review* 55 (October 1996), pp. 638–60 and *Making Sense of War: The Second World War and the Fate of the Bolshevik Revolution* (Princeton: Princeton University Press, 2000).

31. GAGS f. R-79, op. 2, d. 30-a, l. 9.

32. GA RF f. A-150, op. 2, d. 254, ll. 30–48. Stenogram of the 1 March 1950 evening session. Quote ll. 35-36.
33. GA RF f. A-150, op. 2, d. 254, ll. 38–9.
34. 'Vosstanovym rodnoi Sevastopol v 3–4 goda! Novoe v proekte tsentra goroda', *Slava*, 26 Nov 1948, p. 1.
35. RGAE f. 9432, op. 1, d. 50, l. 27. The full text of the discussion is found in ll. 1–31 and RGAE f. 9432, op. 1, d. 243, ll. 191–205. The protocol for the meeting is in RGAE f. 9432, op. 1, d. 154, ll. 300-301.
36. RGAE f. 9432, op. 1, d. 243a, ll. 9–14; GAGS f. R-308, op. 1, d. 21, ll. 22–7.
37. B. Gorskii and B. Bertel, 'Stroit' teatr na udobnom meste', *Slava*, 27 Nov 1948, p. 1; 'Zriteli o stroitel'stve novogo teatra', *Slava*, 3 Dec 1948, p. 1.
38. Four letters have been preserved in the central archives noting the reservations of various groups (RGAE, f. 9432, op. 1, d. 154, ll. 263–8). Workers at the State Khersones Museum, the archaeological museum for 2500-year-old Greek ruins, would obviously have a bias toward tradition and preservation.
39. For a more thorough investigation of the discrepancies between the official press and unreleased materials see Donald J. Raleigh, 'Languages of Power: How the Saratov Bolsheviks Imagined Their Enemies', *Slavic Review* 57, no. 2 (1998), pp. 320–49.

−3−

Living in the Russian Present with a German Past: The Problems of Identity in the City of Kaliningrad.*

Olga Sezneva

Radio Armenia once asked 'Is it possible to foretell the future?'
Answer: 'Yes, that is no problem: we know exactly what the future will be like. *Our problem is with the past: it keeps changing'.*[1]

I recall a spring day in 1984 when, as one of a group of teenagers, I crossed the trestle bridge in the centre of Kaliningrad. This scene is part of a familiar landscape, reproduced on numerous postcards and in tourist guides. As far as one's eye can see there are housing projects constructed from white prefabricated cement panels and erected alongside the second main avenue of the city, Moskovskii Prospekt. Derricks and tip-up lorries occupy the construction site of the House of Soviets (*Dom sovetov*). The memorial to Soviet Sailor Heroes stands on the bank of the river. Suddenly a startling contrast confronts us, the bright white boxes of high-rise blocks encircling the deserted island on which the red brick cavernous walls of old Königsberg Cathedral stand. Black smoke stains the old brick. The roof is shattered. The cathedral's former grandeur is reduced to a sinister skeleton. It was described in this state by a former General Secretary of the Communist Party as 'the rotten tooth of the city'. He had passed away, but his metaphor, thrown in the face of the city's residents, lived on.

'Why don't we live in Königsberg, the real Königsberg! We are the barbarians . . . The city will get its revenge for what we've done to it,' exclaims one of my friends. We keep silent for a while, suffering the impossibilities of our dreams and desires. How did we – children of 'normal' Soviet citizens – acquire this nostalgia for the German past? Where did these naive and radical judgments come from? I returned to the communal apartment where I lived with my family. We shared it with a neighbour whose name sounded enigmatic to me – Udo. We knew he was a German born in Königsberg. He spoke Russian with a slight accent, and had worked as a stoker all his life. He avoided talking about the past even though we were good friends and 'Italian' was written on the 'nationality' line of his Soviet passport. It was definitely not from Udo that I picked up the fever for the city's past. And were my friends and I alone in our nostalgia for the unknown?

The 'Socialist City' and Limits of Theory

The temporal and spatial reordering that has resulted from the demise of the Soviet Bloc has engendered new theoretical approaches to the nature of authoritarian regimes and the relationships between power and its subjects. In Eastern Europe, the socialist past resurfaces in publications of individual recollections of the oppressions of former regimes; in the exhumation of dead bodies, both famous and anonymous; in the renaming of cities; and in the demolition of monuments and memorials. The first two phenomena point to an inextricable link between history, power and its subjects, whilst the rush to rename and remake cities signals the centrality of urban space in the construction of post-socialist identities. This essay will interrogate some of these processes by focusing on the conversion of the former German city, Königsberg, into a Soviet and later Russian one, Kaliningrad.

Space is socially constructed through political and social activity.[2] It can also impose constraints and limitations on human development, sometimes with unexpected twists.[3] It is in this sense that urban space is a repository of memory and history; it has the capacity to carry cultural meanings that may be exchanged among social groups and generations. This observation, however, has not tended to find its way to more conventional analyses of socialist cities. The 'socialist city' has generally been theorized in ways that reveal the legacy of the totalitarian model shaped in political science. The disciplines of urban sociology and social geography have treated the socialist city as a product of centralized state design, and a creation of a single actor, the socialist state.[4] The Soviet city was imagined as a place with a highly controlled organizational structure that provided little space for unsanctioned memories and pasts. This model disregards ordinary people's relationship with a place, the particular lived experience of the quality of life that Raymond Williams has called 'a structure of feelings'. A set of common values, perceptions and conventions developed in a complex negotiation between dominant and oppositional cultural forms can, in Williams's terms, constitute place-specific social experience.[5]

The observations that follow are based largely on an empirical study of the social production of history in the city once known as Königsberg and, since 1946, as Kaliningrad, by the Russian-speaking population.[6] How do these people, who have no direct connection with the former German residents, make use of a foreign past? What might the answer to this question reveal about the relationship between the Soviet (authoritarian) state and its subjects? The case of Kaliningrad shows how polyvocal identifications with place can be produced along the border of national and regional histories, two distinctive frames for collective imagination. My examination of the emergence and contestation of two forms of urban history focuses on the relationship between officially issued representations and unofficial, popular ones. Produced in dialogue with each other, they are highly intertextual and mutually referential.

From Königsberg to Kaliningrad: a brief history

Kaliningrad appeared on the world map at the end of the Second World War on the site of the conquered and annexed German city of Königsberg. The Potsdam Conference in July-August 1945 ratified the transfer of two Baltic sea ports, Königsberg and Memel, to the Soviet Union, and Königsberg became a region within the Russian Federation. In 1946, the city was renamed 'Kaliningrad'. The postwar reconstruction of the city paralleled that taking place throughout the Soviet Union. Despite the particular character of the surviving urban fabric – fragments of German churches, lines of burgher villas, cobblestone roads and distinctively angled, red-tiled house roofs – there was no attempt to emphasize the distinctive architectural character of Kaliningrad. On the contrary, every effort was made to bring it into line with the generic socialist city. Nevertheless, Kaliningrad's proximity to the West and separation from Russia by Soviet Lithuania, together with the restrictions of access placed on foreign visitors determined by the military/strategic significance of the city, distinguished it as different from other Soviet places. In local discourses on the territory's relationship with 'mainland' Russia and Soviet central government, Kaliningrad figures as a 'forgotten land'.

This postwar image of Kaliningrad contrasted sharply with that of the historic, Hanseatic city of Königsberg formed from the unification of three medieval Germanic settlements. The Königsberg castle was erected on the highest point of the city in 1261 and was counterbalanced by Standamm Kirche in 1263. The Königsberg Dom of 1333 hosted the largest collection of books in Central Europe in the sixteenth century and Immanuel Kant was the last university professor to be buried in the cathedral. The significance of the city in European culture was expressed by Ernst Gellner:

> It was in Königsberg that the torch of the Enlightenment burned with its fiercest flame, in the thought and person of Immanuel Kant, who was a universal mind without ever having left the city; and it was there too that the Jewish followers of Moses Mendelssohn systematically transmitted the new secular European wisdom to the East European Jewish community. . . . But this total discontinuity between the Königsberg of Kant and Mendelssohn, and the Kaliningrad of today (whose illustrious sons, if any, remain unknown), is not a contingent external fact. [Its] elimination was the work of two political movements and systems which were unambiguously and conspicuously the fruits, whether directly or by reaction, of that very Enlightenment which had shone on the Baltic shore at least as brightly as it had done in Berlin, Paris, Glasgow or Edinburgh.[7]

It was by antithesis to this image of the city that Kaliningrad was to be built. This was not only a process of physical reconfiguration but, importantly, one based on the acquisition of a new image and new ideology.

The Work of the State in the Construction of History

The authoritarian modernity of the Soviet state was characterized by a prescriptive approach to most spheres of social life including the past. It developed a particular time-consciousness or 'historicity' (not unique to the Soviet state but a feature of Western modernity in general[8]). Characterized by the irreversibility of events, this kind of temporality promoted a linear and progressive view of social change. The teleology of progress was underscored by a vulgar determinism: present-day happenings were viewed as the outcome of preceding patterns of events. Although readily adopted in other Soviet contexts, historicity was threatening in Kaliningrad in that it might encourage unwanted parallels of past and present, as well as invite discomforting predictions. The only solution to the 'problems' presented by Kaliningrad was to adopt the strategy of a 'radical break' with, and erasure of, the past.

Until the late 1980s, the official version of Kaliningrad's history placed great emphasis on the taking of the city by the Red Army in 1945 as a total historical rupture. It identified the past with a particular episode in its history: the fascist period in the decade before the Second World War. A new generation – not only of different nationality but also of a new kind, that of the mythical 'new Soviet person' – took the place of the former German population. A new image of the city was produced and celebrated as a national achievement: 'Today's Kaliningrad is the honoured capital of the Amber land, a port-city, a garden-city, blown by Baltic winds. It is a peace keeper on the western border of our Motherland, a city looking to its future . . .'[9]

Reconfiguring time and defining a new vector of its development was crucial. As a recent official account stresses:

> The new era began in Kaliningrad in April 1945. Half a century ago, the youngest, western-most and the most multi-national province [*oblast'*] of our Motherland arose from the remnants of ruined East Prussia. A former nest of fascist aggression was turned into a peaceful outpost on the border between the Russian Federation and Europe. Literally, every inch of this land is drenched with the blood of Russian soldiers and patriots.[10]

The construction of a new collective framework for the identity of the territory was mediated primarily through the state apparatuses and state agencies, and promoted by those connected with them – local administrators, teachers, officially privileged intellectuals, scholars and journalists. Two dominant representational strategies were employed by the State to incorporate Königsberg into the space of the Soviet Union. One was to create a local history of the Kaliningrad *oblast'*. The other was to attempt to integrate this territory into the general history of the Soviet Union. The image of the new land was publicized primarily through tourist guides and text books for the specialized secondary school course known as 'Regional Studies' (*kraevedenie*). These texts provided geographical information, detailed description of the natural landscape and resources of the region, and of its flora and fauna. They presented an easily comprehensible account of the storming of Königsberg at the end of the Second World War before moving to the industrial and agricultural development of the Soviet period. Furthermore, official art and literature on the theme of Kaliningrad formed a sort of epic genre celebrating the city's repopulation.

On what was effectively an evacuated historical ground and with the almost complete eradication of the city's past before 1945, the State's tactics were designed to instil in the newly arrived inhabitants a 'positive' identification with place. A simultaneous effect of this work was the subordination of the new territory to a hierarchical relationship of centre/periphery, both institutionally and symbolically, within the Soviet Union. Kaliningrad's peripheral position was first and foremost defined by its distinct profile as a military outpost that sealed the region off from foreigners and transport communication.[11] Moreover, the very peculiar administrative organization of the province contributed to its marginality. Kaliningrad was not treated like its neighbours, the Baltic republics, but was subordinated directly to the Russian Federation (i.e. as a province of the Russian Federation).

The construction of Kaliningrad as periphery was designed to erase the notion of a 'unique' German heritage and the sense of the city's historical distinctiveness. Everything that invoked the German past changed its name: cities and villages, streets, areas, and rivers. No historical investigation of the German past could be officially condoned or supported. Archaeological research conducted on the former Prussian territory was oriented toward the discovery of tribal settlements and 'primitive' cultures. Ideological emphasis was placed on the cultural encounters and cooperation between Prussians and early Slavic tribes. Moreover, the political reconstruction of the area required equating the status of the province with other provincial parts of the Soviet Union. From a Western perspective, Kaliningrad was turned into a blank spot on a discursive map of Europe.[12]

The process of de-historicization was conducted through the deconstruction of German remnants and the Sovietization of the cityscape by the application of standardized prefabricated building forms; the ideologically determined design of public spaces; and the wide use of visual propaganda. This reconfiguration did not necessarily reflect a clearly defined project to replan the city. Demolitions in the first decade after the war followed a pragmatic and utilitarian logic. These actions were part of efforts to improve the supply of residential housing. Historical preservation was never advocated in Kaliningrad. Its medieval European character was represented as antagonistic to the values of Soviet city planning. The ideological motivation behind the replanning and rebuilding of the city was directed not only against the specifically German and hence 'fascist' character of the city, but also against those features that were claimed to be generic to all capitalist cities: the uneven development of areas in the city; the poor state of working-class quarters; and the antiquated norms of light and air in office and residential buildings (Figure 3.1). Thus, Königsberg was not only associated with the specific 'guilt' of the German

Figure 3.1 The remnants of the medieval city gates surrounded by the prefabricated panel buildings of the 1980s. German landmarks appear in stark contrast to the later architectural developments, prompting interpretations and commentaries from the city residents

nation, but its roots were proclaimed to lie in the supranational context of capitalist development and were, as such, antagonistic to the Soviet 'way of life'. In 1946 the newspaper *Kaliningradskaia pravda*, asserted:

> It is important to note that the city centre was constructed by Germans un-systematically and in a barbarian way. In general, this is a characteristic of all capitalist cities. There are many streets so narrow that a cable car can barely move along. Wide avenues and tree-lined boulevards will replace these streets and buildings.[13]

Two years later the same newspaper reported:

> A young Soviet city grows and develops at a speed which is unfamiliar and unknown to capitalist cities. This is because only Soviet people are capable of realizing such a grandiose project . . . This is because a wise party of Bolsheviks leads them . . .[14]

Fifty years of planned *and* unplanned destruction had completely changed the image of the city. The ruins of the Standamm Kirche, one of the oldest buildings in Königsberg, were torn down in the early 1950s. The remnants of the medieval castle, despite the protests of a group of local intelligentsia, were blown up in 1969 to be replaced by the House of Soviets (*Dom sovetov*), the tallest building in the city. The new building on the site was, at that time, considered very modern: two towers were connected with a walkway on the level of the fifth floor.

Two of the four bridges across the River Pregel that had survived the war's bombing were destroyed in 1972 to allow construction of a modern trestle bridge. The ruined walls of the cathedral were not restored or preserved until the late 1980s (except where they acted as a supporting wall for the Immanuel Kant pantheon and tomb constructed in 1912–20 by architect Friedrich Lars). Throughout the period, German cemeteries were closed and later razed. Königsberg was used as a source of raw materials for rebuilding cities in Russia: new settlers dismantled its remnants and sent bricks to Russia, where the main tasks of postwar reconstruction were being carried out. Although the radial structure of Königsberg was preserved, the centre was rearticulated and redefined. Streets and avenues were straightened and deprived of their medieval curves. Cobblestone roads were covered with asphalt.

It was a stock Cold War criticism of Soviet city planning that the new districts of modern cities all looked alike, with the kinds of nondescript buildings and memorials that one could find anywhere else in the Soviet Union. The standardization of architectural forms, construction materials, and the organization of public space resulted from the new housing programme announced by Khrushchev and the centralization of architectural and construction agencies in the interest of efficiency. In order to be perceived as omnipresent and 'unavoidable', as Alexei Yurchak has argued, state ideology promoted the 'sameness' of Soviet space.[15] It operated through the 'hegemony of representation', the selection and use of state-determined imagery in the design and organization of city space throughout the country. Predictable and standardized space thus enhanced the incorporation of Königsberg into the ideological space of the Soviet Union. This was achieved both through the organization of city spaces (through buildings, urban planning and the placement of visual representations such as slogans and memorials) and through the representation of the city for others (in, for instance, postcards of city vistas and tourist guides). In each of these projects, reference to the city's German heritage was prohibited. For instance, the depiction of red roof tiles, once widespread in Königsberg, was proscribed: documentary film-makers were compelled to compose their pictures so that these tiles were carefully left outside the frame. My informants stressed many times that there was an official 'canon' of images of the city available for use on postcards and in tourist guides.

However, as I show below, the construction of identity advanced by the State and the particular forms of Soviet patriotism it was intended to engender were not fully embraced by the city's population. The city's specific heritage was turned into a 'weapon' in the struggle for a position in the hierarchy of Soviet cities. The State's attempts to eliminate historical and cultural contradictions through the reconfiguration of the material fabric of the city was challenged by the people's imagination, in which unsanctioned interpretations of history, new and old buildings developed. Official attempts to produce a new sense of place within a unifying ideological frame had to be moderated to accommodate the critical reactions of various social groups.

Memory and Mockery in the Production of Place

In the early 1980s, a group of intellectuals in Kaliningrad organized an underground society, the Prussian club (*Prusskii klub*). The aim of this organization, which today operates officially, was 'to recreate the unity of history'. Its stated goals were to 'compile an inventory of the objects of German architecture; to popularize the heraldry and symbols of East Prussia; and to establish contacts with former residents of Königsberg'.[16] Members of the society adopted Prussian names (in addition to their 'mundane' Russian names) and impersonated Prussian heroes and historical personalities.

The society collaborated closely with a small circle of artists and sculptors, whose common project was the 'historical reconstruction of Königsberg' in paintings. Drawing partially on prewar pictures and other documentary materials but primarily on the artist's imagination, their works romanticized and idealized the no longer extant city of Königsberg. When I asked one of the artists involved in the project why they chose to represent Königsberg in terms of a historical fiction rather than through study of its 'actual' history, he explained: 'it is more pleasing to be an object for a myth or fairy tale than of history, since the product of fantasy is not liable to ideological modification'. Taking a stand against the official view, this form of popular history has attempted to bridge German past and Russian present. The city's landscape has become a terrain on which the battle for recognition of the German heritage as part of the symbolic struggle for place has been fought. It was a covert conflict during the Soviet period, becoming more open in the late 1980s and 1990s. The interpersonal exchange of historical narrative was impossible (the German population had been exiled) and so the pre-Soviet past was silenced. Moreover, a significant part of the city (especially its central districts) had been destroyed. For these reasons such forms of popular history required an imaginary reconstruction of the landscape of the city.

The circulation of alternatives to state-produced history may be interpreted, initially, as the production of urban identities that evaded the official construction of place. The official construction rendered Kaliningrad's history invisible and irrelevant to the Soviet state and its all-Union affairs, unlike other, 'authentically' Russian and, therefore, 'historical', cities. Through the production of a popular history, the residents of Kaliningrad opposed this kind of spatial effacement and fought for a position in a symbolic economy:

> A citizen of Kaliningrad would necessarily point out, first, that we, Kaliningraders, live in the centre of Europe, and secondly . . . oh, secondly, we have European time, an hour later than Moscow. Berlin is closer to us than Moscow. Poland and Lithuania are so close that we can reach out and touch them. And, of course, we are westernmost but we do not brag about it, simply because we are so used to it.[17]

The circulation of popular history illustrates not only the production by the residents of their own unique identity but also the resistance to the hegemonic discourse of the Soviet state. It was an escape, though at times unconscious, from a forced identification with the 'Soviet subject'. Through popular history, it was possible to place Kaliningrad into the history of the West: 'Everybody believed that Königsberg was the second city of Germany in importance, and a major cultural centre of Europe'.[18]

The tensions and controversies of the Sovietization of the German city found expression in various commentaries by its residents. Many of them did not participate in the reconstruction of the postwar city, like another informant, O.D., a thirty-eight-year-old woman:

> O.D.: Too many antagonisms came together in this territory. Maybe, not as much from the German side as from ours. Germans, perhaps, did not object much to our actions here. We, however, treated everything as 'fascist'. For instance, the drainage system. They named it 'fascist' and eliminated it. Or take the cemeteries. What did we do to them? Broke everything, spoiled, opened the graves. Did you see the Jewish cemetery? Tomb stones removed. You can still read German names on them . . . I like that park so much!
> O.S.: Even after such acts of destruction?
> O.D.: No, I don't see it as a destroyed cemetery. When I am there, I try to imagine how it looked before. Or as one would think of ancient ruins. I don't like to think of its reality.

Since an open critique of State policy and actions regarding the city's material culture was impossible, latent resistance to the State's actions took the form of irony and mockery. Consider the following testimony regarding the way the material space of the city was reconfigured:

> I witnessed how an old German cemetery was converted into a park of culture and rest (*park kul'tury i otdykha*). In one of the issues of the newspaper *Kaliningradskaia pravda* of 1948, I encountered an article describing how the architects worked on the development of 'this cultural project'. There was not a word about how this land had previously been used. Afterwards people called this place 'a park of the living and dead'.[19]

> Some time in the 1960s or 1970s, the first *khrushcheby* began to appear in the city, like those everywhere around the country. And then came ugly parodies of Le Corbusier, which were presented as the foundations of the 'enlightened' socialist future.[20]

The last quotation refers to the House of Soviets. People called it the 'Monster' because the still unfinished steel structure resembled a robot. Built on the highest point of the landscape, it remains visible from every other point in the city (Figure 3.2). This building has received a second life in the form of local stories and anecdotes:

Figure 3.2 One of the main avenues of Kaliningrad, Moskovskii Prospekt, with the House of Soviets erected on the site of the former royal castle. The once densely populated historic centre had been destroyed during the war and was rebuilt in the 1980s

It is called 'the would-be Tower of Pisa' because there was a rumour in the 1970s that the building was leaning. It was built partly on the old German foundations, partly on new Soviet ones. The Soviet foundations could not support the weight of the construction and shifted. People also call it 'the wisdom tooth': they are useless but everybody gets them.[21]

German ruins were romanticized, and mysterious stories about them circulated. For instance, the most popular product of collective imagination was the underground Königsberg of sewers, tunnels connecting different parts of the city, and bunkers hiding stolen museum treasures. Soviet constructions, meanwhile, were often lent humiliating interpretations. The Mother-Russia memorial presents an especially interesting case. This important official symbol and object of popular tales was represented in a tourist guide of 1976 in the following way (Figure 3.3):

Figure 3.3 The Mother-Russia (*Mat' Rossiia*) Memorial

The composition depicts a confident woman, walking vigorously and in sprightly fashion. She holds the arms of the Russian Federation in her left hand. Her right hand clearly gestures to the ground, indicating that this land belongs to Russia. The memorial commemorates the foundation of this young Soviet province. The sculpture is 5.25 m high. It is by B. Edunov.[22]

Resisting the official reading, people's imaginations reworked the memorial in another, significantly different way. The memorial was an especially productive subject for this kind of reverie because, accidentally or not, a finger of the right hand, directed down at a certain angle, appears as a particular attribute of masculine anatomy. Such a curious detail produced an alternative account of the memorial's origin and also signalled its ambiguity (Figure 3.3).

As the story goes, at the end of the 1940s a monument to Stalin had stood on this site. In 1957, after the XX Congress of the Communist Party the previous year, it was demolished, but the plinth remained in the centre of the city. At that time the Chief of the Municipal Party Committee had received an urgent order to place something on the pedestal to replace the demolished Stalin, 'something symbolic, meaningful . . .'. Meanwhile, the chief's son-in-law, an architect from Moscow, had been creating a design for a bee-keeping department at the Exhibition of the Achievements of People's Economy. A figure of Demeter, the goddess of the fertility of land, was not accepted by the department. She held a keg of honey in her left hand that had been interpreted as 'historically incorrect'. Through these local contacts, the figure of Demeter was proposed to supersede Stalin on his former pedestal in Kaliningrad. Her name was promptly changed by the authorities and she became 'Mother-Russia'.

That's how a male-looking woman in the square in the centre of the city appeared. She holds the arms in her left hand, and the finger of her right points down. People like to say that 'where the father of the peoples was before, the mother of land stays now . . . but she keeps her masculine essence'.[23]

Importantly, collective imagination together with irony and mockery led to practices that subverted the Soviet state's apparent representational hegemony. Through the production of alternative histories, the residents of Kaliningrad distanced themselves from the Soviet system. The unique history of Königsberg, its geographical specificity, and the imagination of its residents in the context of domination and ideological control by the Party, produced a favourable background for resistance to and subversion of state ideology.

A new *local* identity coincided with *perestroika* and the collapse of the Soviet Union – events that were the catalyst for a more general reconstruction of history. These processes proposed a seemingly new version of history and understanding of the place of Kaliningrad and its contemporary residents in European history. However, this was merely a new perspective on the same problems of identity. This understanding had emerged in the Soviet period in response to the ambiguity of the city's significance and belonging. It was reflected in various movements that developed ideas of historical heredity and continuity. The long-term tension between the state-promulgated representation of a history of Kaliningrad and its popular narration came into conflict with the fall of the Berlin Wall in 1989, and the collapse of the Soviet Union in 1991. At this time, a narrative that revived German heritage surfaced and became dominant, albeit not unproblematically.

Place, Identity and the Meaning of the Past

Kaliningrad's story is about the inventions of the past in a society where 'history writing has been the prerogative of a single-party state and its agents' and where 'monologic historical explanation' reproduced historical orthodoxies.[24] There is nothing new in the idea that new environments produce 'new histories'. A number of works have been written on how the officially promoted 'forgetfulness' of the past transmits forbidden histories into a reservoir of shared rememberings, often turning collective memories into a locus of resistance to official power.

Under Soviet rule, control of historic narrative was explicit and took a multiplicity of forms ranging from rigid guidelines for professional historians to an unapologetic censorship of visual representations, and even going as far as the destruction of physical structures in the city. As a result, the credibility of the official historiography was undermined, with a particular socio-cultural outcome: popular depictions and narratives of local events were often perceived as more truthful, and memories and lived experience became essential elements in the reconstruction of the past. The experience of living in a former German city discredited the official anti-German line and itself undermined the force of the regime's ideology.

The novelty of the case of Kaliningrad is that it yields unexpected glimpses into the role not merely of collective memory but also of imagination in the subversion of the official history. In conclusion, it is useful to review the differences between what was meant to be imagined and what actually was imagined about Königsberg/Kaliningrad.

First of all, the city had to be introduced into the nation (and conceived as an integral part of the Soviet Union, clearly defined in the hierarchy of functions and relations with other parts of the country). Benedict Anderson has suggested a subtle frame for the role of imagination in the history of the nation: he stresses that a nation does not result from predetermined sociological conditions.[25] Neither does it come from a primordial drive. The nation is imagined into existence. Imagination is an everyday social and common practice of citizens in the creation of a sense of unity and the commonwealth.

There are, it should be stressed, two kinds of imaginative practices deployed by the residents of Kaliningrad. One is the kind that, as Anderson's argument suggests, has permitted citizens, particularly during the early occupation of the city after the Second World War, to produce a feeling of shared homogeneous space. At the personal level, it allowed the individual – relocated to this region – to preserve an image of the community from which he or she came: either of a home region, town, village, or a particular ethnic culture. In this sense, the Kaliningrader's imagination worked for the integration of the place into the 'imagined community' of the Soviet Union.

Later, at the end of the 1960s, a new generation of Kaliningrad residents began to imagine the city *into* an imagined European community. This is the second kind of imaginative practice deployed in the city. If official discourse had symbolically removed this former part of Prussia from Western Europe, a parallel one in the imagination of ordinary people reinserted it. In one sense, both imaginative modes were similar to the extent that they took supra-national communities as a point of reference. What is more interesting, though, are the ways in which ordinary people deployed imagination in the representation of the place itself, and how these images contributed to the construction of a local identity. This kind of retrospective imagination of the city functioned like memory to provide material for popular history. However, because actual recall of Königsberg was impossible, memory was superseded by imagination. This resource made it possible to recreate both Königsberg's history and even its no longer extant cityscape. Whilst it is clear that historical narrative can be embedded and transparent in material objects, in the case of Kaliningrad it was a characteristic of buildings that no longer existed. Demolished by the Soviets, for instance, the city's German cathedrals had remained in people's memory.

The reasons why Kaliningraders sought to contest the official version of the city's past relates directly to a crisis in the official framework of Soviet collective identification. The invention of the prewar past, even though represented as a 'recovery' of it, was an act of agency subverting the structure of ideological state domination that aimed at the production of an alternative framework of collective identification.

Zygmunt Bauman, writing about identity, has suggested that the uncertainty in positioning the self, of behavioural styles, and of the ways in which one makes one's own presence proper and significant, encourages people to search for an imagined fixed point, embedded in 'identity'. Hence, identity is 'a critical projection of what is demanded and/or sought onto what *is*, or, more precisely, an oblique assertion of the inadequacy or incompleteness of the latter'.[26] Bauman asserts that identity is realized only at the moment that it springs into discourse as an individual, collective or scientific concern. Its ontological status is always in the present tense: its function is to resolve the tension between 'what is' and what is desired. Hence, 'identity' enters Time in the dimension of the present. Both history and collective memory, although referring to the past, are, in fact, attributes of the present.[27] This gives dynamism and openness not only to historical narrative but also to identity itself.

A clash between 'what is' and 'what is demanded' was characteristic of Soviet society as a whole in the period of 'stagnation' (1972–85). The profound inadequacy found its expression in almost all areas of social life: the 'black market' in an economy of shortage; corruption in a bureaucratic system; and the production of a 'parallel'/underground sphere in ideology and culture. Most of my witnesses' recollections of the revitalization of the memory of Königsberg stem from this period. In Kaliningrad, this overall crisis was deepened by a local schism between the shallow official history of a peripheralized city, and a 'remembered' centrality of the place in European history. The very act of remembrance was a political one: new residents in the city contrasted the imaginary reconstruction of Königsberg to standardized Kaliningrad. By such reconstruction people resisted, even if unconsciously, the hegemonic discourse of state power and the complete dissimulation of their city into the Soviet community.

Notes

* I would like to thank the Foundation for Urban and Regional Studies, London, for its generous support of this project.

1. Radio Armenia (in some versions 'Radio Erevan') was a fictitious voice of ridicule in the Soviet Union. It ridiculed the Communist regime with parodies of state ideology and slogans. Recently, a Polish friend admitted that 'the Radio Erevan series was highly popular in Poland for many years under communism'.

2. Henri Lefebvre, *The Production of Space*, trans. Donald Nicholson-Smith (Oxford and Cambridge, MA: Blackwells, 1991); Anssi Paasi, *Territories, Boundaries and Consciousness* (Chichester, New York, Brisbane, Toronto and Singapore: John Wiley & Sons, 2000); John Agnew and Stuart Corbrodge, eds, *Mastering Space: Hegemony, Territory and International Political Economy* (New York: Routledge, 1995).

3. Keith Basso and Steven Feld, 'Introduction', in Keith Basso and Steven Feld, eds, *Senses of Place* (Santa Fe: School of American Research Press, 1996).

4. G. Andrusz, M. Harloe and I. Szelenyi, *Cities under Socialism – and After* (Cambridge, MA: Blackwell, 1996) exemplifies this trend.

5. Raymond Williams, *The Long Revolution* (Westport, CT: Greenwood Press, 1975). For extended discussion of the 'structure of feelings' see his *Marxism and Literature* (Oxford: Oxford University Press, 1977).

6. My sources include officially printed tourist guides and pamphlets, propaganda in the printed media accompanying administrative campaigns for the demolition of German remains, as well as visual images of the architectural forms of a few German buildings, constructions erected during the Soviet period and altered remnants of German buildings appropriated after the war. I have also examined a collection of urban legends, *Mestnoe vrem'ia: Progulki po Kaliningradu* written by Aleksandr Popadin (Kaliningrad: Iantarnyi skaz, 1998). This collection of popular city legends allows examination of the meanings and interpretations given by ordinary people to Soviet construction. These tales revolve around German buildings as well. Having grown up in Kaliningrad, I can verify that the stories collected here were well known among Kaliningrad's residents.

7. Ernst Gellner, 'For Love of the World. Biography of Hannah Arendt' (book review), *The Times Literary Supplement*, 6 August 1982, pp. 844–5.

8. Anthony Giddens, *A Contemporary Critique of Historical Materialism*, vol. 1 (Berkeley and Los Angeles, CA: University of California Press, 1981).

9. *Znakom'tes': Kaliningrad!* (Kaliningrad: Kaliningradskoe knizhnoe, 1985), p. 3.

10. *Kaliningrad. Iubileinyi al'bom* (Kaliningrad: Iantarnyi skaz, 1996), p. 5.
11. Pertti Joennierni, 'Kaliningrad: A Region in Search for a Past and a Future', *Mare Balticum*, 1998, p. 88.
12. Christian Wellmann, 'Russia's Kaliningrad Enclave at the Crossroads', in *Cooperation and Conflict* (1996), p. 172.
13. *Kaliningradskaia pravda*, 1946, as cited in Iurii Kostiashov, 'Pereselenie glazami pereselentsev', 1997, unpublished manuscript.
14. *Kaliningradskaia pravda*, 1948, as cited in Kostiashov, 'Pereselenie'.
15. Alexei Yurchak, 'The Cynical Reason of Late Socialism', *Public Culture,* vol. 9, issue 2 (1997), pp. 161–88.
16. Regulations of the Prussian Club, 1985, oral version. New regulations, adopted in 1991, include: the study of the original names of the city's districts and streets; popularization of the history of Prussia among school students; opening the Museum of Prussia.
17. Popadin, *Mestnoe vrem'ia.*
18. An artist, personal communication, summer 1998.
19. A journalist, personal communication, summer 1998.
20. An artist, personal communication, autumn 1997.
21. Popadin, *Mestnoe vrem'ia.*
22. *Znakom'tes': Kaliningrad!,* p. 17.
23. Popadin, *Mestnoe vrem'ia.*
24. Andrew Lass and Rubie S. Watson, 'From Memory to History', in Rubie S. Watson, ed., *Memory, History and Opposition under State Socialism* (Sante Fe, NM: School of American Research Press, 1994) pp. 1–3.
25. Benedict Anderson, *Imagined Communities: Reflections on the Origin and Spread of Nationalism* (London: Verso, 1983).
26. Zygmunt Bauman, 'From Pilgrim to Tourist – or a Short History of Identity', in Paul Du Gay and Stuart Hall, eds, *Questions of Cultural Identity* (London: Sage, 1997), pp. 17–20.
27. The presentist definition of collective memory as a reservoir of history, developed in the writings of Maurice Halbwachs, seems the most compelling perspective for explaining the Kaliningrad phenomenon. See Maurice Halbwachs, *On Collective Memory* (Chicago: University of Chicago Press, 2002).

–4–

The Role of Monumental Sculpture in the Construction of Socialist Space in Stalinist Hungary

Reuben Fowkes

The first postwar May Day celebrations of 1945 saw major Budapest public spaces such as Heroes' Square occupied by uncontrolled, heterogeneous crowds. Meanwhile, more orderly public celebrations were held at the Soviet war memorials inaugurated that day on three major public squares. Only seven years later, the carnivalesque element had been completely extinguished; the stage-managed ranks of workers, peasants and soldiers who gathered for the inauguration of the *Stalin Statue* were participating in a mass political theatre that sought to celebrate and cement the bond between the leaders and the led. Building socialism involved changing people's minds and view of history, not just the material conditions of their lives, and new public monuments were expected to play a major educational role in this respect. Equally, the demolition of reactionary monuments was part of the campaign to suppress or eliminate signs of Hungary's bourgeois past. At a time of huge social and cultural change, monuments were designed to proclaim the imminent arrival of the communist utopia and demonstrate the strength and permanence of the new political order.

This essay looks at changes to the public statuary of Budapest between the end of the Second World War and the establishment of Stalinism in Hungary. The intention is to investigate the relationship between politics and public sculpture, and observe the process by which the communist state apparatus tried to use monuments to control public space. I begin by considering the situation during the immediate postwar period of coalition politics, both in terms of the removal of statues of the old regime and the erection of new monuments. An intensification of official efforts to dominate public space and construct a new socialist monumental landscape accompanied the imposition of the Soviet model on Hungary after 1948.

Arguably, the culmination of the attempt to construct socialist monumental public space in Hungary came with the building of the *Stalin Statue*, while its destruction at the hands of angry crowds in 1956 confirmed the failure of the spatial project of the Stalinist utopia.

The Postwar Political Context

In the first provisional government established behind Soviet lines in Debrecen in November 1944, the communists controlled only two ministries, those of agriculture and commerce. The quasi-democratic political context within which the Hungarian Communist Party operated in the immediate postwar period initially limited its ability to control public space and the visual environment. The parliamentary elections of November 1945, in which the centre-right Smallholders Party gained an absolute majority and the communists came third behind the social democrats, resulted in the creation of a coalition government whose three communist portfolios were only secured through the intervention of Marshal Voroshilov, chairman of the Allied Control Commission (ACC), the Soviet-dominated body that administered the military occupation of Hungary until a peace treaty was signed in 1947.

Over the next two years the communists worked aggressively to improve their position through political intimidation, 'salami tactics' to split the other parties, and reliance on tacit Soviet support. Although they quickly became the most important political force in the country, their hands were tied by the influence of non-communist bureaucrats and politicians in local and national government. In the field of public monuments, this restricted their legal powers to remove reactionary statues, and resulted in a politically moderate statue-building programme. The only exception was where Soviet interests were directly involved, for example over the removal of irredentist monuments and the erection of Soviet memorials. In these cases the Soviets intervened directly to achieve their aims.

In addition to the limitations set by the coalition government, the communists were held back in their desire to transform Hungarian society along socialist lines by Moscow, which initially forbade them from copying the Soviet model. The result was a short period of pluralism and a mixed economy. Public space, both in the everyday look and feel of the streets and during public holiday celebrations, bore the hallmarks of coalition politics. At the same time, political momentum was clearly with the communists, and few of the many politically moderate (and aesthetically liberal) monumental projects of the day were actually realized.[1]

Symbols of the Old Regime

The siege of Budapest between December 1944 and February 1945 had resulted in the destruction of many public buildings and monuments, leaving a disordered city to match the chaotic political situation. Altogether, twelve public monuments had been destroyed or seriously damaged, while a further ten had suffered minor damage.[2] As the new authorities began the task of reconstruction, they were faced with the choice of which monuments to reconstruct or allow to remain, which to modify and which to remove. Their work was complicated by the fact that Hungary was an occupied country and under the ultimate control of the ACC.

The first monuments to be removed were those erected in memory of the territories of historical Hungary lost at the Treaty of Trianon of 1920. Since Hungary had been an aggressor state in the Second World War and invaded its neighbours in an attempt to revise the treaty by force, it was natural for the occupying forces to order the removal of monuments that had provided ideological justification and encouragement for Hungarian nationalism. The ACC therefore demanded the removal of irredentist monuments erected by the authoritarian regime of Admiral Horthy, who held power from 1919 to 1944 and led Hungary into alliance with Hitler. The new Hungarian authorities complied with the wishes of the Soviet-dominated ACC, although without much public fanfare.

The most important irredentist monuments were located on Szabadság (Freedom) Square. The first to be removed was the *Sacred Flagstaff*, which was destroyed on Soviet orders to make way for the first Soviet war memorial, inaugurated on May Day 1945. The monument, erected in 1928, was arguably the centrepiece of Horthy-era political symbolism. It consisted of a twenty-metre flagstaff, on the base of which was the following text: 'Our country is the country of the Carpathians, Greater-Hungary. Prince Árpád established it in 896, it will remain until the end of the world.' At the top of the pole was a huge bronze hand, modelled after Admiral Horthy's own hand. The fate of the *Sacred Flagstaff* was decided by the Soviet army. Szabadság Square was chosen as the site of the first Soviet war memorial in Budapest during the final weeks of the siege in early 1945. When the monument was unveiled on May Day 1945, it was on the exact site of the *Flagstaff*, which had unceremoniously disappeared.[3]

Szabadság Square was also the location of four statues representing the borderlands of pre-Trianon Hungary. *North*, *South*, *East* and *West* were removed on the order of the mayor, Zoltán Vas, in August 1945. A report in the magazine of the Soviet-Hungarian Society, *Jövendő* (The Future), explained that the statues had been pulled down 'in the interests of cooperation, peace and friendship with Hungary's neighbours'.[4] The *Hungarian Suffering Statue* had been a gift of the British newspaper magnate, Lord Rothermere, and erected in 1932. It was removed from Szabadság Square in 1947, together with its revisionist plaque decrying the injustice of the Trianon Treaty. The statue itself was re-erected the next year outside a public baths, since without the offending plaque it might just be understood as a bronze nude of a girl in distress.[5] The demolition of the *Sacred Flagstaff* and the erection of a war memorial in its place represented the determination on the part of the Soviet command literally to occupy one of Hungarian nationalism's most holy sites. The square had originally housed a notorious Habsburg barracks where Hungarian political prisoners were held after the defeat of the revolution of 1848. In the 1890s, the hated symbol of Habsburg oppression was demolished and the square became the site of a number of important buildings and monuments symbolizing Hungarian independence, and was renamed Szabadság Square.

The subjugation of this holy site of Hungarian nationalism was underlined by ritual ceremonies first conducted on May Day 1945. In the presence of Field Marshal Malinovskii and hundreds of Soviet troops, members of the new Hungarian government, including the prime minister and the foreign secretary, members of the Budapest National Committee, the mayor and representatives of the political parties were made to listen to the Soviet anthem and speeches in praise of the heroism of the Red Army, before placing wreaths around the monument. The ceremony ended with a cheer for Stalin, led by the Soviet field marshal, and a march by of the various branches of the Soviet armed forces. Ironically, although the *Sacred Flagstaff* had been removed, the four irredentist statues *North, South, East* and *West* and the *Hungarian Suffering Statue* were still in place at the time of the first May Day celebrations. This mixed symbolism was both a result of the chaotic postwar conditions, and the fact that at this stage all Hungarian political parties hoped to retain at least some of the territory regained during the war.

The second category of monuments of the old regime that were removed or not repaired in the immediate aftermath of the liberation were those dedicated to domestic reactionaries. These provoked the wrath of left-wing activists in the communist and socialist parties, and there was an element of crowd justice in their often violent fate. There was also evidence of political manipulation through the employment of 'spontaneous' crowds to demolish statues that could not be removed legally, as well as post-facto invocation of 'crowd action' to confer an aura of democratic legitimacy to destructive acts ordered from above.

The demolition of the statue to the first codifier of Hungarian feudal law, *István Werbőczy*, on 6 May 1945, was a case in point. The sixteenth-century cleric was attacked because his legal work, the *Tripartium*, was enacted after the suppression of György Dózsa's peasant revolt of 1514, enabling him to be symbolically represented as the 'chief defender of Hungarian feudalism and the upper aristocracy'.[6] The destruction was carried out illegally, but in broad daylight and with the apparent connivance of the authorities. A wire cable was fastened around Werbőczy's neck, and after several attempts the statue was toppled and left face down in the grass. The watching crowd held communist placards, while the music played by a uniformed brass band lent atmosphere (Figure 4.1).[7] One year later, to turn the tables completely on the former ruling classes, a plan was announced by the city council to erect a monument to György Dózsa. In the event the project was repeatedly postponed, and a monument to Dózsa erected only in 1961.

Figure 4.1 The Destruction of the *Werbőczy Statue* (May 1945). From János Pótó, *Emlékművek, politika, közgondolkodás* (Budapest: MTA Történettudomanyi Intézet, 1989)

Another early target was the *Monument to the National Martyrs of 1918–1919*. It had been erected in 1934 and consisted of a large stone pillar, topped by a statue of a man killing a monster (representing Bolshevism), and with a base inscription dedicating it to the memory of 'the Hungarian citizens slaughtered by the Proletarian dictatorship'. For the communist authorities, the Republic of Councils, a short-lived revolutionary government established in Hungary after the end of the First World War, was regarded as a heroic, and tragically lost, historical opportunity to establish socialism in Hungary. Those who had defeated the Republic and then carried out a bloody white terror against its supporters were now considered counter-revolutionary reactionaries, not national martyrs. There was no question of monuments dedicated to the memory of the enemies of the Republic of Councils being allowed to remain, and they were ceremoniously demolished in the spirit of a settling of historical scores.

The destruction of the monument provided an opportunity for political propaganda. Although the mayor ordered the removal of the *Monument to the National Martyrs* on 6 August 1945, its demolition was delayed until several days before the municipal elections of 4 October 1945. The monument was eventually removed not by council workmen, as might have been expected, but by activists of the Communist Party witnessed by a large crowd. The left-wing iconoclasts exacted ritual retribution upon the statue by fastening a rope to the figure and pulling it to the ground. The reversal of the historical judgment of the Republic of Councils not only involved destroying the monument to its fallen enemies, but also immediately gave rise to plans for a national pantheon devoted to the martyrs of the Republic.[8]

Monuments that were not removed in the early years included the bulk of the First World War memorials. While irredentist symbols were to be found on many Horthy-era war memorials, the usual policy was to neutralize the revisionist message by removing offending plaques and insignia while avoiding the demolition of the monuments themselves. An order of the Budapest city council from 1947 confirmed the practice by which 'irredentist symbols should be removed, although the monuments themselves should not be demolished'. The justification was that: 'the relatives of the fallen of the 1914 war are still alive, and it would be wrong to hurt their feelings, especially since the soldiers fought in the erroneous belief that they were defending their country'.[9] As well as older war memorials, monuments to historical figures with no direct political significance were, if undamaged, allowed to remain for the time being. If they had been destroyed or severely damaged in the war, they were not reconstructed.

New Monuments of the Coalition Period

Large-scale monuments erected in Budapest in the immediate postwar period were exclusively devoted to the honour of the Soviet army. Other statues were planned, both by city authorities and civic groups, though these projects failed as the political horizon narrowed and the Communist Party tightened its control of public space. As the most important monument erected in the coalition period, Budapest's *Liberation Monument*, inaugurated on 4 April 1947, shows clearly the importance of political considerations of the effect of sculpture on public space. Soviet memorials had already been erected on the site of the *Sacred Flagstaff* on Szabadság Square, as well as on two other central Budapest squares, yet the need was felt for another monument that would be visible throughout the city clearly to express the glory of the Soviet army. The *Liberation Monument*, depicting a female figure or victory holding a palm leaf guarded by a fierce Soviet soldier and flanked by two allegorical sculptures of progress and the triumph over fascism, was designed as a constant reminder of the Soviet victory. Hungary was initially regarded as a defeated enemy nation; the monument demonstrated Soviet control of the conquered territory by dominating Budapest public space.

The initiative for the monument, its planning and erection were all directly or indirectly controlled by the Soviet army. The sculptor, Zsigmond Kisfaludi Strobl, was personally chosen by Marshal Voroshilov during the last weeks of the war on stylistic grounds, despite the fact that, as the former court sculptor for Admiral Horthy, he was disliked by most progressive artists and left-wing politicians. The official commission that followed, in the name of the Hungarian government, thus went directly to Kisfaludi Strobl without a competition. Two possible sites for the statue were suggested by the city authorities, but these were overruled by Voroshilov, who insisted on the commanding position offered by Budapest's Gellért Hill.[10] This prominent location had been the site of another military barracks, the Citadella, which had functioned as an instrument and symbol of Habsburg repression in the mid-nineteenth century. Like the first Soviet war memorial erected on Szabadság Square, the site of the *Liberation Monument* had specific symbolic connotations for Hungarians. It is remarkable that the Soviets deliberately located their two most important war memorials in places that had previously been sites of Habsburg oppression.

In July 1947, a month before the first rigged national elections, the Public Art and Culture Committee of Budapest city council met to draw up a list of statues to be commissioned and erected in the city. They called for monuments to the composer Béla Bartók, the sixteenth-century peasant rebel György Dózsa, the Jacobite revolutionary Ignác Martinovics, the 1848 rebel Mihály Táncsics and the working-class poet Attila József.[11] Despite the announcement of various competitions and campaigns of public subscription, none of these monuments was erected in the period because, as projects, they became mired in ideological disputes.

The failure to erect a statue to Attila József is a clear case in point. The campaign to erect a statue to the acclaimed poet of working-class origins, who committed suicide in 1937, began in May 1947. The Attila József College announced a joint competition with the Hungarian Arts Council to erect a monument in his memory on 15 March 1948. The first round of jury deliberations in September 1947 was inconclusive; the winner of the second round in November was András Beck, who had been a jury member on the original panel. Political upheavals in the art world, in particular the institution of dogmatic Socialist Realism, led to the rejection of Beck's

Figure 4.2 András Beck's monument to Attila József against the backdrop of a new housing estate in the Budapest suburb of Angyálföld (1952). Reproduced from Károly Lyka, *Budapest szobrai* (Budapest: Képzőművészet Alap, 1955)

winning design and the shelving of the project, since he 'failed to express the poet's revolutionary élan, his unbreakable faith in the victory of the working class and hatred for capitalist exploitation'.[12]

The *Attila József Monument* was finally erected in 1952, after two more inconclusive rounds of competition that forced András Beck, the eventual winner, to completely revise his original model to take into account ideological criticisms. The finished statue showed Attila József in the unmistakable guise of party agitator, complete with cloth cap and working boots. The poet was represented gesticulating decisively and gazing into a distant, egalitarian future (Figure 4.2). It had originally been planned to erect the monument on Eskü Square, by the Danube close to the *Sándor Petőfi* statue. In the event, the monument was erected on a different site, far from the centre in the new industrial suburb of Angyálföld. This was not necessarily a demotion, as the statue of the poet was ideally placed to hold sway over the new working-class inhabitants of the model Stalinist housing estate, and to symbolize the Party's efforts to overcome the divide between art and the masses.

Returning to the coalition period, the major challenge for public celebration and opportunity for monumental memorialization in the immediate postwar years was the centenary of the Hungarian Revolution of 1848. Planning for the symbolically charged anniversary began as a civic movement, but was taken over and centralized by the Ministry of Communications in spring 1947. In the evolving political context, an increasingly limited conception of the centenary took hold, in order to stop the movement from getting out of hand and to empty the celebration of 'nationalist' or even anti-Russian content. In the end, the memorialization of 1848 was limited to a bust and a statue of the revolutionary poet Sándor Petőfi, an iron *Hungarian Youth – Centenary* memorial gate, and a granite block engraved with '1848–1948', all of which were erected in the outer suburbs of the city.[13] In the background to the government's attempt to play down the celebration of 1848 were Soviet accusations of nationalism against their Hungarian comrades. Thus, in March 1948 the Hungarian Party was severely criticized by a high-ranking Soviet delegation for having images of Petőfi and Kossuth on their placards and for 'preferring the colours of the Hungarian national flag to red'.[14] Russian sensitivity over 1848 had its roots in popular consciousness of the role played by tsarist troops in helping to defeat the revolution in 1849 and the potential for unhelpful contemporary parallels.

There was only one case of a statue commissioned and erected through the actions of civic organizations in the postwar period. This was the *Wallenberg Statue*, Wallenberg being the Swedish diplomat who saved hundreds of Jewish lives during the German occupation of Budapest. The bizarre fate of the statue, however, marks the end of the coalition period and any inclination on the part of the communists to share public space democratically. In November 1945 the Wallenberg Committee, whose backers included prominent bankers and the director of the Hungarian Oil Company, asked for and received permission from the mayor to have a street renamed and a monument erected in his honour. In March 1949 the sculpture, by Pál Pátzay, was erected in Saint István Park. However, the morning before its intended inauguration on 9 April 1949, council work-men removed it in a secretive dawn raid.[15] The reason was that the statue had come to the notice of the Soviet authorities, who had abducted and later murdered Wallenberg in the last weeks of the war, and were obvi-ously displeased by his memorialization.

The failure to establish democratic public space through the erection of statues of broad public appeal in the coalition period had much to do with the narrowing of the public sphere as the communists gradually took over all the reins of power. Since it usually took at least two years to build a major monument – a process involving the drawing up of a commission and organization of a competition, the work of the sculptor, the examin-ation (and often correction) of his or her design, preparation of the site and, in the case of bronze, casting – execution often lagged behind pol-itics. This explains why very many projects conceived during the coalition period were unceremoniously dropped once the communists had a mon-opoly of power; the ideological criteria became so strict as to rule out their completion on grounds of both style and content.

The Political Transition of 1947–9

The election in August 1947 resulted in victory for the 'four party coal-ition' led by the communists, and was soon followed by the elimination of all remaining political opposition. The culmination of the political transformation came with the elections on 1 May 1949, the first in which no political alternative to the ruling party was offered to the voter, and the subsequent adoption of a Soviet-style constitution declaring Hungary to be a People's Democracy. The communist political steamroller went hand-in-hand with an acceleration of the programme of social and economic change. The go-ahead for socialist transformation was signalled at the founding meeting of the Comintern in Poland in September 1947, at which the Hungarian party was criticized for its slowness. The split with Tito and the expulsion of the Yugoslav Communist Party from the Comintern in

June 1948 increased the pressure on the Hungarian leadership to prove their loyalty to the Soviet Union, setting in motion a chain of events that would lead to the establishment of fully-fledged Stalinism in Hungary. By 1949 the changed atmosphere had worked its way through to all areas of public life, including the cultural and artistic spheres.

The radical shift in cultural politics in this period had far-reaching consequences for public sculpture and public space. Institutions such as the universities, the Academy of Fine Art, the Artists' Union, and even the Ministry of Religion and Culture, were restructured and placed under the control of communists. The change in personnel was matched by a new demand on sculptors to produce monuments that reflected and popularized the new ideology. Statues took on a new role as focal points for mass demonstrations of loyalty and unity under the banner of Stalin, and all treacherous signs of symbolic opposition were eliminated, for fear they might encourage reaction.

The Second Wave of Statue Removals

Several monuments that had survived the war, the Soviet occupation, and the anger of left-wing crowds, later fell victim to the organized iconoclasm of the years of transition. While, during the first wave of destruction, association with revisionism or the discredited Horthy regime was often the reason for demolishing a monument, in the subsequent period of communist rule, the motives for removal were often more intangible, and ranged from political vindictiveness and hysteria to hunger for recyclable bronze.

Monuments could be taken down because of their association with contemporary political forces. As such, their removal could be understood as a tactical move against opponents of communist power. It was thus that on 27 April 1947 the statue of Bishop Ottokár Prohászka was pulled down by 'unknown elements' the morning before crowds arrived to remember the twentieth anniversary of his death. The decapitation of the statue of a bishop gave a clear message to the Catholic hierarchy of Hungary to end its opposition to the nationalization of church schools. As it happened, the demolished statue showed signs of itself becoming a site of ritual opposition, as crowds gathered to lay flowers around his head. The statue was then removed and repaired by the city council, before being placed in storage.[16]

The *Monument to General Bandholtz* also fell victim in the intensifying ideological atmosphere, this time on the international front. The statue had been erected in 1936 in memory of an American general who helped save the collection of the National Museum from marauding Romanian troops after the defeat of the Republic of Councils in 1919. Damaged in the war, it was repaired by the city council and returned to its original location in 1946. In 1949, a letter to the party newspaper asked the rhetorical question, how could a statue to a 'counter-revolutionary, foreign imperialist' be allowed to remain on Szabadság Square?[17] The mayor took advice from the Foreign and Defence Ministries before proceeding with the removal of the statue, which caused offence through its association with both pro-American and anti-Romanian feeling.

During the transition to full-blown Stalinism, the removal of monuments of the old regime often had a practical character, even if the public justification was ideological. The demolition of the monument to *Jenő Rákosi*, a conservative newspaper editor, is a case in point. In August 1948, the head of the art section of the Ministry of Religion and Popular Culture (VKM) wrote to the mayor, asking for permission to use the bronze from the *Rákosi* statue 'to make 8,000 small statues of figures from artistic and national life'. The mayor agreed, as long as the VKM organized the removal of the statue and that the town hall be assigned an acceptable number of the small statues created from it. Subsequently, a letter appeared in the *Szabad Nép* demanding the removal of the 'reactionary' statue. It was removed by workmen on 1 December 1948.[18]

As in the case of *General Bandholtz*, the instrument of an outraged letter from a member of the public was used to give the removal a popular veneer. The demolition of unwanted public statues was no longer entrusted to left-wing activists among the people, but carried out by the authorities who claimed to be acting on their behalf. Democratic legitimacy for changes to public space was sought in these cases by the manufacture of demands 'from below' in order to justify actions taken by the authorities.

There were cases of monuments removed not specifically because they were irredentist or reactionary, but because of their constellation in public space. The *First Infantry and National Uprising Regiment Memorial* had the fate of surviving the siege and initial wave of removals of the coalition period, only to be demolished in October 1948, a victim of the increasingly paranoid political atmosphere. The monument included a statue of a grenade thrower; unfortunately, if you stood behind the statue it lined up perfectly with the *Liberation Monument* on Gellért Hill. It was perceived to 'threaten' the Soviet soldier on the lower plinth of the *Liberation Monument*.[19] It was destroyed because it provided people with the opportunity to mock the Soviet army and think iconoclastic thoughts, and thereby to undermine the established spatial order.

Stalin's Seventieth Birthday and the Birth of the Cult

Sculpture had a highly visible role as an instrument in the public idoliz-
ation of Stalin in Eastern Europe. Beginning with the orchestrated mass
celebration of Stalin's seventieth birthday throughout the Bloc on 21
December 1949, the image of Stalin infiltrated into all aspects of public
life in Hungary. Mass-produced busts for display in factories and offices
created the impression of the omnipresent leader, while huge outdoor
Stalin monuments provided the focus for carefully stage-managed public
rituals on national holidays to demonstrate the people's and the local
communist leaders' loyalty and love for the Generalissimo. In previous
years the event had been marked with a congratulatory telegram to Moscow
and a flurry of newspaper articles: the celebrations of 1949 were on a
completely different scale. In the weeks leading up to the anniversary, the
Politburo of the Hungarian Communist Party discussed the progress of
preparations five times, including devoting a whole session to 'literary
and artistic preparations for Stalin's birthday'.[20] Plans were laid for the
inundation of public space with images of Stalin, both to prove the loyalty
of the Party in a time of widespread accusations of treason, and to complete the transformation of Hungary into a leading country engaged in the
building of socialism.

The event itself was marked by frenzied Party celebrations in town
halls and theatres throughout Hungary. In Budapest, the mayor made the
following 'spontaneous' declarations: that 'Budapest's most beautiful
street, Andrássy Avenue, be renamed Stalin Avenue'; that 'a statue of
Generalissimo Stalin, of fitting artistic quality and size, be made and
erected in the most worthy and appropriate place in our capital – within
a year'; and that a copy of the statue, *Gratitude*, be erected in Budapest
by 4 April 1950.[21] The *Gratitude* [*Hála*] *Statue* was the centrepiece of a
train-load of Hungarian birthday gifts to Stalin that were first exhibited in
Budapest and then in the Pushkin Museum in Moscow, along with gifts
from the rest of the socialist Bloc. *Gratitude* was a marble group composition depicting a smiling, bare-chested worker and his peasant wife, and
their two small wreath-bearing children, in other words, the ideal nuclear
family of the communist utopia. The inscription in Russian read: 'To the
Great Stalin – the Grateful Hungarian People, 1949'. Kisfaludi Strobl,
who was also the creator of the *Liberation Monument* on Gellért Hill,
made a stone copy of *Gratitude*, which was erected on Szabadság Square
in 1950. This completed the square's transformation from a holy site of
Hungarian nationalism to one of public devotion to socialist internationalism and loyalty to Stalin and the Soviet Union.

The celebration of Stalin's birthday led to the creation of a genre of mini-shrines decorated with mass-produced busts and iconic portraits of the Generalissimo surrounded by red flags and slogans in factories and offices throughout the country. Clearly, the aim was to infiltrate Stalin's image into all corners of Hungarian life. 200 plaster and ten bronze copies of a Stalin bust purposely commissioned that autumn, 1,000 bronze Stalin medallions, 5,000 large portraits, 30,000 smaller portraits and 5,000 eight-picture wall posters of Stalin's life were produced and widely distributed.[22]

The Party attached great importance to the popular reception of the propaganda attached to the celebration of Stalin's birthday. The reaction of visitors to the exhibition of Stalin's gifts and to an exhibition about Stalin's life were carefully monitored, and reports drawn up for the Party leadership on the popular mood. A report from the Budapest Party Agitation and Propaganda Department to the Secretariat on 'lessons from the organized celebration of comrade Stalin's birthday' laid particular stress on the positive popular reception of the exhibition: 'The celebration of Stalin's birthday began with the exhibition of gifts from the Hungarian working people. The exhibition was held in the Palace of Exhibitions and was highly esteemed by the workers. Huge crowds visited the exhibition without a break, they waited with discipline and without complaint until their turn came.' Individual workers' comments were noted, a certain Comrade Molnár from the Hungarian Cloth Factory had written in the visitor's book that: 'these gifts are truly valuable, because they are given by the working people, the working people who have Stalin to thank for everything.' The report concluded that the success of the exhibition demonstrated 'the love and attachment of the Hungarian people towards comrade Stalin'.[23]

The second exhibition, on 'Stalin's Life and Works', was judged by the Budapest Party Propaganda and Agitation Section to have been poorly organized. Workers had complained of having to wait outside for hours before being rushed through the exhibition, some apparently needing to go three times to view it properly. Nevertheless, a common working class opinion was that: 'if I'd read about Stalin's life and work for a whole month, then still I would remember less than after visiting this exhibition.'[24] The exhibition, organized by the Soviet-Hungarian Society and held at the National Museum, was visited by 200,000 people. Smaller scale travelling exhibitions on the theme of 'The Great Stalin's Life of Struggle' were shown in 900 places around the country to a staggering one-and-a-half million people.[25]

The Climax of Hungarian Stalinism: the Building of the Stalin Statue

The years after 1949 saw further consolidation of the communist dictatorship and the attempt to create a more stable and institutionalized system. Having succeeded in eliminating the other Hungarian political parties, the leadership began a purge of the Communist Party, targeting both those who had originally been social democrats and the so-called 'home communists' who had spent the war years in Hungary rather than in the Soviet Union. In addition to the poisonous political atmosphere, living standards fell drastically as resources were diverted into a military and industrial build-up required by the first Five-Year Plan. It was in this context that the mayor's costly promise to erect a huge *Stalin Statue* was fulfilled.

The building of the *Stalin Statue* clearly indicated the importance of the potential 'monumental effect' of statues on the masses. The competition, organized jointly by the city council and the Ministry of Culture, was announced on 16 March 1950. Twenty-five sculptors were given two months to make 1:10 scale plaster cast models of the statue, which was to be erected on 15 December 1950. The materials used were to be bronze or marble, the statue was to be between five and six metres tall, and the site was unspecified.[26] As was so often the case, none of the twenty-four designs submitted were judged satisfactory, necessitating a second round of entries by four of the sculptors.

A winner was finally chosen by the Politburo in December 1950. Mikus Sándor owed the lucrative commission both to institutional connections and his success in creating a Stalin that could act as a cultic focus for demonstrations. It was claimed that its formal simplicity and economy of gesture allowed people to forget for a moment that it was an artistic creation and to feel the presence of the great leader (Figure 4.3). Mikus commented to this effect: 'The huge figure is standing still, but with such motion, as if he was about to speak to the people gathered around him.'[27]

During the planning of the Stalin monument, leftist elements within the Party argued that it should be erected on the site of the *Millennium Monument* in Heroes' Square. That monument, built between 1896 and 1929, memorialized Hungary's greatest leaders from the pagan chieftain Árpád, through Saint István to the Habsburgs. The square lies at the end of Andrássy Avenue (which as has already been mentioned was renamed 'Stalin Avenue' in 1949), and was already a favoured site for public celebrations on dates such as the anniversary of the liberation of Hungary on 4 April and May Day. During these highly stage-managed public ceremonies, a tribune for the Party leaders was erected around the central

Figure 4.3 The Stalin Statue, Budapest (1951–6). Reproduced from Károly Lyka, *Budapest szobrai* (Budapest: Képzőművészet Alap, 1955)

column and decked out with portraits of Stalin, Lenin and Rákosi, to act as a focus for the military and civilian parades. It may have seemed to some a natural step to displace the Archangel Gabriel and the pre-feudal Magyar chieftains in order to make way for a statue to the crowning figure of Hungarian history. The precedent of the 1919 Republic of Councils, when the Habsburg statues were taken down from their pediments in the arcade around the back of the square and a plaster statue of Marx and Engels was erected in the centre, was still in living memory.

Cooler heads prevailed, and it was finally decided to locate the *Stalin Statue* on Felvonulási Square, a few hundred metres away. The perceived advantages of the chosen site included the fact that tens of thousands of workers went there on workdays, and 'the area is suitable for the accommodation of more than 100,000 people'.[28] The Politburo went further, and decided to widen Marching Square by knocking down the buildings on the edge of the city park, and also to turn the monument's base into a tribune from which the leaders could watch parades 'as on Red Square'.[29]

On 16 December 1951, a year behind schedule and two years after it was announced, the Budapest *Stalin Statue* was inaugurated. 80,000 workers gathered before the tribune to hear the Hungarian and Soviet national anthems and listen to a speech by the Minister of Culture and chief ideologue, József Révai. In his speech he linked the inauguration of the statue with the removal of offending reactionary prewar statues and the subsequent erection of statues to progressive Hungarian historical figures. The *Stalin Statue* was therefore the crowning achievement of the communists' interventions into public space. Révai invoked the notion that 'this statue has arisen from the soul of the Nation, this statue is a Hungarian statue', and elaborated the point by describing Stalin as the climax of Hungarian history. The Party newspaper went on to clarify the meaning of the statue, which lay in the fact that 'to love one's country and to be faithful to the Soviet Union, to be a patriot and to be a proletarian internationalist, are one and the same'.[30]

Contemplating the statue, and the mass rituals of which it was the focus, it is indeed impossible to ignore the aura of religious adoration that surrounded the monument. There are echoes of the practices of the pre-modern era and even of paganism. The *Stalin Statue* resurrected the ancient habit of venerating images as if they were identical with the person they represented. The aim of the cult was to make the populace feel the eyes of the leader upon them everywhere, at home, in the workplace and around the city.

Epilogue: The Demolition of the Stalin Statue

The death of Stalin and rise to power of Nikita Khrushchev led quickly to the curtailing of the Stalin cult within the Soviet Union. At the Twentieth Party Congress of February 1956 Khrushchev denounced the cult of Stalin in his 'Secret Speech', which included the statement that: 'It is impermissible and foreign to the spirit of Marxism-Leninism to elevate one person, to transform him into a superman possessing supernatural characteristics akin to those of a god.' It was followed in June 1956 by a Central Committee decree: 'On Overcoming the Cult of Personality and its Consequences.'[31] Later that year, the Hungarian uprising of 1956 exacted revenge for years of Soviet and communist oppression on the massive Stalin icon, in an act of retribution that went far beyond the controlled destalinization advocated by the Soviet leadership.

The destruction of the *Stalin Statue* was a key event in the outbreak of the Hungarian Revolution. On the evening of 23 October 1956, crowds that had spent the day occupying other key public spaces, such as Kossuth Square and Bem Square, gathered in Felvonulási Square and decided collectively to take action against the statue. It took more than an hour to pull it down, despite the use of wires, blowtorches and heavy machinery. The toppling of the statue was a ritualized act of crowd justice that marked the crossing of a revolutionary threshold, and came shortly before the outbreak of shooting around the state radio building. Eyewitness accounts collected by the 1956 Institute provide valuable insight into a rare case of mass iconoclasm in the twentieth century.

One witness to the events was Ervin Kaas, a thirty-one-year-old Catholic activist and clerk, who spent the rest of the 1950s in the notorious Recsek labour camp:

> We arrived at Felvonulási Square between 7.30 and 7.45 pm. There was a very large crowd. I climbed a tree and saw a truck around 30–40 metres from the statue, and just at that moment a wire cable was being attached to the statue by its neck, then the truck reared up a little, and you could feel that it was straining, then the sound of the engine went down a little, I looked at the statue, and saw that it hadn't moved at all.[32]

The difficulty the iconoclasts faced in pulling down the statue is confirmed by other accounts. Mihály Nagy was another observer-participant in the action:

> Several lorries had already tried to pull down the statue; even the strongest wire cables gave way, because from inside it had been strengthened with a huge great arch-shaped iron bar, so it really was no easy business to pull down the statue. The constructors had given it some thought, they wanted it to be a lasting creation. It would even have been hard to blow it up.[33]

Rezso Bóna, a worker and participant in the revolution who was later sentenced to ten years' imprisonment, confirms the accounts of many other witnesses in his explanation of how the statue was finally brought down: 'This is how the Stalin statue was brought down; they cut it at the boots with these blowtorches, and fixed ropes to some Csepel 350 trucks, which they attached to the Stalin statue, and then toppled it from its base.'[34] The description of how the statue actually fell from István Kállay, a goldsmith who ran an underground radio station in 1956, sounds remarkably unmonumental: 'Now, the way it came down, really, it was like a rubber ball, it jumped up a couple of times before coming to rest.'[35]

After the statue's successful demolition, which according to one witness took place at precisely 9.21 pm, people sang the Hungarian national anthem, then someone stood on the base and made a short speech saying to the effect that it symbolized the end of tyranny in Hungary.[36] The next

The Role of Monumental Sculpture in Hungary

day the crowd dragged the remains of the *Stalin Statue* across the city to Blaha Lujza Square, where it was broken up into small pieces that were taken away as souvenirs. One of Stalin's hands was taken by the actor Sándor Pécsi, who, after the restoration of Soviet power, buried the relic in his garden where it remained until the late 1980s. It was eventually unearthed and bought by the Hungarian History Museum.

Notes

1. Éva Standeisky *et al.*, eds, *A fordulat évei: politika, képzőművészet, építészet, 1947–49* (Budapest: 1956 Institute, 1998).
2. János Pótó, *Emlékművek, politika, közgondolkodás* (Budapest: MTA Történettudományi Intézet, 1989), p. 20.
3. László Prohászka, *Szoborsorsok* (Budapest: Kornétás, 1994), pp. 72–7.
4. 'Ledöntötték a gyulölet szobrait', *Jövendő* (15 September 1945), p. 13.
5. Pótó, *Emlékművek*, p. 32.
6. 'Ledöntött nagyságok', *Képes Világ* (19–25 May 1945).
7. Prohászka, *Szoborsorsok*, p. 52.
8. Pótó, *Emlékművek*, p. 25.
9. BFL (Budapest city archives) XXIII/114 and BFL 3835/219/1950/ XI/b.
10. Prohászka, *Szoborsorsok*, pp. 144–7.
11. *Kis Újság* (26 May 1947), p. 3.
12. Minutes of jury meeting, 11 June 1951. BFL XXII 114/3835/295-1951.
13. Levente Hadházy, András Szilágyi and Ágnes Szőllőssy, eds, *Negyven év köztéri szobrai Budapesten. 1945–1985* (Budapest: Budapest Gallery, 1985).
14. Standeisky, *A fordulat évei*, p. 205.
15. Pótó, *Emlékművek*, p. 60.
16. Ibid., p. 29
17. Ibid., p. 39.
18. Ibid., p. 34.
19. Prohászka, *Szoborsorsok*, p. 60.
20. Minutes of the Hungarian Politburo, 22 November 1949. MOL (Hungarian State Archive) KS-276-54/ 72 ő.e.

Reuben Fowkes

21. *Szabad Nép* (21 December 1949).
22. Minutes of the Hungarian Politburo, 22 November 1949. MOL-KS-276-54/ 72 ő.e.
23. Excerpt from the report of the Budapest Party Propaganda and Agitation Department to the MDP Secretariat, 7 January 1950. MOL-KS-276-108/26 ő.e.
24. MDP Secretariat, 7 January 1950. MOL-KS-276-108/26 ő.e.
25. Report of MDP KV Agitation Department on the Hungarian-Soviet Society, 15 May 1950. MOL-KS-276f. 108cs /22 ő.e.
26. Pótó, *Emlékmüvek*, p. 76.
27. 'A legboldogabb magyar szobrász', *Magyar Nemzet* (24 December 1950).
28. Minutes of 7 March meeting of art section of city council. BFL 3835/ 59/1950-XI.
29. Pótó, *Emlékmüvek*, p. 80.
30. 'Sztálin elvtárs szobra', *Szabad Nép* (16 December 1951), p. 3.
31. Matthew Cullerne Bown, *Socialist Realist Painting* (London: Yale University Press, 1998), p. 305.
32. Interview with Ervin Kaas. Oral History Archive of the 1956 Institute, vol. 442–3.
33. Interview with Mihály Nagy. Oral History Archive, vol. 495, p. 21.
34. Interview with Rezso Bóna. Oral History Archive, vol. 228, p. 6.
35. Interview with István Kállay. Oral History Archive, vol. 282, p. 23.
36. Interview with Ervin Kaas. Oral History Archive, vol. 442–3.

–5–

Wandering the Streets of Socialism: A Discussion of the Street Photography of Arno Fischer and Ursula Arnold

Astrid Ihle

Our understanding of East German society in the 1950s has been shaped by the propaganda images of heroic national reconstruction that were circulated in the press and state-sanctioned media of the day. In these photographs, the city features prominently as a sign of national progress and development. Throughout the 1950s, newspapers and magazines in the German Democratic Republic – such as the daily *Neues Deutschland* or the journal *Neue Berliner Illustrierte* – abounded with photographs glorifying the process of urban reconstruction in the war-ravaged city centres. Documentations of major building projects such as the Stalinallee boulevard in Berlin were seen as symbolic of the people's collective effort towards the building of a new socialist society. Representations of construction activists, worker brigades, apprentice masons and enthusiastic volunteers formed the stock-in-trade images of this *Aufbau* (reconstruction) iconography, which, with the introduction, in 1951, of a state-governed reconstruction programme, the *Nationales Aufbauprogramm* (NAP), was integrated into a broad propaganda campaign. Beneath the surface of this ubiquitous propaganda photography, however, lay multiple photographic voices that brought to light an alternative view of everyday life in the cities of postwar East Germany. Coming of age in the 1950s, young photographers such as Arno Fischer (b. 1927) in Berlin and Ursula Arnold (b. 1929) in Leipzig embarked on independent photographic explorations of their immediate urban environment, focusing on disregarded aspects of city life such as the ruined cityscape or the mundane activities of day-to-day survival in postwar East German society.[1] These photographs differ sharply from the state-sanctioned *Aufbau* photography. Exposing the gap between the State's rhetoric and the daily experiences of ordinary East Germans, they speak of a radically different urban experience.

Among the better-known independent ventures is Arno Fischer's documentary project *Situation Berlin*. A photographic autodidact, originally trained as a sculptor, Fischer produced a series of acclaimed photographs during the 1950s, which recorded the disparate social, political and economic developments in Berlin's eastern and western sectors prior to the building of the Berlin Wall in 1961. Focusing on banal scenes of everyday life – many of which took place on the margins of the great political events of the day – Fischer's photographs allow the viewer a critical glimpse behind the façade and pathos of postwar reconstruction, both East and West, in the ideologically, if not yet geopolitically divided city. Fischer's photographs were produced '*im eigenen Auftrag*', i.e. they were not commissioned by a newspaper or state agency, but grew independently out of the photographer's personal interests and concerns. Despite its critical attitude, a sympathetic bias towards the developments in the eastern sector prevailed in his work. In 1961, a selection of Fischer's photographs was to be made available as a book, entitled *Situation Berlin*. However, with the building of the Berlin Wall and the official eradication of the West Berlin sector from GDR maps, Fischer's documentation, which had also included photographs of West Berlin, took on an undesired political edge and was dropped by the cultural authorities.[2]

In the mid-1950s, Ursula Arnold, a photography graduate from the Hochschule für Grafik und Buchkunst (HGB; College for Graphic and Book Arts) in Leipzig, embarked on a similarly controversial exploration of the socialist city-in-the-making. Photographing in the dilapidated neighbourhoods of postwar Leipzig, Arnold's work highlights those aspects of urban life – ruins, urban plight, social outsiders – that were commonly ignored by the ambitious photojournalist of the period. Her photographs of Leipzig street life present an arresting documentation of postwar urban culture in the GDR that confronted the images of heroic national reconstruction that were circulated in the mass media. Most of Arnold's street studies were produced during the photographer's brief involvement with freelance photojournalism between 1955 and 1956. Significantly, though, none of them was ever published in the contemporary press. Focusing on familiar, yet officially repressed aspects of city life, Arnold's photographs articulate an altogether different urban consciousness. Her street studies remain enigmatic and self-contained fragments of a 'hidden world' beyond the reach of state propaganda. They are, as I wish to argue in this essay, the products of an acute observer of city life: a female *flâneur* – *flâneuse* – rearranging the urban scenes through the lens of gender as she strolls through the streets of the socialist city.

Rethinking the concept of the *flâneur*, which is generally associated with a quintessentially male urban consciousness, in what follows I want to analyse Arnold's photographs in terms of woman's access to the streets of the socialist city and her 'rightful' place within the emerging social order. This raises the following questions at the outset: what were the conditions of *flânerie* in 1950s Leipzig as they presented themselves to a young woman photographer? Is it possible at all to speak of a *flâneur/flâneuse* in the socialist city?

Born on the streets of nineteenth-century Paris, the urban persona of the *flâneur* is, by definition, inextricably linked to the processes of emerging capitalism, industrialization and urban transformation of that period. His 'natural' habitat is the Paris of the arcades and (later) department stores, the city of restaurants, boulevards and gardens, of crowds jostling in public spaces. An urban stroller and observer, the *flâneur* rejoices in the fleeting and transitory nature of the urban spectacle, without participating in it. He is the 'man *of* the crowd', invisible but all-seeing.[3] His mastery of the gaze and social detachment identify the *flâneur* as male and of superior social status (if downwardly mobile), while his ostensible idleness is said to conceal intense intellectual activity.[4] In the writings of his contemporaries, he emerges as a sort of seismograph of modernity, a quality that has made him into the emblematic figure of modern urban creativity, Baudelaire's 'hero of modern life'.[5] However, as a producer of texts (literature, painting), the *flâneur* eventually becomes a commodity himself and, in seeking a marketplace for his productions, gets caught up in capitalist commodity circulation. Therein lies the *flâneur*'s ultimate drama.[6]

Since his early days on the streets of Paris during the Second Empire, the *flâneur* has surfaced in various locations and in many different guises: as idle dandy and bohemian, detective, journalist, or sociologist, he has been spotted in 1920s Berlin, on Manhattan's Upper East Side, and as far away as São Paulo.[7] In an attempt to make sense of the changed and changing social and cultural landscape, writers have recast this ambiguous figure of modern urbanity and creativity in the image of their own changing conceptions of the social order and their place in it.

Much has been written about the limits and constraints, if not the impossibility, of a female *flâneur* or *flâneuse*.[8] Women's presence in the city has traditionally been subject to strict regulations and clear demarcations of space, which have prevented them from taking part in the leisurely activity of anonymous, ostensibly purposeless strolling – unless as objects of the urban spectacle and/or the male gaze. In his book *Imagining the Modern City*, James Donald has commented upon scholars' persistent search for the elusive *flâneuse* whose 'spectral presence . . . haunt(s) the discussion'.[9] By asking what is really at stake in this story, Donald has challenged contemporary investments in that concept. For him, it is first and foremost a question of desire and identification, which is likely to be more revealing of today's feminist agendas than of women's actual desires in, for instance, nineteenth-century Paris.

> Women in public have (I assume) always had their own purposes and itineraries, and have simply wanted to be allowed to get on with them. That wish, so far as I can see, need not entail taking on *any* imaginary identity, and certainly not that of the *flâneur*. It *does* entail at least an implicit claim to a right though: the right to act in a self-chosen way, the right to be an agent, the right to walk the city streets unmolested and unchallenged.[10]

Given the loudly proclaimed gender equity of the new East German state, one would have expected that the last obstacles barring women's full and free access to the streets were finally removed with the advent of socialism, making the need for a 'resurrected' or fictive *flâneuse* redundant. However, while traditional preconceptions relating to gender roles were, at least seemingly, discarded, new sets of normative female role models were put into place, which clearly prescribed women's visibility and mobility within the public sphere of the socialist city. In order to assess the actual conditions of women's access to the streets – in terms of 'the right to act in a self-chosen way, the right to be an agent' – within the context of 1950s East German society, the ideological division of the socialist city needs to be analysed along the lines of geography and gender. It is in this process, I suggest, that we might encounter a *flâneuse*.

At first sight, the socialist cities-in-the-making of 1950s East Germany could not be further from the nineteenth-century Paris of consumption, commodification and spectacle. However, urban renewal on a grand, national scale, and the social and economic changes brought about by socialist reconstruction, left many artists and intellectuals in the GDR with a sense of uncertainty, and in need of an urban practice to make sense of the changing social, cultural and political landscape. In his essay 'The *Flâneur* in Social Theory', David Frisby has put forward the notion of *flânerie* as an urban practice involving the activities of observation, reading/interpretation and the production of texts.[11] For Frisby, *flânerie* offers, not least, a chance of reflecting upon the worlds we inhabit. By inviting the *flâneur/se* onto the streets of 1950s East Germany, I want to examine what it meant to assume the power of the gaze and articulate an independent worldview within a culture that closely monitored individual expression and autonomy. I am not assuming that Arnold (or Fischer, as it were) referred to themselves as *flâneur/se*. However, as an analytical category, the concept of *flânerie* allows us to place the work of these GDR photographers within a wider discussion of urban practices that have shaped our understanding of the modern urban experience through literature and art.

As a plane of projection for the country's proclaimed ideals and values, the concept of the socialist city advanced to political prominence in the postwar period. Conceived as a positive counter-image to the alleged decadent Western metropolis, its function was, first of all, to assert the social, moral and political superiority of the socialist state. At the Third Party Conference of the SED (Sozialistische Einheitspartei Deutschlands; Socialist Unity Party of Germany) in July 1950, Walter Ulbricht, the Party's First Secretary, proclaimed the rebuilding of the country's war-ravaged cities a political priority. 'Monumental buildings should be erected', announced Ulbricht, 'to assert the power and strength of the national building effort (*Aufbauwille*) and express Germany's great future'.[12] City-planning objectives were laid down in the 'Sixteen Principles of Town Planning' (*Sechszehn Grundsätze des Städtebaues*).[13] As with all other aspects pertaining to the social, cultural and political reconstruction of the East German state, it was the Soviet model that was to determine the architecture of the new city. This model favoured a pompous urban style of high-rise buildings, wide squares and grand boulevards (*Magistralen*), with an emphasis on order, symmetry and the magnificence of public buildings to represent the grandeur of the socialist state.[14] Structurally, the new building guidelines conceived of the city as a hierarchical, strictly zoned and centrally organized system, whereby the city centre was accorded pre-eminence as the locus of state power.[15] Underlying this imagined 'totalization' of space was a perceived need for control and surveillance as an integral part of GDR urban planning. With its plain grids, neat statistics and clear set of social norms, the 'concept-city' (Michel de Certeau) of the socialist utopia bespeaks the wish 'to make the city an object of knowledge and so a governable space'.[16] Against the diversity, randomness and dynamics of urban life, it sets the fantasy of a transparent text, in which 'all practices and all relationships are subject to surveillance and the law'.[17]

According to the 'Principles', the East German city was perceived, both in its structure and architectural form, as 'the expression of the political life and the national consciousness of the people', that is as a 'truthful reflection of the new power relations'.[18] The ideals and values of the East German state (which were understood to be identical with those of its citizens) were seen to be directly inscribed in the reorganization of urban space. Guided by the utopian belief that the masses could be transformed by the urban environment in which they lived, the socialist city was conceived as a public space designed to support the process of social integration and the formation of the new socialist citizen. A decree by the Central Committee of the SED, published in the newspaper *Neues Deutschland*, emphasized the disciplining power of the new architecture, which was to educate the East German people in the spirit of a 'unified, democratic, peace-loving and independent Germany, the fulfilment of the Five-Year Plan, and the fight for freedom'.[19] As an expression of state ideology, organized urban reconstruction in the GDR actively contributed to contemporary discourses pertaining to the redefinition of social role models and identities, including women's function and 'rightful' place in the emerging order. By negotiating the changes in women's status and their everyday lives, as well as how they appeared in the public sphere of the city, urban practices helped reshape the relationship between space, gender and identity in the socialist city-in-the-making.

Following a call by the Central Committee of the SED in November 1951, the *Nationales Aufbauprogramm* (NAP) was launched, an ambitious state-sponsored programme of national reconstruction that relied on the mass mobilization of the population.[20] The construction of Berlin's Stalinallee – a grand inner-city boulevard displaying opulent 'workers' palaces' (*Arbeiterpaläste*) – was the first major building project initiated within the framework of the NAP, construction starting as early as 1952. Within the rhetoric of NAP propaganda, the Stalinallee boulevard came to stand for peace, national unification, a new Germany and the victory of socialism. This symbolic significance was powerfully brought home through a pervasive propaganda campaign, whose declared goal was the active recruitment of large sections of the population for the task of socialist reconstruction. As Stalinallee advanced to a political symbol that stood for the creation of a new and better society, active participation in the construction of this very society became postulated as an educative measure that helped shape the new socialist being of the future.[21]

Photography – as chief 'ideological tool' – played a critical role within this carefully devised propaganda scheme, not least because the majority of the State's agitprop material of those days – posters, brochures, postcards, daily newspapers – relied on the medium for its production and mass circulation. Writing in *Die Fotografie*, the critic Ernst Nitsche elaborated on the significance of the photographic image within the framework of national reconstruction, emphasizing that it enabled millions of people to experience directly the raising of 'our new buildings of freedom, our apartment blocks, factories and cultural institutions', which he saw as vivid evidence of 'our new and better society'.[22] The photojournalist tackling the field of socialist reconstruction was faced with a real challenge, however. It was his (rarely her) task to transform the bleak and scarred urban landscape of Germany's postwar inner cities into optimistic images of national growth and progress, which were to inspire hope and confidence, as well as a feeling of national pride and duty, to a mostly disillusioned, tired and deeply humiliated people. It was therefore not enough to record the activities of urban reconstruction in a straightforward 'documentary' style, based on observation and understanding. Rather, the photographer's mandate was to create a *potential reality* to fit the sloganeering and rhetoric of party politics. This was mainly achieved by staged or manipulated photographs, which were specifically designed to produce the desired effect in the viewer. The result of this practice was an avalanche of recurrent motifs: journeymen masons diligently building brick by brick as they smile into the camera; male and female construction workers, their tools displayed like weapons, their gazes proudly lifted towards the future; as well as the numerous honoured activists and worker brigades. These portraits of 'typical' role models – which regularly appeared in propaganda brochures such as *Wir bauen die Stalinallee* (published by the Nationales Komitee, 1952) or on the cover of the *Neue Berliner Illustrierte* – were invariably pictured against the backdrop of cranes, scaffolding, banners and rising buildings, which acted as potent social signifiers of national growth, progress and development. In these photographs, the city is generally revealed in wide horizons or long vistas, which give powerful expression to the panoptic claims of the socialist city.

Women were particularly prominent in the imagery of NAP propaganda. Whether as apprentice mason, construction worker, or as diligent *Trümmerfrau* ('rubble woman'), *Aufbau* photography played a crucial role in fixing female role models that determined women's visibility and mobility within the socialist city. One image that was incessantly circulated in the postwar media was that of the *Trümmerfrau* (Figure 5.1). In these photographs, the tedious and monotonous work of clearing away the rubble and breaking stones, often performed by elderly women with no other income, was rendered as a cheerful and perfectly orchestrated choreography of collective urban labour, which effectively veiled the complex realities of female existence in those harsh years of postwar deprivation. The image of the heroic 'rubble woman', dedicating herself to national reconstruction, set a pattern for subsequent female role models that emphasized women's indispensable, yet subordinate, role in socialist

Figure 5.1 *Trümmerfrauen* (Rubble Women), ADN-Zentralbild, 8 March 1952. ('Am 8.3.1952, den Internationalen Frauentag, halfen die Frauen von Groß-Berlin auf den Enttrümmerungsschwerpunkten des Nationalen Aufbauprogramms am Wiederaufbau Berlins.') Photo: Bundesarchiv Koblenz (Bild 183/19 000/1337 N)

production. Defying both the hardship as well as the seductions and tribulations of urban existence, it also continued a tradition of urban thought that neatly divided female urban types into the opposing categories of 'virtuous womanhood' and the 'fallen woman'. Through her active participation in socialist reconstruction, the East German woman was given a chance to redeem herself from her Nazi past and become a new and better socialist citizen.[23]

Arno Fischer's photographs documenting the developments in postwar Berlin could hardly be more antagonistic to the official genre of *Aufbau* photography. Travelling between the eastern and western sectors on a regular basis, Fischer sharpened his eye for the particularities of everyday life in the divided city.[24] From 1954 onwards, he started recording his impressions with the discreet and portable, small-format camera. His photographs do not show the 'heroes' of national reconstruction, but ordinary people – spectators, passers-by, children; people engaged in the act of looking or waiting. The actual event is never depicted, however; the action is perpetually postponed. Fischer was not interested in the grand, pathetic gestures of his period; his attention was for the little, unspectacular episodes of everyday life, many of which took place on the margins or in the shadow of public events or political demonstrations. However, in their seeming innocence, the depicted scenes often exposed the pathos and arrogance of postwar German society, both East and West, even more blatantly. Snapshots of military parades and war veteran meetings in West Berlin, for instance, seemed to reveal the fallacy of Adenauer's peace rhetoric, while the photograph of a deserted building site at Bersarin Platz (the uppermost end of Stalinallee) would appear to belie the myth of thriving socialist reconstruction. (Figure 5.2) Another photograph of 1956 (Figure 5.3) shows a group of spectators at a May Day Parade in East Berlin, lined up in front of the ruins of the Kronprinzenpalais on the boulevard Unter den Linden. With their unfocused gazes, and indifferent, sceptical expressions, these individuals are a far cry from the cheering crowds of official propaganda. Tightly framed, Fischer's photograph transforms the urban scene into a stage-like setting, with the crumbling architecture as backdrop. The boundaries between inside and outside

Figure 5.2 Arno Fischer, *Ostberlin* (East Berlin), 1957. Photo: Courtesy of the artist

Figure 5.3 Arno Fischer, *Ostberlin* (East Berlin), 1956. Photo: Courtesy of the artist

become somewhat blurred. Significantly, there are no long vistas or extended horizons to help locate the scene in its wider urban context – only through a crack in the dilapidated wall do we get a glimpse of the city (of ruins) beyond. The overall impression is one of enclosure.

Working from outside the official academic establishment and institutions, Fischer's work developed somewhat untouched by the formalism/realism debate that raged throughout the 1950s.[25] As with all other aspects of cultural production, photography was subject to strict regulations and political demands set by the aesthetic and ideological doctrine of Socialist Realism.[26] The exact nature of Socialist Realist photography was hotly debated on the pages of the magazine *Die Fotografie*. Emphasizing photography's political mission as an ideological tool, leading commentators such as Ernst Nitsche and Kurt Eggert – while they did not deny the medium's aesthetic qualities – left no doubt that formal considerations had to be set aside in favour of the 'right' political content. 'In order to develop a realistic art', Nitsche wrote, 'the social conditions in the GDR must be considered; our life must be properly portrayed in its progression.'[27] The photographer actively assisted the coming into being of a new society and a new socialist people, and this had to be adequately conveyed by concentrating on what was postulated to be 'typical'. 'Realism, therefore', Nitsche concluded, 'is the laughing, happy life; it is our proud youth; it is our workers; it is our beautiful German homeland. Abstract formal visualization in which nothing can be recognized only evokes false emotionality, the kitsch photography of old; it means isolation from the people, a furthering of imperialism.'[28] Discredited as 'naturalistic', the socially engaged documentary style of the immediate postwar period was also no longer encouraged due to its perceived lack of a clearly articulated sense of party loyalty (*Parteilichkeit*). Instead, photographers were encouraged to make an 'imaginative and critical choice' of reality – based on firm Marxist-Leninist principles.[29] Formal experimentation, textual ambiguity as well as the articulation of a subjective view were not encouraged.

Fischer's practice, by contrast, distinguished itself through the photographer's spontaneous reaction to events on the streets, an approach that, stylistically, was (often) marked by bold compositions and unusual cuts and perspectives. For inspiration, he turned to international developments such as Edward Steichen's exhibition *The Family of Man*, which toured West Berlin in 1955 and which Fischer helped to install.[30] Popularising the notion of 'human interest' and 'life photography', the compassionate and egalitarian humanism of Steichen's show seemed to offer an alternative model of photographic practice for many young photographers in the GDR.[31] But it was Robert Frank's work *The Americans*, which Fischer discovered in an issue of *U.S. Camera Annual* in 1958, that confirmed his photographic vision: like the Swiss photographer, Fischer found symbolic meaning in little, dislocated moments of everyday life, which he translated into a radically subjective formal language. His exposure of the false optimism and arrogance of German postwar politics, East and West, bears many parallels to Frank's deconstruction of the post-Second World War American façade of idealism.[32] Above all, however, Fischer's work testified to the photographer's critical inquiry into the nature of human life versus state political systems. Whether East or West, the individual in his photographs does not figure as an active agent in his or her own right. Instead, people appear as passive pawns in a wider ideological game in which they have no say.

A self-taught photographer, Fischer's public persona was not easy to assimilate into existing categories of professional photographic practice. His brand of observational street photography was a far cry from the academic aestheticism of Socialist Realist studio photography; nor could it be likened to the ambitious, ideologically committed work of the professional GDR photojournalist. In his 1957 article 'Fotoreportage' Kurt Hartmann described the photojournalist of the period as the man 'in the centre of the action' who strives to capture, in a split second, the decisive and 'typical' moments of an event.[33] By contrast, Fischer's focus was on the disregarded incidents backstage, and he always maintained a critical distance from that which he observed. His photographs have been described as the 'findings of a passer-by' who strolls through his natural habitat, the city.[34] This image of Fischer as a solitary stroller, who, with his camera, collects impressions of the urban spectacle, brings to mind the urban persona of the *flâneur*. To be sure, Fischer's critical gaze – his incisive social analysis of the urban scenes he witnessed – was essentially alien to his historical antecedent who roamed the streets of nineteenth-century Paris. However, there is a sense in which both Baudelaire's 'hero of modern life' as well as Fischer, a 'concerned photographer' in 1950s East Germany, were driven out onto the streets by an existential need to make sense of the changing social, cultural and political landscape as it became inscribed in the urban environment. Exploring the rituals of city life, they both, as *flâneurs*, asserted the right to define for themselves the meaning and order of things, 'rather than allowing things or appearances to be defining of themselves'.[35] Insisting on seeing for himself, Fischer bestowed his own personal meaning on the scenes he picked out of the kaleidoscope of urban life in an attempt to lift the mystifying veil of state ideology.

To be sure, the lonely figure of the *flâneur* did not fit with contemporary cultural discourses, which could not possibly account for this highly individualistic urban persona – unless he walked the model boulevard of Stalinallee under the watchful eye of the authorities. The very activity of solitary, seemingly purposeless strolling was perceived as highly suspicious in view of the officially encouraged striving for collectivity and social integration. When people walked the streets of the socialist city, then, it was not alone, but preferably – as countless photographic records suggest – as part of a demonstration or some other type of collective urban activity. However, what made the figure of the photographer as *flâneur* truly controversial was the articulation of a personal world view in his (or her) work. Fischer's endeavour to set up an alternative perception of social reality – based on the photographer's subjective evaluation of the urban phenomena he witnessed – represented an interrogation of the State's claim to omniscience and truth, which was unacceptable within the ideological framework of state socialist discourse.

After graduating from the Hochschule für Grafik und Buchkunst (HGB) in Leipzig in 1955, Ursula Arnold worked as a freelance photojournalist for the magazines *Zeit im Bild* and *Neue Berliner Illustrierte*. While still a student at the HGB, Arnold had completed an extensive documentation of Leipzig's secular building tradition that traced the city's envisaged transformation from a bourgeois city of commerce into a socialist metropolis. In her freelance work, however, the photographer distanced herself more and more from the dictate of the 'centre', both geographically as well as ideologically speaking, as she embarked on a highly personal exploration of her immediate urban environment.

Rejecting the grand pathos of official *Aufbau* photography, in her street studies Arnold explored the mundane activities of everyday life on the streets of postwar Leipzig. Her photographs of children playing under the protective gazes of grandmothers, working women picking up groceries on their way back from work, and widows roaming the narrow alleyways around the Thomaskirche in Leipzig's historical city centre, conjure up an altogether different world beyond the official discourse of the socialist city. This is, above all, a women's world; one whose protagonists bear little resemblance to the heroines of state propaganda. Most of Arnold's street studies were taken in Leipzig's city centre; through the photographer's focus, they reappropriate the urban environment from a decidedly 'gendered' perspective. One of Arnold's most striking photographs of the period is the portrait of an old newspaper woman (Figure 5.4). Dressed all

Figure 5.4 Ursula Arnold, *Zeitungsfrau* (Newspaper Woman), Leipzig, 1956. Photo: Courtesy of the artist

in black, deeply bent under the heavy weight of her burden, only her brow, nose and cheekbones protrude as the frail person painfully climbs up a flight of stairs towards the viewer. In the background, a woman in a light trench coat is just about to ascend the staircase opposite. This juxta-position sets up a sharp contrast, which is further accentuated by a dramatic play of light and shadow imbuing the scene with symbolic meaning. While the young woman walks towards a ray of sunlight, the destination of the older woman's ascent appears sombre and uncertain. The photo-graph's vertiginous perspective (with the newspaper woman photographed from a high angle) produces a destabilizing spatial effect, which adds to the imbalance of this chance encounter. The picture was taken in Leipzig's central district 'am Markt', yet all references to the outside world are avoided; the scene is presented within a closely contained architectural space, cut off from the teeming city crowd. With this photograph, Arnold captured the bitter social reality of a generation of widowed working-class women who, after the war, had to make ends meet through back-breaking and tedious labour. The contrast to the cheering *Trümmerfrauen* of NAP propaganda could hardly be more striking.

Another photograph from that same year (1956) opens up on the mun-dane, yet imposing view of a dilapidated backyard that occupies the entire picture plane (Figure 5.5). Before the backdrop of a crumbling façade, a bridal couple proudly strides towards the camera while friendly neigh-bours watch from their windows. The scene is brightened by capturing the couple just at the moment they step into a streak of gleaming sunlight that bathes the otherwise bleak courtyard setting. The semi-public courtyard setting blurs the distinctions between outside/inside, public/private. The framing creates a stage-like, theatrical effect, which gives the impression that we are glimpsing another, 'secret' world. (A solarized person in the foreground adds to the surreal, almost dream-like quality of the depicted.) Against the grand vistas and totalizing representations of the socialist city, Arnold's photograph sets an intimate view of a commonplace, non-descript urban locale beyond the reach of panoptic power. Conceived as a positive image of hope and new beginnings, the photograph was never-theless rejected by the newspaper editors, presumably for its portrayal of urban ruins and poverty.[36] Besides the decaying quality of the depicted architecture, the signs of a spontaneous makeshift life, which prospered in the back streets of the war-ravaged city, might also have caused a decided discomfort among the editorial staff. By focusing on those aspects of urban existence that were self-consciously ignored by official prop-aganda, Arnold effectively confronted the viewer with the repressed 'other' of postwar urban reality. Her photographs evoke the 'unspeakable

Figure 5.5 Ursula Arnold, *Hochzeit* (Wedding), Leipzig, 1956. Photo: Courtesy of the artist

aspects of the city' – the (potential) chaos and disorder, flux and change, which lay just beneath the polished façade of the socialist urban imaginary.[37] They reveal another world – or, to use Elizabeth Wilson's words – a 'second city' within and yet beyond the perimeters of the grand streamlined boulevards and ordered spaces of the socialist utopia.[38]

In her book *The Art of Taking a Walk*, Anke Gleber has argued that 'the female flaneur embodies marginal facets of life in the street often overlooked by other, more comfortable, mostly male flaneurs whose positions have been less exposed, less on the edge of their societies'.[39] This assessment of the *flâneuse* certainly holds true for Arnold's articulation of a 'gendered' perspective in her work. By tracing women's day-to-day trajectories in the socialist city, her photographs map a distinct urban experience, one based on a specifically female negotiation of the city that official accounts tended to neglect. To be sure, images of *Trümmerfrauen* and female construction workers proliferated in the East German press and mass media of the postwar period, testifying to women's pervasive presence in the public sphere of the city. Yet, these representations are only partial accounts, based on very specific interests and perspectives. They tell us little about the complex realities of female urban living in the postwar period, or the actual conditions of women's autonomy and right to self-definition within the socialist city. To judge from official records, women's access to the streets was primarily defined through the officially promoted striving for collectivity and social integration. The woman in the public sphere was not perceived as an active agent in her own right, but, above all, as an indispensable element of a wider social apparatus and its operations. She remained an object, if not of the individual male gaze, then of the omniscient gaze of the (imagined) socialist father.

The extensive documentation of women's life in the socialist city – which included the creation of certain female role models and stereotypes that were circulated across a wide network of discourses and signifying systems throughout the 1950s – bespeaks the wish to fix women in their 'rightful' place within the emerging social order. The solitary woman stroller, by contrast, embodies the promise of freedom, autonomy and self-definition, that is 'the right to act in a self-chosen way, the right to be an agent, the right to walk the city streets unmolested and unchallenged' (Donald). Equipped with a camera and an independent, critical mind, she assumes the right to walk, see and make meaning of and for herself. Certainly, it is no coincidence that Arnold's photographs have been described by the German photo historian Enno Kaufhold as the 'results of a greater sense of autonomy'.[40] Venturing into the 'back streets' of the socialist city, Arnold not only turned her back on notions of 'correct' subject matter, but defied the limited (and limiting) range of urban female types that did not allow for women to roam the streets on their own and actively and independently assume the power of the gaze. Arnold's intimate documentation of urban life in postwar Leipzig is extraordinary, not least because it presents us with the first instance of a perception of the East German city through a female perspective. Her street studies reinscribe women's daily lives into the narratives of East German social history. Significantly, her brand of observational street photography goes beyond the critical, at times cynical, detachment of many of her (mostly male) colleagues to express a sympathy for those whom she portrayed.

Notes

1. Arno Fischer and Ursula Arnold, together with Evelyn Richter, can be considered pioneers of a critical, socially engaged tradition in GDR

photography. Coming of age in the Stalinist period of the 1950s, they were among the first to articulate an independent photographic practice against the propagandistic demands and restrictive aesthetic codes of Socialist Realism. Of the three photographers, Ursula Arnold is probably the least well-known, her standing among the most disting-uished photographers of the former GDR being only recently officially acknowledged through a retrospective exhibition and critical reassess-ment of her work. See Franziska Schmidt and T. O. Immisch, *Belle Tristesse – Ursula Arnold – Photographien* (Berlin: ex pose Verlag, 2000). While Fischer and Richter pursued active careers as contro-versial photographers and inspiring teachers throughout the GDR's existence, Arnold withdrew from the photographic scene in the late 1950s to dedicate herself to a profession in television, photographing only in her free time. For an introduction (in English) to the work of these photographers see Karl Gernot Kuehn, *Caught. The Art of Photo-graphy in the German Democratic Republic* (Berkeley, Los Angeles and London: University of California Press, 1997). The most compre-hensive overview of Fischer's work to date is provided by the catalogue that accompanied his retrospective exhibition at the Staatliche Galerie Moritzburg Halle in Halle an der Saale in 1997, *Arno Fischer – Foto-grafien*, edited by T. O. Immisch and Klaus E. Göltz, with texts by Andreas Krase, Stefan Raum and Jutta Voigt. For further reading see Ulrich Domröse, ed., *Nichts ist so einfach wie es scheint. Ostdeutsche Photographie 1945-1989* (Berlin: Berlinische Galerie, exh. cat., 1992); Ulrich Domröse, ed., *Positionen künstlerischer Photographie in Deutschland seit 1945* (Berlin: Dumont, 1997); Gabriele Muschter, ed., *DDR Frauen fotografieren. Lexikon und Anthologie* (Berlin: ex pose Verlag, 1991).

2. In 1957, the newly founded publishing house Edition Leipzig appro-ached Fischer to publish a book of his Berlin photographs, with texts by Günter Rücker and Heinrich Göres. However, Fischer's critical perception of the postwar situation as well as the idiosyncratic style of his photographs proved highly controversial. The building of the Berlin Wall in August 1961 eventually served as an excuse to drop the print-ready project altogether. With West Berlin eradicated from the geographical (if not socio-psychological) map of East Berlin and the GDR, officially, there was no longer *one* Berlin. For many years, Fischer's photographs only circulated within a small, private circle of friends and students. In 2001, the East German photo historian Ulrich Domröse of the Berlinische Galerie in Berlin published a book on Fischer's project *Situation Berlin*, which, for the first time, assembled

all the photographs that were originally to be published in Fischer's cancelled book project of 1961. See Ulrich Domröse, ed., *Arno Fischer. Situation Berlin – Fotografien 1953–1960* (Berlin: Nikolai Verlag, 2001).

3. Keith Tester, 'Introduction', in Keith Tester, ed., *The Flâneur* (London and New York: Routledge, 1994), p. 3.
4. Priscilla Parkhurst Ferguson, 'The *flâneur* on and off the streets of Paris', in Tester, *Flâneur,* p. 26.
5. Tester, *Flâneur,* p. 6.
6. See Walter Benjamin, *Charles Baudelaire. A Lyric Poet in the Era of High Capitalism* (London: New Left Books, 1973).
7. While some scholars have argued that the *flâneur/flânerie* ceased to exist with the advent of an invasive consumer society that precluded creativity, others have appropriated and transformed the urban persona of the *flâneur* from a historical figure into an analytical category of investigation that emphasizes different aspects of *flânerie* as an urban practice. See the essays in Tester, *Flâneur*; see also Elizabeth Wilson, *The Sphinx in the City. Urban Life, the Control of Disorder, and Women* (Berkeley, Los Angeles and Oxford: University of California Press, 1991).
8. See for instance Janet Wolff, 'The invisible flâneuse. Women and the literature of modernity', in *Feminine Sentences: Essays on Women and Culture* (Cambridge: Polity Press, 1991); Griselda Pollock, 'Modernity and the spaces of femininity', in *Vision and Difference* (London and New York: Routledge, 1988).
9. James Donald, *Imagining the Modern City* (Minneapolis: University of Minnesota Press, 1999), p. 112.
10. Ibid., p. 112–14.
11. David Frisby, 'The *flâneur* in social theory', in Tester, *Flâneur*, p. 82.
12. Walter Ulbricht, report at the Third Party Conference of the SED, 20.07.1950, cited from Werner Durth, Jörn Düwel and Niels Gutschow, *Architektur und Städtebau in der DDR*: *Aufbau: Städte, Themen, Dokumente* (vol. 2) (Frankfurt and New York: Campus, 1998), p. 83.
13. 'Die Sechzehn Grundsätze des Städtebaues vom 27. Juli 1950, mit Erläuterungen von Lothar Bolz ', in Durth, *Architektur und Städtebau* (vol. 2), pp. 84–7.
14. Stylistically, Socialist Realism prevailed as the only approved form. Rejected as 'formalist' and therefore reactionary, the modernist architecture of the 1920s and 1930s – such as Bauhaus, International Style and Russian Constructivism – was to be replaced by an eclectic mixture of recycled historical styles, drawing on regional and local

traditions from Germany's cultural heritage. In Berlin, for instance, a neoclassical style was encouraged, in imitation of the buildings of the German architect Karl Friedrich Schinkel (1781–1841).

15. See 'Die Sechzehn Grundsätze des Städtebaues (Grundsatz 6)', in Durth, *Architektur und Städtebau* (vol. 2), p. 86.

16. Michel de Certeau, *The Practice of Everyday Life* (Berkeley, Los Angeles and London: University of California Press, 1984), p. 95; Donald, *Imagining the Modern City*, p. 14.

17. Frédéric Rouvillois, 'Utopia and Totalitarianism', in *Utopia. The Search for the Ideal Society in the Western World* (New York and Oxford: New York Public Library/Oxford University Press, 2000), p. 318.

18. See 'Die Sechzehn Grundsätze des Städtebaues (Grundsatz 1)', in Durth, *Architektur und Städtebau* (vol. 2), p. 84.

19. 'Der Kampf gegen den Formalismus in der Kunst und Literatur, für eine fortschrittliche deutsche Kultur', *Neues Deutschland*, 18 April 1951.

20. 'Wäre es nicht schön? Es wäre schön!', *Neues Deutschland*, 25 Nov 1951.

21. On this issue see for instance Doris Müller, 'Die Stalinallee in der politischen Propaganda im ersten Jahr des "Nationalen Aufbau-programms Berlin 1952"', in *Parteiauftrag: Ein neues Deutschland. Bilder, Rituale und Symbole der frühen DDR* (Berlin: Deutsches Historisches Museum, 1997).

22. Ernst Nitsche, 'Realismus und Formalismus in der Fotografie', *Die Fotografie*, no. 4 (1953), p. 112.

23. For a discussion of the phenomenon of the East German *Trümmer-frau* see for instance Ina Merkel, . . . *und Du, Frau an der Werkbank. Die DDR in den 50er Jahren* (Berlin: Elefanten Press, 1990).

24. Between 1947 and 1953, Fischer studied sculpture in Berlin, first at the Hochschule für Angewandte Kunst, Berlin-Weißensee, in the eastern sector; then, from 1952–3, at the Hochschule der Künste in West Berlin. In 1952, he moved to East Berlin. After breaking off his studies in 1953, he worked in a photo lab. In 1956, he was appointed teaching assistant at the Hochschule Berlin-Weißensee.

25. The campaign for Socialist Realism reached its most aggressive and overtly politicized articulation in a declaration by the Central Com-mittee of the SED on 17 March 1951 entitled 'Der Kampf gegen den Formalismus in Kunst und Literatur, für eine fortschrittliche deutsche Kultur', in which various forms of prewar modernism were identified as 'formalism' and set up as examples of an alternative reactionary political framework.

26. Stylistically based in nineteenth-century history painting, Soviet-style Socialist Realism had its ideological foundation in Andrei Zhdanov's declaration at the Soviet Writers' congress in 1934, in which he had identified 'ideological commitment' (*ideinost'*), 'party-mindedness' (*partiinost'*) and 'national/popular spirit' (*narodnost'*) as indispensable elements of socialist art.

27. Nitsche, 'Realismus und Formalismus', p. 113.

28. Ibid.

29. Kurt Eggert, 'Fotografie und Realismus', *Die Fotografie*, no. 5 (1953), p. 118.

30. Kuehn, *Caught*, p. 90.

31. Organized by Edward Steichen, Head of Photography at the Museum of Modern Art, New York, in 1955, *The Family of Man* was conceived as an international touring exhibition, which capitalized heavily for its popular appeal on a sentimentalized, multinational humanism. On the impact of this exhibition in the GDR see Wolfgang Kil, 'Faszination des Beiläufigen', *Bildende Kunst*, 2 (1987); for a western perspective see Roland Barthes, 'The Great Family of Man', in *Mythologies* (London, 1973).

32. Robert Frank's work *The Americans* was first published in book form in France in 1958 as *Les Americains* (with an introduction by Jack Kerouac).

33. Kurt Hartmann, 'Fotoreportage', *Die Fotografie*, no. 6 (1957), p. 162.

34. Andreas Krase, 'Die Zeitlosigkeit des Moments oder die Aufhebung des Alltäglichen im Alltag: Der Photograph Arno Fischer', in Immisch and Göltz, *Arno Fischer*, p. 137. ('*Fischers Photographien sind Fundstücke eines Passanten, der sich durch einen städtischen Raum bewegt, der in diesem Fall sein eigener Lebensraum war.*')

35. Tester, *Flâneur*, p. 3.

36. Interview with Ursula Arnold, Berlin, 27 July 2000.

37. Wilson, *Sphinx in the City*, p. 54.

38. Ibid., p. 8.

39. Anke Gleber, *The Art of Taking a Walk. Flanerie, Literature and Film in Weimar Culture* (Princeton: Princeton University Press, 1999), p. 201.

40. Enno Kaufhold, 'Auf freudlosen Gassen', *Frankfurter Allgemeine Zeitung*, 7 June 2000.

–6–

Soviet Exurbia: Dachas in Postwar Russia
Stephen Lovell

Space was a state project for the Soviets. The post-revolutionary order was designed to create a new man by remaking his environment in the broadest sense: not only by eliminating political and social opposition, building factories and creating institutions, but also by ripping apart the fabric of everyday life and then weaving it anew. Soviet people were required not just to acknowledge discursively, but also to feel and see, the 'sovietness' in which they were enveloped. The energies of a great number of intellectual workers were mobilized to this end: engineers, film-makers, artists, architects and many others combined to create a visual and material culture in which we can see encoded the ideology and practice of Soviet socialism. Vladimir Papernyi, in an excellent and influential study, has argued that architecture – one important aspect of the Soviet appropriation of space and the material world – can productively be viewed as the struggle between two principles: a dynamic, decentred 'Culture One' (corresponding roughly to the avant-garde spirit of the 1920s) and a static, monumentalist 'Culture Two' (crudely speaking, the culture of Stalinism).[1] More recently, Emma Widdis has seen a similar trajectory – from 'decentred' to 'recentred' principles of spatial organization – in the first twenty years of Soviet cinema.[2]

Whatever opinion one holds of such ambitious structuring binaries (my own view is that they have done more good than harm), they do not at first glance appear overly accommodating to the dacha (the Russian weekend or holiday house). For dachas are an intermediate phenomenon par excellence: they are owned and inhabited by urbanites, and so are not properly embedded in the rural landscape, yet they also represent a rejection (albeit temporary and partial) of dynamic modernism in favour of a more wholesome exurban life. The dacha is a space out of town that depends on the city for its functions and meanings. Both before and after the Revolution, it has been charged with lacking the authenticity of dwellings more deeply rooted in the soil such as the manor house, the *izba* or the homestead. To some extent, therefore, Russian exurbia shares the social and spatial marginality of (petit) bourgeois suburbia, which has regularly been the object of disdain in English society.[3] On the one hand, the dacha gestures towards rural tranquillity and immersion in nature while failing to sever its links to the city. On the other hand, it is considered to be a cowardly betrayal of urban life and conspicuously rejects the principles of modernity that tend to be valued, or at least to get noticed, by intellectuals. The dacha, then, straddles perhaps the most fundamental, and controversial, spatial divide of modern civilization – that between the country and the city – and it does so in a society where the metropolis and the rural hinterland have had an exceptionally polarized relationship.

In the Soviet context, moreover, there were several further reasons why dachas might excite disfavour. They were liable to be branded a despised 'remnant of the past' for their association with the pre-revolutionary 'bourgeois' lifestyle. They were synonymous with private life and domesticity, both of which were regarded with great suspicion in the early Soviet period. They were associated with leisure rather than physical toil and productive work. As a setting for family life, they were gendered female at a time when masculine proletarian virtues were all the rage.[4] The very appearance of a dacha plot was offensive to the Soviet gaze. It laid claim to a portion of state-owned land without offering the payback of agricultural labour. Worse still, it fenced off this land for the private use of a single household that, strictly speaking, did not 'need' the extra accommodation: dachas were by definition second homes for people ordinarily resident in urban flats. The dwellings that stood on dacha plots were profoundly alien to the Soviet communal ethos: they represented enclaves of unsocialized existence that were impervious to the penetrating collective gaze.

Given all these drawbacks, it is striking that the dacha did after all carve out a reasonably secure niche in Stalin-era culture.[5] In part, this was a matter of simple economic expediency: the desperately overworked new state did not have the wherewithal to administer the pre-revolutionary dacha stock, and any way the population found to relieve the housing shortage without making claims on state resources could only be welcomed. Dachas were also useful as a perquisite for the emerging Soviet elite. But equally, and rather less obviously, they found a place in the iconography and ideology of the 1930s. As Papernyi and others have shown, the Stalin period marked a decisive turn away from the deurbanizing (and often anti-urbanist) projects of the 1920s and a move towards urban monumentalism. The city – and especially the great metropolis of Moscow – was to be bolstered by new principles of urban planning and by grand architectural projects, and – no less importantly – it was to be separated from the rural hinterland by the thick wooded boundary of a 'green belt'. Stately, high-rise construction was to be preferred to suburban sprawl or the grubby fade-out of city into surrounding countryside; the 'decentring' principles advanced by some radical architects and planners were to be rejected in favour of 'recentred', hierarchical spatial arrangements.

Dachas fit this project rather well, because they were located safely on the other side of the green belt. Far from undermining the distinction between urban and rural settlement, they actually made it more secure. Urbanites were able to breathe fresh air and to establish a short-term bond with the soil (even after the industrialization drive of the First Five-Year Plan, Soviet ideology maintained a residual attachment to the ideal of an organically whole 'new man' equally at home on potato patches as on the factory floor); yet, crucially, this bond did not weaken the Soviet citizen's sense of his public, urban responsibilities. Rather, the use of a country house brought him closer to the values of Soviet civilization: dachas could be accommodated within the much-trumpeted ethic of 'culturedness' (*kul'turnost'*) that was promoted as an attribute of Stalin-era domesticity and so brought ideology to bear on everyday life and material culture.[6]

Yet one should not exaggerate the prominence or prestige of the dacha in Soviet public discourse. While holiday houses had been widely tolerated since the 1920s, they contained within them the seeds of their own vulnerability: they were 'second homes', and as such were 'inessential', not to say luxurious, items. In practice, Soviet bureaucrats and citizens usually sidestepped this difficulty by presenting the dacha as an object of legitimate 'personal' consumption, not as a luxury or (worse still) a source of proscribed unearned income. Dachas were to be welcomed as long as they served merely as evidence of the rising living standards of the Soviet 'masses'; but as soon as they began to give free rein to bourgeois 'proprietorial' instincts, they were discursively cut down to size. By the early 1960s, in an atmosphere pervaded by Khrushchev's 'austere consumerism', hostility and suspicion competed with encouragement of dacha settlement.[7] Building regulations became strict, and infringements were sometimes punished severely; tales abounded of inspectors sending in bulldozers to demolish houses that had broken the rules. Infringements were easy to find, as building regulations were so restrictive as to frustrate even the least ambitious Soviet dacha dweller. Dachas became an easy target for Soviet satirists: the magazine *Krokodil*, for example, contained a healthy sprinkling of cartoons holding up to scorn the propensity of dacha owners to turn their dwellings into tastelessly decorated small castles, or the tendency of dacha proprietors to squeeze the last available kopeck out of their tenants instead of devoting themselves to gainful agricultural tasks (most landlords were, of course, year-round rural dwellers). Dacha folk were particularly suspect because they strove always to partition space (either inside their dacha dwelling or on the surrounding plot of land) so as to safeguard it from the intrusions of neighbours or relatives or to extract from it income of some kind. Such partitional impulses were deeply suspect in a society that, in public at least, placed a premium on the values of openness, collectivism, and hospitality dispensed with the appearance of disinterest.

The negative stereotypes of the dacha outlined above were articulated with greatest intensity during the Khrushchev period. By the early 1970s, dachas had grudgingly been accepted as a fact of life for the population of Russia's major cities, and public discussion of them became rather more restrained in tone. They were not embraced wholeheartedly, however, until the very last years of the Soviet period, when plots of land for out-of-town construction became much easier to obtain than at any stage previously.

This concludes my survey of publicly expressed Soviet attitudes to the dacha. In what remains of this chapter, my attention will shift to less 'official' discourses (namely, those heard in memoirs, interviews and fiction) and to the ways in which individual Soviet people made habitable, and hence gave meaning to, their own dacha spaces.[8]

From about the 1960s onwards, what Soviet people called 'the dacha' was in fact a composite phenomenon made up of four main elements. The first was the 'official' dacha (*kazennaia dacha*) made available to people occupying positions in party-state organizations or in enterprises. Next came a village house (*sel'skii dom*) built as a dwelling for a family permanently resident in a rural area, but subsequently bought or rented by urbanites as a holiday home. The third category was a dacha 'proper': a holiday house built with that function in view, most commonly under the auspices of a cooperative sponsored by an organization or enterprise (Figure 6.1). The final, and by the late Soviet period much the most common, type was the upstart 'garden plot dacha': a house built on a plot within a 'garden association' (*sadovodcheskoe tovarishchestvo*) or 'garden cooperative' (*sadovodcheskii kooperativ*).

Each of these four types had implications for the way people used their dachas. The available accounts suggest strongly that the occupants of 'official' dachas resembled hotel guests. Their houses were often fitted out luxuriously (by Soviet standards); at the upper end of the scale of privilege, they might come complete with such desirable features as

Figure 6.1 A dacha 'proper': This picture was taken in Komarovo, north of St Petersburg, one of the more desirable dacha locations for the postwar Leningrad intelligentsia. Although the house is by no means large or grand, it stands in a spacious plot that is not given over to vegetable growing

housekeeper, billiard table and real stone fireplace, and they tended to be located in settlements equipped with a good shop, a canteen, even a cinema. The mentality of the residents also differed fundamentally from that of 'individual' *dachniki* (dacha folk). They were able to enjoy comfortable holidays while at the same time protecting themselves from charges of 'petty bourgeois' materialism; for, after all, these dachas were not even their 'personal', let alone 'private', property. They received their dacha perks, so the largely unspoken rationale went, not for who they were but for the post they held. In some settlements nomenklaturists (members of the party-state privileged class) were reminded of this fact by the official inventory numbers that were stamped on the furniture. It was apparently bad form for them to buy their own dacha or even to show too proprietorial a concern for the dachas provided for them by the State.[9] The village house, by complete contrast, was part of a pre-existing rural architectural ensemble, and, in the eyes of the intelligentsia especially, benefited greatly from its radical separation from the world of Soviet officialdom. The owners or tenants of such a house were taking over a lived-in, domesticated space, and would usually expect to maintain it in the same spirit.

The other two categories – the 'dacha plot dacha' and the 'garden plot dacha' – are rather less easily distinguished. Dachas 'proper' tended, for one thing, to be older than houses on garden plots: they could be part of a Soviet dacha cooperative dating from the 1920s or 1930s, or they might even be holiday houses built before the Revolution. In general, they also stood on plots that were larger than those allocated to members of garden cooperatives. The most important distinction, however, concerned not the age of the house or size of the plot, but rather the nature of their use. Dacha plots were allotted on the understanding that their recipients would build, or have built, a dwelling that would enable them to spend portions of the summer there; the surrounding plot might also be cultivated for vegetables, fruit or flowers, but that was not its primary purpose. Garden plots, by contrast, were intended to be units of agricultural production: members of garden collectives were explicitly required to contribute their own labour in cultivating the plot.[10]

What I want to argue here is that the postwar history of Soviet exurbia is best regarded as a story of convergence between the 'dacha plot dacha' and the 'garden plot dacha'. On the one hand, dachas 'proper' became rather more agricultural in the ways they were used. On the other hand, garden plots became ever more 'dacha-like' in the sense that people were increasingly able to build on them houses that became alternative dwellings for the summer period. By the late Soviet period, the 'dacha' designation was conferred on a dwelling not for its formal legal status but for the practices and spatial arrangements that it made possible. From the 1950s onwards, out-of-town dwellings were a defining element in the everyday experience of hundreds of thousands of Soviet urbanites: although often modest in their dimensions and their facilities, they infused people's lives with new meanings, gave them new opportunities to pursue 'private' activities, yet also enabled them to cultivate a sense of community that was largely independent of party-state institutions.

Garden plots first emerged as an amenity widely accessible to the population of the major cities in the postwar period. Along with allotments (*ogorody*) they performed above all a subsistence function in the hungry years of the late 1940s and early 1950s. Although in practice they seem often to have overlapped, garden plots and allotments were notionally distinct concepts. Allotments were closer to the city, came in smaller plots, and were used above all to grow the staples of the Soviet diet: potatoes and cabbage. Garden plots were larger, located further from people's city homes, and offered a wider range of produce (including fruit as well as vegetables).

There was, however, one basic resemblance. Neither allotments nor garden plots were intended by the authorities to contain dacha-style dwellings: they would offer Soviet urbanites the opportunity to supplement their meagre postwar diet, but they were emphatically not supposed to become second homes. To allow gardeners to build dwellings on their plots would be to sanction de facto private property. In order to avert this possibility, many early garden settlements were organized along 'collective' lines. Plots were relatively large (usually between 400 and 800 square metres) and cultivated not by individual households but by many different members of the cooperative.

The authorities may have intended to prevent the partitioning of Soviet space – the subdividing of agricultural territories into individual family plots – but this aim was soon subverted in practice. Correspondence between the sponsor organizations of garden settlements (factories, enterprises, and other employers), the trade unions, and the city and regional authorities shows clearly that Soviet urbanites overwhelmingly preferred to work on their own plots instead of contributing labour to what were in effect collective farms for urbanites. The territory of garden settlements was soon split up into individual sections: even in the early 1950s, this seems to have been the standard practice, although it was rarely mentioned directly.

An even more controversial issue was the permissibility of dwellings on garden plots. To begin with, in the immediate postwar period, they were absolutely forbidden, but the interdictions soon started to lose their force. Factories and enterprises lobbied local soviets, pointing out that gardeners could not do without simple shacks in which to store tools and seek shelter in bad weather. In time, over the 1950s, the restrictions loosened still further: garden settlements, and individual members of those settlements, became more self-assertive in marking off separate plots and putting up modest single-family dwellings on those plots. By the Khrushchev era – a time when land for all kinds of construction was widely distributed through organizations – garden plots were generally coming to be understood as the poor man's dacha.

Garden plot holders were now free to build themselves a quasi-dacha, but they did not receive much in the way of official encouragement or practical support as they did so. The tasks of making the plot fit for habitation, laying the foundation, obtaining building materials, and putting up the house were left to them. Some people brought in paid labourers to help, but many relied on their own efforts and those of their family members. At the same time, they had to contend with severe official regulations that sought to box in the property instincts of Soviet citizens.

Houses were to have no more than one storey, they were to be unheated, and their floor area and number of windows were always restricted.

Even so, the case of garden plots provides a striking illustration of the ways in which official regulations and other public normative statements could leave room for manoeuvre 'on the ground'. As garden settlements were originally conceived, they precluded any appropriation by individuals of the communally used and maintained space. But over time, and in practice, people made the official regulations more elastic, or simply ignored them. By the 1960s the right of 'collective' gardeners to cultivate their own plot and to build their own dwelling on it was not seriously disputed; the more adventurous of them might now test out or second-guess the regulations by putting up outbuildings, making improvements to the interior, or even risking an extension. And cultural values seem to have shifted in line with social practices. It is from about this time that people began to elide 'dacha plot dachas' and 'garden plot dachas' in linguistic usage: the word 'dacha' served for both these types of dwelling.

The new terminology was symptomatic of changes in the attitudes of Soviet urbanites towards their exurban patch. Most obviously, even garden plot holders now had that precondition for domesticity: a house. As Aleksandr Vysokovsky has convincingly argued, dacha-style dwellings were the nearest Soviet city-dwellers came to a private home and tended to elicit in them warm feelings. Dachas provided a home environment tied closely to people's aspirations, activities and emotions; urban apartments, by contrast, were received as a handout from the State and could not be created and moulded by their owner-occupants to anything like the same extent.[11] To be sure, dachniki were constrained in the type of dwelling they chose both by the shortage economy and by official restrictions: building materials were always hard to obtain, and houses were not in any case allowed to exceed certain set dimensions. But the very fact of having to overcome such obstacles seems to have played a large part in developing in people an emotional and experiential bond with their exurban environment. By all accounts, the affective power of the dacha or garden plot was felt even in the earliest attempts to make it habitable; many of my informants recalled the significance of building a temporary shack (*vremianka*), and several emphasized the importance of an even more fundamental piece of domestic architecture: the short-drop toilet encased in a flimsy lean-to. The main building on the plot would follow in as short a time as the family's resources permitted: in some cases a few weeks, in others several years.

To an uninitiated eye, garden plot dwellings perhaps differed little: most of them were of the same size and followed very similar designs.

But the very fact that most garden plot holders built their own houses meant that these dwellings, and their associated spaces (both internal and external), soon acquired an extremely personalized history. In many cases, the peripeteias of a dacha's biography were preserved in very visible and tangible form: the dwelling was gradually adapted and extended as more building materials became available or official regulations loosened. The interior of the dacha dwelling was made not only habitable but also domesticated. Furniture and other artefacts (books, crockery, record players) were recycled from city flats, walls were painted and papered, internal partitions were used to generate further rooms, and attics (*mansardy*) were converted into a sleeping space. Outbuildings – sheds, shower huts, chicken coops – might provide the finishing touches to a fully equipped and properly functioning garden plot.

The acquisition of a garden plot became a fundamental structuring event in the life stories of Soviet citizens. As one of my respondents, a garden plot holder since the early 1980s, reflected: 'There were my student years, the years of military service, the years of my professional career. Now my "garden plot" years have arrived, and they will clearly last as long as I live.' Many of the 'dacha biographies' that I have heard or read stress the subject's initial resistance to the idea of an out-of-town landholding. Dachniki in the 1960s and 1970s were commonly able to obtain a plot only in middle age and were often dismayed by the prospect of bureaucratic and other practical difficulties, as well as by the sheer investment of time that dacha construction and garden cultivation represented. Yet they had little choice but to take what they were offered: a second home, however modest, was just too great an amenity to be spurned by Soviet families whose three generations often lived in as many rooms (or fewer) in their city flats.

Garden plots were soon found, moreover, to have positive attractions of their own. The cultivation of the plot and the construction of a dwelling were arduous but engrossing and satisfying. The ability to overcome the problems thrown up by the shortage economy brought with it a healthy rise in social status: the owner of a dacha was a 'man who knew how to live'. The achievement of post-Stalin dachniki was all the greater given that in general they did not bring in workmen even for the more specialized jobs: the members of dacha and garden cooperatives tended to do all the building themselves. In fact, for two generations of Soviet men, the ability to construct and kit out the family dacha was an important means of self-validation. It also enabled them to measure themselves against their peers: given that the size, shape and design of the house were restricted by legislation, 'good' dachas would be distinguished from 'bad' dachas not by the number of floors or rooms, but by how the windows had been fitted or the cement laid. One St Petersburg man, born in 1933, recalled in the late 1990s the satisfaction he had gained from joining a garden cooperative relatively late in life (at the age of fifty):

> You go along, have a look, there are plenty of people you know in the cooperative, they're building houses, so you go up to them, take a look, ask them about how they do things. It's a real job building a dacha yourself, you lay the bricks, you mix the cement, you do the carpentry. Makes you both academician and hero, as they say [. . .] It gives you a kind of moral satisfaction when you're making something with your own hands.[12]

When he stood back and contemplated his endeavours, the Soviet garden plot dachnik could construct for himself a gratifying self-image. In the words of one of my respondents: 'The owner of a dacha stands out from those around him: he is practical, industrious, determined and full of optimism in his anticipation of regular contact with nature.' Such sentiments, and the stock narratives of dacha life to which they gave rise, can be traced not only in interview and memoir material, but also in mainstream Soviet fiction, which in the post-Stalin era became increasingly concerned with, and informative on, questions of everyday life. The same gendered proprietorial impulse as in the quotation above informs a short story of the 1980s where the hero, a welder at the local factory, finds his vocation (and thereby abandons the bottle) by building his own house:

> Three years Kondrat spent building his allotment house, building it thoroughly and without haste, and the house came out a real marvel: it was spacious, light and cosy. It reminded you of a traditional Siberian izba, where there's nothing superfluous, where everything has been thought through and made to last. [. . .]
> He'd done the house, the gates, the little veranda and the greenhouse according to his own taste: solidly, in the peasant manner, without any excessive dacha-style showiness. Next to over-elaborate two-storey mansions and houses with strange roofs cut away to make room for attic windows, his estate [*usad'ba*] was most likely the finest of all, in the way a person with inner spiritual grace is fine.[13]

Here an attempt is made to reclaim the country house as an attribute of an authentic, patriarchal rural world; the dacha, persistently feminized in Russian culture since the nineteenth century, is invested with spartan male virtues. The word 'dacha' acquires some quite different connotations – as a plot of land to be looked after, not as a place of idle repose.

Kondrat steadfastly resists any incursion of cluttering 'feminine' artefacts into his austere new home. His wife tries to prettify their dwelling by laying out a flowery oil-cloth on the table, but is told off severely for doing so: 'Don't even think of it! You hold sway at home in the flat, but don't go setting up a stupid perfumery here.'[14] But she is happy to be tolerant: the 'dacha' has cured Kondrat of his alcoholism and given him a sense of purpose and pride. As another fictional character reflects in a moment of villagerly revelation, with her family about to revoke its decision to place its dacha on the market, 'city flats don't seem to be for living in but for passing time'; the dacha, by contrast, brings a sense of purpose and participation in community life. Neighbours in urban apartment buildings are largely indifferent to one another; dacha owners, on the other hand, form a mutual-aid 'brotherhood' that cuts across social boundaries such as that between manual and intellectual workers.[15]

We see here how the dacha could be accommodated within perhaps the most powerful cultural trend of the post-Stalin decades: a growing awareness of the economic predicament and cultural potential of the Russian village. In its literary manifestations this was known as 'village prose' (*derevenskaia proza*). Narratives infused with this rusticizing spirit treated dachas approvingly if they could be construed as a return to village roots or as an adoption of patriarchal values.[16] But dacha folk qua holidaymakers were consistently contrasted unfavourably with year-round residents in the same settlements. On occasion this led authors to the conclusion that dachas were doomed not only morally but physically: one conventional way of bringing closure to narratives of exurban life was to reveal on the last page that the settlement in question was shortly to be removed in order to make way for a rest home or a suburb.[17]

Dacha texts tended nonetheless to treat the exurban impulse with sympathy: the willingness of city-dwellers to confront serious obstacles in order to satisfy their thirst for land was viewed as praiseworthy; and their urge to own property was assessed in various ways but rarely subjected to outright censure. One exemplary case is *Dacha for Immediate Sale*, a lengthy story set in a provincial city in the 1970s or 1980s. Nina Pavlovna Kalugina, recently retired, leaps at the chance to snap up a dacha sold cheap due to the owners' sudden departure. Her husband Igor' Petrovich, stuck in a middle-aged rut of television and detective novels, is unenthusiastic. Nina Pavlovna gets to work on him by stressing the benefits of the dacha for their health and domestic economy, but also by pointing out that having a dacha is quite accessible even to ordinary people like them: 'here [i.e. in this town] what people call dachas aren't just suburban villas or izbas bought up in villages, but also the most ordinary little houses in collective garden associations.'[18]

Igor' Petrovich is eventually won over and, on acquiring a plot in a garden settlement, quickly finds himself forming a bond with the soil. Then, amazingly, he hits on the idea of building a new house from scratch himself. As he ponders his options on a walk around a neighbouring settlement, he catches sight of a dacha that matches his ideal:

> The house contained an unimaginable variety of architectural styles of different eras and peoples. There were European blinds on the windows, the roof was crowned by a gothic tower, there were north Russian carved window surrounds and cornices, a porch under an awning, once again carved. And all this had been painted as if the decorator, finding that one tin of paint had unexpectedly run out, had grabbed another, the first one that came to hand, and when he'd finished that, took yet another, and carried on painting without thinking about how the colours sky blue, orange, green and raspberry were coordinated. But the point was that the colour coordination lay precisely in this apparent lack of coordination. The house was alive, it breathed, it made inspired play with the colours, entrancing passers-by even at a fleeting glance.[19]

This passage is extremely expressive not only of Soviet Russian standards of taste, but also of an ostensibly un-Soviet concern with domestic space and pride in personal property. The owner of this dacha – who, it transpires, is a mouse-like work colleague of Igor' Petrovich's – has, like another fictional dacha-owner mentioned earlier, been saved from alcoholism by the acquisition of a plot of land. In a conversation with Igor' Petrovich, he expounds on the destructive effects of *beskhoziaistvennost'* (the neglect of property brought on by the absence of ownerly instincts), claiming that no word for this concept can be found in non-Soviet dictionaries.

The dacha's difficult connection to the property issue in Soviet Russia is often identified as one of its main features. Although in theory most dacha or garden plot holders were members of a collective, in practice they were able to dispose freely of their individual dwellings. Dacha settlements may not have been the only places where Soviet citizens could indulge their proprietorial urges, but such urges found unusually visible, not to say spatialized, expression. Individual plots were very publicly partitioned off from the public areas of the settlement. And even within the limits of a single plot, space might be further subdivided. It was common for a single extended family to use the same plot, sometimes dividing the dacha dwelling into two or more distinct parts. Plots might also be shared by people with no such blood relation. In the immediate postwar period especially, individual dachas seem quite often to have been subdivided into separate flats – to the extent that a government circular of December 1953 had to offer specific instructions on the correct way to proceed if land disputes arose between people sharing a single plot within a dacha cooperative.[20] The aim of 1950s legislation on dacha cooperatives was to regularize the procedures whereby people acquired and transferred their plots and houses and to put an end to 'abuses' involving the de facto sale of patches of land or of rooms in the dacha. A building in a dacha cooperative could be transferred to another person on condition that that person was accepted as a member of the cooperative.[21] But the fact that proscribed informal arrangements persisted was reflected in the quantity of advice given on the legal resolution of conflicts arising from shared use of dachas.[22] The documentary evidence I have seen suggests that family disputes – especially those surrounding divorce settlements – could have extremely messy consequences; in some cases, internal partitioning was ordered by a court as the only way of reconciling the plaintiffs' conflicting claims.[23]

Such goings-on in dacha settlements were a mild embarrassment for a society that proclaimed to be advancing steadily towards harmonious collectivism; not for nothing did the *Krokodil* satirists draw readers' attention to avaricious dacha landlords and to fenceside disputes between dacha neighbours. Yet the available evidence strongly suggests that official pronouncements on property had a basic congruity with the concepts employed by people 'on the ground'. Both these discourses, when exploring the basis for property rights, attached most importance not to a contractual relation between people and things or even to blood relations between people (although these factors were of course not ignored), but rather to the ways in which labour was performed. Quite simply, the person who had made the largest contribution to cultivating the dacha plot or building the dacha dwelling deserved the largest share. An impassioned justification of the property impulse on these grounds is found in another piece of dacha fiction where the hero, deeply offended by his wife's less than enthusiastic response to the house he has gone to enormous trouble to build, explains to himself the attraction it has for him. In contrast to the rented accommodation where he has spent his whole life up to now:

> [h]ere he had built a dwelling himself, with his own hands, he'd poured his own soul into this house. And even if it wasn't much to look at, even if it wasn't a grand residence or a villa, it was at least his, every last log in it had been nurtured by him, every detail had been polished and warmed in his hands a hundred times over. And this house wasn't official [*kazennyi*], nothing here was slapdash. The desire to have your own house, either held openly or kept to yourself, can probably be found in every person, and it is indestructible.[24]

Yet the same character who here so passionately defends the dignity of personal ownership is tormented just a few lines later by the various deceptions he has had to perpetrate in order to complete his house. He has committed theft of state property many times over, which makes him no different from millions of other Soviet citizens, but which he nonetheless finds deeply shameful to admit. Dachniki, as we see clearly in this story, were caught between their aspiration (by the 1970s generally regarded as legitimate) to build a house of their own and the wholly illegitimate means that were required if this aspiration was ever to be met.[25]

My account has tended to present the late Soviet dacha as an embodiment of an awakening domesticity, as part of the post-Stalin 'discovery' of private life. But it is also possible to interpret the dacha phenomenon in a quite different light: to see the garden settlements that mushroomed from the 1960s onwards as collective farms for underprovisioned urbanites, as open-air communal flats. For, on the face of it, these garden settlements, which might easily number one thousand or more separate plots, offered little privacy and drew people willy-nilly into forms of collective life. The planning authorities usually offered the least hospitable parts of their region to garden collectives, and all members of the new garden collective could be mobilized to help make the territory fit for habitation – by clearing trees or draining marshy land, and then by marking out plots and roads. Smaller mutual aid networks seem often to have been formed in order to accomplish specific tasks: notably, to obtain building materials. Most people, moreover, did grow vegetables in their garden, and the very fact of spending several hours every day in the open air and in public view drew them into the local community – and, perhaps more pertinently, into the public gaze.

So how exactly can we categorize the late Soviet dacha? And behind this question lurks a more general issue: how can we conceptualize the relationship of 'public' and 'private' spaces in Soviet Russia? A useful first step, I think, is to recognize that this relationship was not fixed: the 'dacha' of the 1930s was very different from that of the 1970s. In the Stalin period, dachas were still very much a minority phenomenon even in the major cities, while by the Brezhnev era they had become available to a significantly greater proportion of the urban population (and in the late 1980s their social constituency would expand dramatically). In the 1930s the communal flat had been the main domestic arena for social interaction in the major cities, but by the 1970s the separate flat and the garden settlement were becoming the most prominent domestic spaces for Soviet urbanites. And this change is indicative not only of an improvement in living standards but also of a shift in the practices and unwritten rules of everyday life.

The communal flat, quite apart from being a grim reality in the lives of millions of Soviet people in the 1930s and afterwards, can serve as a powerful metaphor for Stalin-era society: a social microcosm where basic human ties have been severed, where trust between people has broken down, where the household unit has been destroyed and coercively reformed, and where surveillance of the individual by the collective is consequently greatly facilitated. The *kommunalka* was a worm's-eye panopticon where only 'public privacy' was possible.[26] When we turn to the late Soviet dacha, however, it seems possible to reverse this formulation and argue that garden settlements were characterized by an altogether more benign 'private publicness'. For, although members of garden cooperatives were tied explicitly to an organization and never out of range of the collective eye, they were at least able to retreat to a plot of land, and to a modest dwelling, that they could without too many qualifications call their own. And, although there remained (especially in the Khrushchev period) a risk of unheralded intrusions by the State, in general dacha folk were able to gain a sense of the permissible and to achieve some limited agency in pushing back the limits of the legitimate. The genealogy of the late Soviet dacha suggests, therefore, that the grand structuring narratives of Soviet space can be supplemented – and qualified – by the smaller stories of everyday habitats. The postwar garden plot provides a pleasingly demarcated and spatialized test site for studying the interplay of state 'project' and individual and group action in postwar Russia.

Notes

1. V. Papernyi, *Kul'tura 'dva'* (Ann Arbor: Ardis, 1985).
2. E. Widdis, 'Projecting a Soviet Space: Exploration and Mobility in Soviet Film and Culture, 1920–35' (Ph.D. dissertation, Cambridge University, 1998).
3. See for example J. Carey, *The Intellectuals and the Masses: Pride and Prejudice Among the Literary Intelligentsia, 1880–1939* (London: Faber, 1992), pp. 46–70.
4. Note again the parallel with Anglo-American suburbia, which was persistently 'feminized' in public discourse from the mid-nineteenth century onwards.
5. A much fuller treatment of this question, and of the social and institutional history of the early Soviet dacha, can be found in my article 'The Making of the Stalin-Era Dacha', *The Journal of Modern History*, June 2002.

6. *Kul'turnost'* is extensively glossed in C. Kelly and V. Volkov, 'Directed Desires: *Kul'turnost'* and Consumption', in C. Kelly and D. Shepherd, eds, *Constructing Russian Culture in the Age of Revolution, 1881–1940* (Oxford: Oxford University Press, 1998).

7. The apt phrase 'austere consumerism' is drawn from D. Crowley and S. Reid, 'Style and Socialism: Modernity and Material Culture in Post-War Eastern Europe', in their edited volume of the same title (Oxford: Berg, 2000), p. 12.

8. A word on sources: besides archival and published materials, I draw on numerous informal ethnographic interviews and on a set of twenty unpublished memoirs. The latter were elicited by 'dacha biography competitions' that were advertised in the newspapers *Vechernii klub* (Moscow) and *Sankt-Peterburgskie vedomosti* in 1999.

9. See for example M. Voslensky, *Nomenklatura: Anatomy of the Soviet Ruling Class* (London: Bodley Head, 1984), pp. 205–6.

10. This was clearly stated in the statutes (*ustav*) of garden settlements.

11. A. Vysokovsky, 'Will Domesticity Return?', in W. C. Brumfield and B. Ruble, eds, *Russian Housing in the Modern Age: Design and Social History* (Cambridge: Cambridge University Press, 1993).

12. I am grateful to Irina Chekhovskikh for sharing with me the transcript of this interview.

13. V. Zikunov, 'Kondratova dacha', in idem, *Rodinskie kolodtsy: Rasskazy* (Krasnoiarsk, 1990), pp. 41 and 44.

14. Zikunov, 'Kondratova dacha', p. 42.

15. These quotations are taken from another piece of standard-issue late Soviet fiction: T. Nikolaeva, 'Prodaetsia dacha', in idem, *Na malen'koi stantsii: Povesti i rasskazy* (Gor'kii, 1987), pp. 114 and 94 respectively.

16. A striking example is G. Popov, 'Dacha' (1965), in idem, *Gusi-lebedi: Rasskazy* (Minsk, 1968).

17. On the counterposing of dachniki and permanent residents, see A. Chernousov, 'Vtoroi dom', *Nash sovremennik*, no. 1 (1983); N. Kozhevnikova, 'Dacha: Povest'', *Oktiabr'*, no. 12 (1983); G. Shergova, 'Zakolochennye dachi', *Novyi mir*, no. 3 (1978); Iu. Trifonov, 'Starik', in idem, *Sobranie sochinenii v chetyrekh tomakh*, 4 vols (Moscow: Khudozhestvennaia literatura, 1985–7), vol. 3.

18. O. Pavlovskii, 'Srochno prodaetsia dacha', in idem, *Srochno prodaetsia dacha: Povesti* (Kaliningrad, 1989), p. 7. This point is echoed later (p. 19) in an ironic observation by their eighty-year-old neighbour: 'It's only lately that they've started calling them dachas, afore that they were just allotments like any others'.

19. Ibid., p. 63.
20. 'O poriadke pol'zovaniia zemel'nymi uchastkami v dachakh DSK' (22 December 1953), in T. D. Alekseev, comp., *Zhilishchnye zakony*, 3rd ed., expanded (Moscow: Izdatel'stvo Ministerstva kommunal'nogo khoziaistva RSFSR, 1957). The recommended procedure – that such disputes be settled before 'comrades' courts' within the dacha cooperative – was discussed in more detail in a later article: see B. Erofeev and M. Lipetsker, 'Sudebnye spory ob ustanovlenii poriadka pol'zovaniia zemel'nymi uchastkami', *Sotsialisticheskaia zakonnost'* (hereafter *SZ*), no. 4 (1959).
21. This policy is spelled out in *SZ*, no. 5 (1950): in the cautionary case cited (from the late 1940s), a cooperative member had sold an outbuilding on his plot without consulting the administration; it then transpired that the outbuilding was liable for removal as it had been put up without the necessary permission. The original sale agreement was accordingly declared annulled.
22. For examples, see 'Iz praktiki prokuratury SSSR', *SZ*, no. 9 (1951), p. 93; Ia. Ianovskii, 'Pravovoe regulirovanie zhiloi ploshchadi chlenov zhilishchno-stroitel'nykh i dachno-stroitel'nykh kooperativov', *SZ*, no. 8 (1955); A. Mel'nikov, 'Sudebnaia praktika po sporam s dachno-stroitel'nymi kooperativami', *SZ*, no. 10 (1958); *Sovetskaia iustitsiia*, no. 7 (1959), pp. 83–4.
23. Cases of this kind can be found in Tsentral'nyi munitsipal'nyi arkhiv g. Moskvy, f. 819, op. 3, dd. 2, 192, 293.
24. Chernousov, 'Vtoroi dom', p. 90.
25. Two further, contrasting, treatments of the theme are: I. Davydov, 'Dacha v Malakhovke', in idem, *Devushka moego druga* (Saratov, 1965), where the dacha property urge is seen as wholly destructive and debasing, and V. Lukashevich, 'Zimniaia dacha', in idem, *Doroga cherez zarosli: Povesti i rasskazy* (Moscow, 1972), where it is treated with considerably more sympathy.
26. The characterization of the communal flat as an arena for 'public privacy' is taken from Katerina Gerasimova's chapter in this volume.

Weekend Getaways: The *Chata*, the *Tramp*, and the Politics of Private Life in Post-1968 Czechoslovakia[1]

Paulina Bren

In August 1968 the Soviet-led Warsaw Pact invasion of Czechoslovakia brought an end to the Prague Spring – and with it, to any hopes of reforming communism – and placed a pro-Moscow, politically orthodox regime in power. This post-Prague Spring communist leadership initiated what was officially referred to as 'normalization' – a programme for political consolidation, social conformity, and a return to 'normal, socialist life'. But what exactly was 'normal, socialist life' to be in the aftermath of the political tumultuousness and experimentation that had been the Prague Spring?

The country's future communist leader, Gustav Husák, offered an answer soon after the invasion. He explained: '[A] normal person wants to live quietly, without certain groups turning us into a jungle, and therefore we must appeal to people so that they condemn this. This party wants to safeguard the quiet life.'[2] If the reform communists of the 1960s had wrought havoc and brought disorder, now, under 'normalization', the quiet life would rule supreme: a quietness in large part dependent on a nationwide amnesia about the recent past as well as a wilted ambition for a socialist utopia. As such, the 1970s and 1980s would look radically different from the earlier two decades of postwar communism that had encompassed first Stalinism and then political liberalization.

This essay explores the ways in which the recreational use of the Czech countryside intersected with the ideologically motivated endorsement of the 'quiet life', intended by the Party as an antidote to the resurgence of any political activism reminiscent of the Prague Spring. I will focus on two opposing uses of the outdoors: *chata* culture and the *tramping* movement. *Chata* culture entailed the ever-expanding Czech pastime of long weekends spent at a private country cottage in the Czechoslovak countryside, and while not always applauded by the regime, this activity became a part of public discourse during the 1970s and 1980s. In contrast, the far less publicized, and frequently censured, *tramping* movement involved young people gathering in groups and venturing into the countryside with little more than a small backpack of supplies. Both movements embodied distinctly different notions of community, citizenship and political resistance, and yet, with varying degrees, both contributed to the disruption of the sought-after 'quiet life'. By juxtaposing the *chata* movement and the *tramping* movement, I further wish to show how conflicts played out under communism were frequently layered with memories and experiences rooted in the pre-communist period and should not automatically be viewed as self-contained episodes of postwar history.

Chata Culture

In 1969, as the 'normalization' leadership acquired full control of the government, as the country's borders were once again sealed off for travel, and as a large-scale purge against reform communists was set in motion, the public, retreating into their homes, sought solace amongst friends and family. It was at this time that the Czech pastime of the weekend escape into the countryside also acquired a renewed popularity. The typical destination for this weekend getaway was a so-called *chata*: a simple, recreational cottage in the Czech countryside, either a newly built structure or else a renovated peasants' cottage. The *chata* and the weekend getaway had existed earlier, but its popularity exploded after 1969. The result was a large increase in the purchase of already existing cottages as well as the land on which to build new structures. According to an analysis made in the early 1980s by the Czech Institute of Interior Design, 31% of Prague households owned a *chata*, 25% of Prague households otherwise had access to one belonging to friends or relatives, and 5–10% of Prague households used *chaty* belonging to their workplace. On average people were spending 100 to 120 days a year at their country retreat.[3]

By the early 1970s, the official press was openly referring to the phenomenon as '*chata*-mania'.[4] Curiously, this was a peculiarly Czech obsession, making far less headway in the Slovak part of the country.[5] Very quickly, the *chata* became part of the physical and cultural landscape of the Czech republic, with cities emptying on Friday afternoons as everyone set out to the countryside for a long weekend. As one expert on Czechoslovakia noted in the 1980s, the timbre of the 'normalization' period resonated in the commonplace image of an 'early escape on Friday afternoon in a private car laden with stacks of precooked Wiener schnitzel for a weekend away from it all at a private country cottage'.[6] The epitome of this trend, frequently parodied in film and television, were the *chata* colonies – clusters of new, often aesthetically unattractive, recreation cottages, with rows of Trabant and Škoda cars parked out in front.[7]

Despite such ostentatious displays of materialism, the regime did not, by and large, rail against this self-contained, private activity, nor against the emphasis on consumerism that came with furnishing the insides of the *chata*. Although private property still remained for the most part unavailable and indeed taboo in the cities, as befitted Party ideology, restrictions on owning small-scale private property in the countryside had always been much looser and less likely to be investigated. Enthusiasm for the *chata*, therefore, also represented an unconcealed pleasure in the acquisition and use of otherwise 'forbidden' private property. That the regime did not discourage this weekend pastime and its use of the Czech countryside is suggested by the existence of an official monthly magazine dedicated to the interests of the *chata* enthusiast.

Chatař (The *Chata*-Owner) offered its readers a do-it-yourself paradise: the bulk of articles in the magazine were centred on home improvement, offering detailed explanations, including blueprints, on how to build a sturdier roof, a straighter staircase, thicker walls, etc. For the times when the precooked Wiener schnitzel had run out, each issue of *Chatař* provided recipes built around the canned meats one could easily transport to the *chata* in the family car, and even puzzles and games to entertain the children in case the weather turned inclement. Everything that *chata* owners might possibly need was inside the magazine's pages, just as everything they needed was also within the four walls of their weekend cottage. Occasionally, the Party did demand that people explore opportunities for more communal getaways, such as work-sponsored outings, but, despite the rhetoric, it took no consistent measures to constrain the blossoming *chata* culture.

There were, I would argue, two reasons for the regime's unspoken consent. First, burdened with an intransigent public after the 1968 invasion, and needing to seek some sort of consensus with them, the Party leadership was quick to promise an improved standard of living that could even duplicate the lifestyles spied by the Czech public during the 1960s when they were able to travel for the first time in large numbers to 'the West'.[8] The weekend retreat into the Czechoslovak countryside – while not comparable to a trip to Italy – promised to deliver on a regular basis the sort of rewards that communism and the communists had been promising for so long. People were given the go-ahead to focus on satisfying their material needs, especially within and around the home.[9] In fact, the regime's acquiescence might have been best explained by William Levitt, creator of the history-making postwar American suburb of Levittown, when he claimed that, 'No man who owns his own house and lot can be a Communist. He has too much to do.'[10] Because while the normalizers wanted their citizens to be communists, they did not want them to be politically active, only politically compliant. The demands of acquiring and maintaining a *chata* conveniently detracted from the practice of politics during this period of late communism when, as the cultural theorist Slavoj Žižek has said, the last thing any communist regime wished to see was for its citizens to actually act out communism.[11]

The second reason I want to suggest for the 'normalization' government's collaboration in the burgeoning *chata* culture was the obvious political advantages to be gained if the cities emptied out during the weekends, splintering urban inhabitants amongst different country locales. As the regime had learned from the experience of the Prague Spring, political discontent translated into political resistance not in the villages but in the cities; dissatisfaction was transformed into political action not by agricultural workers but by the cities' intellectuals and intelligentsia. Thus, *chata* culture could ostensibly provide for a depoliticized, government-mediated escape into pastoral Bohemia and Moravia for those who sought solace from the trauma of 'normalization'. There the regime allowed its citizens a modicum of self-realization in the area of consumption as compensation for the lack of independence permitted in politics.

'Normalization' and Privatized Citizenship

Altogether, the 'normalization' government's support of the *chata* culture could be conceptualized as what Michel de Certeau referred to as 'strategy' – 'the imposition of power through the disciplining and organization of space'.[12] The 'normalization' regime and the official press never stated directly, yet implied constantly, that to own a *chata*, to spend weekends in the countryside, in the tamed outdoors, meant to participate in the current success of what was now called 'real socialism';[13] to be a *chata*-owner was to be a good communist. A communist citizen who defined himself within the contours of his private life and not his public self was seen as preferable, as more likely to conform to what Party leader Husák had referred to early on as 'the quiet life'. Grand gestures – once portrayed poster-size by communists riding joyously atop combine harvesters, joined in a communal embrace – were now too politically inflammatory to contemplate.

The Prague Spring and its calls for reform communism had poisoned the notion of public politics, of street-level political argument, for the orthodox communists now in power. The political ideology that became the cornerstone of 'normalization' was, therefore, quite different: it aimed to define and locate communist citizenship within a publicly shared private world. Public life was cast out in favour of what Lauren Berlant, writing on 1980s Reagan America and the infantilization of citizenship, has called 'simultaneously lived private worlds'.[14] The *chata* culture perfected just such a vision in that citizens were encouraged to define and locate themselves in a private world, one that was at the same time being replicated by others around them, thus offering the pretence of public life while avoiding its dangers.

Chata culture thrived on the fantasy of the weekend getaway as a private retreat where one was left to one's own devices, beyond the ideological radar range of the 'normalization' regime. This supposedly individual escape from ideological demands and political pressures was however being shared by millions of other citizens, while also being promoted by the government. Throughout the 1970s and 1980s, the *Chatař* magazine played to this very fantasy, always featuring on its front cover a photograph of a single, solitary, unpeopled *chata* surrounded only by trees and grass. It was an image that immediately suggested isolation, separateness and self-sufficiency.[15] The weekend exodus to the country cottage has been read most often, by both its practitioners as well as by its commentators, as a defiant gesture: to get away to the *chata* was to act on the desire to escape into the depoliticized private sphere, into the embrace of family and friends where political jokes and anti-communist sentiments were freely voiced. For example, Czech sociologist Lenka Kalinová has argued that the *chata* culture was an expression of disillusionment with collective recreation.[16] Yet it cannot be overlooked that the *chata* culture centred on a decidedly state-endorsed escape, whereby a person in fact participated in 'normalization' and the government's desire for 'the quiet life'. In this sense, the Czech countryside had ceased to be 'elsewhere', although the desire for it to be so remained.

The *Tramping* Movement

The regime's acceptance – even if grudging – of *chata* culture can be surmised from the way in which this pastime figured vividly in the public discourse. In contrast, the so-called *tramping* movement – an alternative and less politically agreeable use of the Czech countryside – remained shrouded in secrecy and silence. Unlike the *chata* culture, the *tramping* movement had been founded on preserving the notion of the countryside as 'elsewhere', as beyond the reach of state control. Furthermore, the movement strove to retain its history at a time when the preservation of 'history' and 'memory' had come to be seen as a defiant gesture by a regime intent on forgetting the past: as Milan Kundera would write in *The Book of Laughter and Forgetting*, '[I]t is 1971 . . . The struggle of man against power is the struggle of memory against forgetting.'[17]

According to the chroniclers of the movement, *tramping* had first taken root after the First World War in the newly founded, democratic Czechoslovak Republic. It began as a Saturday afternoon ritual among Czech working-class youth, particularly those living and working in Prague. With their working week done, these young men and women would pack a small rucksack and head into the Czech countryside, spending the remainder of their free weekend together in the outdoors. Their intention was to unshackle themselves from the restrictions imposed on them in the city by their employers and their circumstances; for a short while, at least, to leave the reality of their lives behind and to live instead according to their own rules in the outdoors. More clearly than in the case of the later *chata* culture, the *tramping* movement represented an unmitigated escape into the Czech countryside as a form of resistance against the dominant political ideology of capitalist, conservative, bourgeois values.

The history of the *tramping* movement should have been an attractive piece of propaganda for the Communist Party, which was keen to demonstrate that class-based cleavages and political radicalism had been a central component of the independent, 'democratic' interwar republic for which many citizens continued to feel a deep nostalgia. Yet references to the movement were almost non-existent in the official histories of twentieth-century Czechoslovakia. This interwar youth movement was largely absent from the annals of the reimagined past, at most reduced to a memory of the songs once sung by the *trampové* around their campfires. Stanislav Motl, a member of the interwar *trampové*, confirmed this historiographical absence. In the preface to the 1990 reprinting of Josef Peterka's 1940 chronicle of the movement, *A History of Tramping*, Motl wrote that silence closed down around the movement after the 1948 communist takeover of Czechoslovakia, was temporarily lifted during the liberal Prague Spring period, and then reinstated under 'normalization'. It only became possible to discuss *tramping* openly after the 1989 'velvet revolution'.[18]

Not surprisingly, this policy of censure was never directly explained by the communist regime, but one can guess at the reasons for it, especially as the details of this movement emerge. During the interwar years, the *tramping* movement became closely intertwined with a fascination for American Wild West lore. In the early 1920s, as young, urban Czechs began to congregate in the countryside at weekends, they called themselves 'wild scouts' to distinguish between their pastime and the institutionalized scouting movement that was then also taking root. Over time, these wild scouts began to assemble at specific points along the rivers and the valleys of Bohemia and Moravia, setting up camp settlements which they named, in admiration of the American Wild West, 'Rawhide', 'Hiawatha', 'Yukon', 'Utah', 'Uragan', (*sic!*) 'Liberty', and 'Kansas'. The wild scouts' surroundings were similarly renamed so that the Vltava river, which runs through Prague under the Charles Bridge, was now 'Big River', while smaller tributaries took on names such as 'Old River', 'Gold River' and 'Snake River'.[19] And just as these young men and women sought to carve out new identities in the 'wilderness' of the Czech countryside, so they also renamed themselves. In his 1940 chronicle of the movement, Josef Peterka (aka 'Bob Hurikán') recalled: 'Overnight, Anička, Manička and Boženka became Annie, Mary, Bobina or Daisy, Betsy, Virginia; and with the men it was even worse: Jarda became Harry, Pepík became Bob, Ota became Brandy, Zdeněk Iron Fist or Winthrop, Edie and sometimes even Swenny, Grizzly . . . Bill, Old Shatterhand, Farnum, Dawson, Jack, etc.'[20] In the late 1920s, the 'wild scouts' permanently adopted the epithet 'tramps' (*trampové*), and began to refer to their outings as 'going on the tramp', or going 'tramping'. The word 'tramping' was apparently taken from the literary work of Jack London who used the term to describe a way of life practised by the American 'hobo'.[21]

The Czech *tramping* movement was thus an eclectic appropriation and reimagination of the North American pioneering days and ways. With the end of the First World War, Europe was flooded with American Wild West films. *Red Ace* was one of the first to be shown in Czechoslovakia and, according to Bob Hurikán, it 'shook the souls' of the wild scouts.[22] The American-style hero and the romanticism of the Wild West projected onto the film screen – and further supplemented by the popular novels of the American writer J. F. Cooper and the German writer Karl May – instantly spoke to these young men and women. Trapped in the repetitiveness of factory work and everyday life, these workers and students carved out their freedoms in the landscape of the Czech countryside, using the images of a romantic pioneering America to live on their own terms during the weekends before returning to the aesthetic greyness and the social restrictions that awaited them in the city.[23]

A second likely reason for censure of the movement's history under communism was related to the movement's politicization, which came as a response to the sort of government-initiated harassment that was now reminiscent of the communist regime's own tussles with dissidents. In April 1931, Hugo Kubát, the Czech regional administrator, had declared that persons of the opposite sex could not share a tent or hut if they did not possess a marriage certificate. This government decree was the last in a series of ongoing attempts to control the unfettered wanderings of the cities' working-class youth and, in this case, further to shape their morality. Every Saturday following the declaration of this infamous 'Kubát decree', police descended onto the countryside, chasing the *trampové* from their makeshift accommodations. The *trampové* recognized the political implications of this morality campaign, and pointed to the contradictions in the government's sanctioning of middle- and upper-class immorality while punishing the *trampové's* way of life. As an article in the leftist magazine, *Tramp*, explained to its readers:

> Without a marriage certificate, you're prohibited from going into the woods with a girl! That, however, does not apply for those made-up girls in the automobiles because the decree does not affect countryside hotels. Let's not even talk about the massage parlours and bar rooms. Because there the gentlemen employers are paying to be 'refreshed', with money that you earned for them.[24]

Over the next few years the *trampové* continued to defend their rights under the movement's increasingly radical leadership, and eventually the decrees were rescinded in May 1935.[25] With their political consciousness shaped during these struggles with local authorities, many of the movement's members went on to fight against Franco in the Spanish Civil War and as partisans against the Nazis during the Second World War.[26]

There was also a third reason why the 'normalization' regime had no desire to publicize the interwar *tramping* movement: while gesturing toward leftist radicalism, it, like so many of Eastern Europe's communist parties during this period, was more at ease with the political passivity that bourgeois lifestyles established. Ironically, by promoting *chata* culture, the communists were not building a proletarian society, as they might claim, but creating the sort of middle-class 'settlements' that, during the 1930s, the left-wing second-generation of *trampové* had regarded as the sorry sign of the *embourgeoisement* of a once self-consciously working-class movement. Deriding the increasingly petit-bourgeois habits of ageing first-generation *trampové*, as well as the ways in which the middle classes had taken to imitating the weekend *tramping* life, a 1930 article in *Tramp* sardonically described the current state of affairs:

> Just ten years ago the valley had thundered with volleys of revolver bullets, metal sheathed sombreros shone in the sun, harmonicas ran rampant and nowhere were there signs of a thought about having a roof over one's head. Until there appeared the first cabin made from brushwood. And then a tent. And, well, that was the end . . . And then came Father Time, who sucked out the brains from the boys' skulls and spat them back into their palms; and looking about themselves they said: 'Ha! We're men? Far from it! Are our women girls? Far from it! We are professors and engineers, our girls have become madams and chaste young women – we are ladies and gentlemen![27]

This 1930 description paralleled the very sort of leisure time and use of the outdoors that the communist authorities in the 1970s and 1980s were endorsing because, unlike *tramping*, it did not detract from political compliance but bolstered it.

In short, the *tramping* movement's association of personal freedom with American lifestyles and symbols (no matter how layered with misconceptions and misidentifications) was none too welcome to the communist regime. Nor did the 'normalization' leadership wish to publicize the fact that the conservatism practised by the Czech regional chief Kubát during the 1930s 'bourgeois-democracy' was troublingly similar to the Communist Party's own prurient demands for wholesome socialist citizens. Furthermore, while political left-oriented activism was, in theory, the mainstay of the Communist Party, the communist movement was intolerant of competition from other leftist ideologies, as its 1950s programmatic destruction of social democracy and its supporters showed. It was for all of these reasons that the *tramping* movement went largely unmentioned during communism.

One further explanation, however, can be offered for the communist-imposed silence on this otherwise verdant episode of interwar political radicalism. The *tramping* movement clearly represented a different definition of citizenship and its relationship to space from that promoted by 'normalization'. From the outset, the very essence of *tramping* lay in its emphasis on community. It was both a fluid and yet a tightly-knit community that, during the 1930s, was further transformed into a politically conscious body, becoming, when necessary, a vehicle for resistance. In contrast, the success of the *chata* culture rested on an entirely opposite set of premises; here the goal – for both its participants as well as the regime – was a private, atomized citizenry. It was for this reason that *chata* culture, while sometimes derided by the normalizers for its distasteful displays of materialism, remained acceptable. At the same time, not only the memory of the interwar *tramping* movement but the contemporary *tramping* movement itself remained off-limits to the public.

Tramping as Resistance

In 1978 an article about *tramping* appeared in an issue of the newsletter of the dissident organization Charter 77, regularly sent out to its members to keep them abreast of the government's violations of human rights. The article was written by Vladimír Oborský, a young participant in the ongoing, contemporary *tramping* movement. Oborský used the opportunity to relate the recent experiences of the *trampové*. According to his account, following the onset of 'normalization' in 1969, the communist authorities, anxious not to alienate youth outright, did not immediately eliminate *tramping*. They tried, in the first instance, to bring it under the control of the official Socialist Youth Union, which itself had recently been purged of any cravings for the sort of institutional independence that it had begun to enjoy in the 1960s. By the mid-1970s, it had become evident to the Party that this policy of 'co-option' was failing, and that the *trampové* were remaining free from government control, their movement further bolstered by the influence of the 'Western' hippie movement. The official policy of accommodation was therefore replaced with one of repression.

Oborský argued that the latest course of repression, which intersected with the government's actions against the recently founded Charter 77 dissident group, even outdid the infamous 1931 Kubát decree which had allowed police to hound the *trampové* under the pretext of upholding morality laws. In February 1977, for example, just a month after the official founding of Charter 77, the police had burned one *tramp* campsite to the ground. The destroyed structures included historically significant huts from the early *tramping* movement. This physical destruction was then followed by a press campaign, which charged that, among other things, the *trampové* were organizing orgies in their camps. Interestingly, it was not just the repression that was familiar; the accusation of immorality in 1977 was remarkably reminiscent of the 1931 Kubát decrees that had made it legally possible to arrest *trampové* for sharing lodgings with members of the opposite sex. In addition to the press campaign, Oborský continued, a more covert campaign against the present day *trampové* was also being waged: its young members were being brought in for random police questioning and threatened with the removal of what the police referred to as 'privileges' – including high school matriculation, university enrolment, and career options.[28] *Tramping* evidently continued to play on the same anxieties as it had in the 1920s and 1930s; it stirred fears that young people were taking weekends off from their assigned roles and identities to congregate as a community with its own rules in the unregulated expanse of the Czech countryside.[29] *Tramping* was seen by the authorities as subterfuge disguised as leisure.

Tramping seemed all the more intolerable to the normalizers because, with working-class grievances theoretically resolved, there should have been no need for such activity. And the physical evidence of that resolution was to be found in the existence of the ubiquitous *chata*. A 1974 article in *Tribuna* (The Tribune), the weekly newspaper of the Communist Party's Central Committee, smarted at the unwillingness of the *trampové* to be tamed by the material benefits ostensibly offered to them by communism. The author of the article related her experiences and observations during a recent train ride into the countryside. Sharing the train compartment with her was a group of young *trampové* who, she wrote, pleasantly surprised her with their exemplary behaviour: 'They were not rude or rough, they addressed each other with romantic names, as if picked from some Western.'[30] Even though their manner was not intimidating, the author's sense of order was nevertheless threatened by their appearance: she could not understand why, even if their families were unable to afford a *chata*, these otherwise reasonable young men and women could not keep themselves clean and well groomed. This seemingly innocent remark took on a much larger significance with the author's conclusion of the incident: why, she asked, had the communist government spent so much time and energy ridding the gypsies of their former lifestyles only now to have these children 'from respectable families' adopt the gypsies' lifestyle? As anyone in Eastern Europe well knew, 'gypsy' was the catch-all word for a disregard of political rules, social order, spatial boundaries and modern hygiene. Further, by referring to the *trampové* as children of 'respectable families', the author implied that, in her view, they did indeed have access to a *chata* but were consciously choosing not to make use of it. The point was that so long as they were unable to tame the *trampové*, who insisted on sleeping under the communal stars rather than under the private roof of a *chata*, the communist authorities would never be able to bring the countryside entirely under their jurisdiction, to police its expanse, and to break up the sort of community-building to which *tramping* aspired.

The *Chata* Culture as 'Ruse'

Contrasted with the *tramping* movement, the regime's acceptance of the *chata* phenomenon becomes clearer. In fact, it is only against the background of the anti-state opposition potentially percolating through the *tramping* settlements that the government's endorsement of the atomizing *chata* experience can be situated. I would argue that *chata* culture could only be considered 'acceptable' by the 'normalization' regime if judged solely by the benefits gained from the political passivity it encouraged. If judged by any other criteria, *chata* culture repeatedly fell short because it brought with it more problems than it solved. For example, the infestation of *chaty* and, even more so, of *chata*-owners, into the Czech countryside was soon producing damaging effects on the environment; *chata*-owners tossed their garbage on the ground, and washed their cars outdoors, letting the soapy water drain into the rivers.[31] In addition, as more people increasingly had more money but less to spend it on, *chata* expansion also became a necessary pastime, and included the addition of consumer luxuries such as television antennas, swimming pools, and saunas, also often acquired on the black market.[32] And yet the regime's criticism of the environmental damage, aesthetic vulgarity and blatant materialism associated with *chata* culture remained muted or, at most, gently admonishing, even as it came provocatively close to resembling the much-feared 'petit-bourgeois' mentality seen as typical to 'the West'.[33]

Chata culture further overlapped with the already pressing problem of labour discipline. On Friday afternoons, Czechoslovakia's roads were congested with traffic as everyone made their way to their *chata*. So as to avoid the inevitable traffic jams, people began packing up for the weekend after only a couple of hours of work on Friday. Similarly, they were arriving late to work on Mondays. The working week shrank to little more than three full days of work. Furthermore, plumbers, electricians, builders and other trained craftsmen were not to be found during the four-day weekends because they were off moonlighting on other people's *chaty*, making a sizeable secondary income outside of official state structures.[34] Many people, however, decided to forego hiring professional labour and took on the necessary do-it-yourself tasks themselves, using the instructions and blueprints in *Chatař* as their guide. Through the media, the government thus further implored the public not to treat their workplace as an opportunity to rest after a weekend of hard work fixing up their *chata*.[35] As if labour issues were not enough, *chata* culture further tested the boundaries of the strict morality that the Party ideologues insisted upon: it was common knowledge that *chaty* were popular sites for sexual trysts and extra-marital affairs.

The equally troubling issue of state property theft further intersected with *chata* politics. As rural land for recreational purposes became more scarce, the government insisted that those first in line for purchasing a *chata* should be the politically active members of socialist society, those who 'give more to society'.[36] Such threats were of no use, however; the reality was that those with money, and not ideological dedication, had the means to 'buy' themselves some land, thus further encouraging bribery and corruption. It also became a national joke that *chaty* were being built from stolen state property. One popular film by the director Petr Schulhoff – whose comedies poked fun at the money-grubbing, petit-bourgeois habits of socialist citizens – showed a middle-aged, married couple in their car on the way to their *chata*. They pass by a state construction site where a pile of bricks sits out in the open. As wife and husband scamper out to gather the bricks and toss them quickly into the back of their car, the husband exclaims: 'I can't believe no one's guarding these!' The wife responds happily: 'A few more and we've got ourselves a garage.'[37] In their eyes, it would have been criminal *not* to have taken the bricks to improve their *chata*.

In the process of building, renovating, decorating and enjoying their *chata*, most *chata*-owners, whether consciously or not, stole time and goods from the communist state, and transgressed its rules. It would be overstating the case to suggest that these were acts of outright anti-communist resistance, although the justifications heard most often – that communist property was by definition public property or that theft and truancy damaged only 'them' and not 'us' – sometimes seemed to suggest so. Instead, the actions of so many of the participants in the post-Prague Spring *chata* culture could be understood as what de Certeau called 'tactics', the counterpoint to 'strategy', 'the "ruses" that take the predisposition of the world and make it over, that convert it to the purposes of ordinary people'.[38] Such 'tactics' are the means used by those without power to erode or else subvert the creations of the powerful: to make space ('tactics') within place ('strategy'). As de Certeau noted, 'In these combatants' stratagems, there is a certain art in placing one's blows, a pleasure in getting around the rules of a constraining space . . . Even in the field of manipulation and enjoyment.'[39]

The 'tactics' employed in the 1970s and 1980s by Czech *chata* enthusiasts resembled those of the interwar *trampové* in that both aimed to create a world of make-believe in their outdoor 'settlements', to construct a temporary refuge where at least the illusions of freedom could be entertained. On the one hand, the communist regime repressed remnants of the *tramping* movement, seeing in it the seeds of genuine opposition and dissent. On the other hand, it stood by as the popularity of the *chata* grew. *Chata* culture was tolerated and even encouraged because, in many ways, it exemplified the sort of relationship between the state and the 'ordinary citizen' that the post-Prague Spring regime wished to endorse. By the 1970s, official communist culture no longer promoted a nation of eager, publicly active communists. Instead, it sought to create a nation of private persons joined together in their mutual quest for the good life, which, the regime insisted, could best be had under communism. It was the vision of a deeply conservative communist regime that had 'convinced a citizenry that the core context of politics should be the sphere of private life'.[40] In contrast, the *tramp* harked back to the kind of leftist radicalism and public community spirit that the regime now considered dangerous for its own survival.

Thus, the post-1968 Czechoslovak regime tolerated, in the name of 'normalization', the excesses of the *chata* culture and allowed these excesses to continue even as they further chipped away at the country's already declining economy, exacerbating labour shortages and corruption. Ironically, the rise of state-sponsored private citizenship had decidedly public consequences: although *chata*-owners were not consciously using their weekend activities to resist the regime, they were acting as creative 'users' of state-sponsored cultural products. By taking advantage of what was on offer, and the regime's reluctance to disallow it, the Czech *chata* enthusiasts were affecting their political environment. Consequently, the use of the outdoors, which the 'normalization' regime set out to control, had, to a certain extent, become uncontrollable.

Notes

1. Research for this article was generously funded by the Fulbright-Hays Program and the Social Science Research Council.
2. As quoted in Kieran Williams, *The Prague Spring and its aftermath. Czechoslovak politics, 1968–1970* (Cambridge: Cambridge University Press, 1997), p. 175.
3. *Práce*, 5 January 1984, p. 3.
4. Open Society Archives, Budapest: *RFE Czechoslovak Situation Report*, 11 July 1973.
5. Official statistics from the 1970s and 1980s revealed that the number of *chaty* built in Slovakia were only 10% of the number built in the Czech lands. Similarly, *chaty* were found not to be as prevalent in

other East European countries. *Chata* culture was, therefore, an especially Czech phenomenon. As to the discrepancy between Slovakia and the Czech lands, I would add that since Slovakia had been largely agricultural until then, most Slovaks living in cities still had family in the countryside whom they could visit.

6. Vladimir Kusin, 'Husak's Czechoslovakia and Economic Stagnation', *Problems of Communism*, May-June 1982, p. 28.

7. For example, the front page of the satirical cartoon magazine, *Dikobraz*, no. 26, 26 June 1973.

8. The notion of a 'social contract' is frequently evoked in the existing literature on post-1968 Czechoslovakia. See, for example, Timothy Garton Ash, *The Uses of Adversity* (Cambridge: Granta Books, 1989); Grzegorz Ekiert, *The State Against Society: Political Crises and their Aftermath in East Central Europe* (Princeton: Princeton University Press, 1996); Vladimir Kusin, *From Dubcek to Charter 77: a study of 'normalization' in Czechoslovakia, 1968–1978* (New York: St Martin's Press, 1978); and Milan Simecka, *The Restoration of Order: The Normalization of Czechoslovakia* (London: Verso, 1984).

9. See Milan Otáhal, *Opozice, Moc, Společnost 1969/1989* [Opposition, Power, Society 1969/1989] (Prague: ÚSD AV ČR, 1994), pp. 31–3.

10. As quoted in Karal Ann Marling, *As Seen on TV: The Visual Culture of Everyday Life in the 1950s* (Cambridge, MA: Harvard University Press, 1994), p. 253.

11. Robert S. Boynton, 'Enjoy Your Žižek!', *Linguafranca*, October 1998, pp. 44–5.

12. Mike Craig, 'Relics, places and unwritten geographies in the work of Michel de Certeau (1925–86)', in Mike Craig and Nigel Thrift, eds, *Thinking Space* (London and New York: Routledge, 2000), p. 137.

13. In answer to a 1976 query from a distraught policeman from the Czech town of Terezín, state television responded with an explanation of the new term 'real socialism' (*reálný socialismus*): 'In today's real world, in the world in which we live, there exist many opinions about socialism, even within the international workers' movement. So as to differentiate from utopian expectations, it is stated that in the countries of the socialist camp, where socialism is being built, the emphasis is not on a socialism fashioned out of expectations or speculations, but based on reality, on the fact that we're dealing here with the reality of developing socialist life and society.' (Czech Television Archives, Prague: Ve Fond; k. #120; ev.j. 811; sign. Zelenka: 'Dopisy diváků 1976–77': Letter from Ing. Jaroslav Bažant, ČsT, to Miroslav Bock, Útvar SNB, Terezín, 28 June 1976.)

14. Lauren Berlant, *The Queen of America Goes to Washington City: Essays on Sex and Citizenship* (Durham, NC: Duke University Press, 1997), p. 5.

15. It was finally after the 1989 'velvet revolution' that for the first time issues of *Chatař* had photographs of people partaking together in social activity on the front cover. See, for example, *Chatař*, 6/1990.

16. Lenka Kalinová, *Sociální vývoj Československa 1969-1989* [The Social Development of Czechoslovakia 1969–1989] (Prague: ÚSD AV ČR, 1998), p. 52.

17. Milan Kundera, *The Book of Laughter and Forgetting*, trans. Aaron Asher (New York: Harper Collins Publishers, 1999), p. 4.

18. Stanislav Motl, preface to Bob Hurikán, *Dějiny trampingu* [The History of Tramping] (Prague: Novinář, 1940; 1990), p. 6.

19. *Chatař*, 8/1989, pp. 6–7.

20. Hurikán, *Dějiny trampingu*, pp. 16–17.

21. Ibid., p. 21.

22. Ibid., p. 16. The interwar *tramping* movement passed through several 'thematic' phases, including the wild scouts era, the cowboy era and the Canadian era. Each was accompanied by its own costumes, slang and fireside songs.

23. Marek Waic and Jiří Kössl, *Český tramping 1918–1945* (Prague: Ruch, 1992), pp. 12–13. While Hurikán's history of tramping is based on his own recollections, Waic and Kössl's study is archival-based.

24. Waic and Kössl, *Český tramping*, p. 56.

25. For different accounts of and opinions about the responses to the Kubát decrees, see František Mores, *Trampské hnutí ve středních Čechách (Příspěvek k poznání jeho pokrokové orientace)* [The Tramping Movement in the Central Czech Lands (A contribution toward exploring its avant-garde orientation)], *Středočeský sborník historický*, no. 12 (1977) (one of the rare official articles on *tramping* during the communist period); Hurikán, *Dějiny trampingu*, pp. 246–50; and Waic and Kössl, *Český tramping*, pp. 50–60.

26. In his account of the movement, Bob Hurikán claims to have led an effective partisan group, operating out of his former 'settlement' in the Czech countryside. The archives, according to Waic and Kössl, reveal a less effective Hurikán who was, nevertheless, arrested in the spring of 1945 when the Gestapo began to fear a large-scale *tramp* offensive. Waic and Kössl, *Český tramping*, pp. 91–8.

27. *Tramp*, 12 September 1930: as quoted in Mores, *Trampské hnutí*, p. 58.

28. Libri Prohibiti Archives, Prague: Vladimír Oborský, 'O trampimgu' [*sic!*], *Info o Chartě 77*, no. 10, July–August 1978.
29. The Czechoslovak Communist Party often fretted over the ability of young people to assemble informally, and to pledge their loyalty to these self-created groups. In the mid-1960s, for example, a government report about contemporary youth saw warning signs in this younger generation's tendency to ignore party-organized activities and instead to assemble in informal groups whose members 'create their own norms for behavior which they then strictly hold to and enforce'. (State Central Archives, Prague: fond 10/5; sv. 6; aj. 23: *Problematika současné mladé generace* [Issues Surrounding Today's Young Generation] (Materials for the 17th meeting of the Central Committee's Ideological Commission), 7 October 1965, p. 38.
30. 'Trempové', *Tribuna*, no. 13/74, 27 March 1974, p. 6.
31. Special government ordinances were issued in 1971 that allowed for the construction of private recreation facilities only within the framework of district land development plans. But individuals nevertheless had no problem in making private deals with local agricultural cooperatives that sold off land to anyone willing to pay under the table for it. In 1972, Radio Prague criticized the vast profiteering taking place between sellers of land, buyers of land, and corrupt regional government committees – all for the purposes of building *chaty*. (Open Society Archives, Budapest: *Radio Prague*, 10 July 1972, 07:10).
32. Some of the newly built or expanded *chaty* were such a blot on the landscape that the Prague Research Institute for Building and Architecture compiled an illustrated handbook of the aesthetic dos and don'ts of *chata* construction. The handbook was sent to all regional government committees as a guide to the sort of *chaty* considered an aesthetic eyesore. If judged to be aesthetically unacceptable, the owner would theoretically be forced to make improvements. (Open Society Archives, Budapest: *RFE Special Report*, 27 April 1973: based on *The Economist*, 27 April 1973.) At the same time, the monthly *Chatař* magazine instituted a section called 'Architecture in Practice' where photographs of real *chaty* were printed and then critiqued.
33. For more on representations of 'the West' during late socialism in Czechoslovakia, see Paulina Bren, 'Looking West: Popular Culture and the Generation Gap in communist Czechoslovakia, 1969–1989', in Luisa Passerini, ed., *Representations and Cultural Exchanges Across the Atlantic: Europe and the United States 1800–2000* (Brussels: PIE Lang, 2000).

34. In the 1980s, moonlighting income was estimated at 6 billion crowns a year, with three billion crowns coming from jobs related to the construction of family houses and *chaty*. (Kalinová, *Sociální vývoj*, p. 51.)
35. *Vlasta*, no. 12, 16 March 1984, p. 28.
36. *Tribuna*, 31 May 1973.
37. Petr Schulhoff, director, *Co je doma, to se počítá pánové* . . . [Gentlemen, what's at home counts . . .] (Prague: Barrandov Film Studios, 1980).
38. Craig, 'Relics, places', p. 137.
39. Michel de Certeau, *The Practice of Everyday Life* (Berkeley: University of California Press, 1984; 1988), p. 18.
40. Berlant, *Queen of America*, p. 3.

–8–

Khrushchev's Children's Paradise: The Pioneer Palace, Moscow, 1958–1962

Susan E. Reid

In this house the walls will teach.

Komsomol'skaia pravda, 2 June 1962

Stepping out in the party's footsteps,
Defending peace and truth,
Keep to the path, knowing no bounds
Into the distance of the radiant years –
Be prepared!

Pioneer Oath, *Komsomol'skaia pravda,* 19 May 1962

Should you ever be in Moscow, take a trip across the river to the green and pleasant area in the south-west of the city known today by its picturesque, traditional name, the Sparrow Hills (*Vorob'evye gory*), but for much of the Soviet era as the Lenin Hills (*Leninskie gory*). There, you cannot miss the triumphal tower of Stalin's 'Palace of Science', Moscow State University, which commands a splendid panorama over the city and a privileged sight-line to the Kremlin towers. But only if you take time to wander down towards the River Moskva will you come upon, nestling unostentatiously in a hollow beneath its shadow, another monument to the ideals of communism – the Moscow Pioneer Palace. Or rather, an anti-monument. You might be forgiven for failing to notice this modest and informal complex, or for dismissing it as a Soviet version of the generic, postwar modernist school building so familiar and, hence, unremarkable in Britain and America.[1] The upbringing of children was, indeed, its purpose. But this was no ordinary educational establishment; it was a special zone for the incubation of the future communist society, at once a built embodiment of the promised radiant future, and a means to bring it about.

The Moscow Pioneer Palace was built to house the after-school activities of the Communist Party's children's organization – the Pioneers.

Susan E. Reid

When it opened in June 1962, at the height of the Khrushchev Thaw, it was hailed as the prototype for the communist city of the future. Far more than just a building, it was an entire environment – a 'City of Happiness' or 'Pioneer Republic' – designed to facilitate the socialization and ideological formation of children, their aesthetic and scientific education, play and fantasy.[2] Access was to be free, voluntary, and, in principle at least, open to all children of appropriate age. This exemplary 'socialist space' was to promote their self-realization as fully rounded individuals, at the same time as developing their communist consciousness and collective spirit. As the team of young architects and artists who built it claimed, their design gave visual and spatial expression to the joyfulness of the new life being created within.[3]

The Pioneer Palace was, furthermore, a landmark in the destalinization of Soviet architecture and its realignment with international modernism, which Nikita Khrushchev had instigated in 1954 (Figure 8.1). Denouncing Stalinist architectural 'excesses', historicizing, eclectic forms and expensive one-off solutions, Khrushchev called on architects to develop standardized plans for different building types, and to utilize economical, technologically advanced construction, prefabricated panels and synthetic materials such as pre-stressed, reinforced concrete.[4] Contemporaries articulated the design of the Pioneer Palace – a dispersed, horizontal construction of glass, reinforced concrete and prefabricated panels picturesquely integrated with its natural surroundings – in terms of freedom, truth to function, transparency, dynamic use of space, and the absence of a single dominant façade. These were, of course, central principles of the Modern Movement. But they took on specific, Soviet, meanings here, in

Figure 8.1 Ceremonial parade for opening of the Pioneer Palace, 1 June 1962

relation both to the ideology of Khrushchevism, which proclaimed modernity and rejuvenation of the socialist project, socialist 'democratism' and humanism;[5] and also to the palace's designation as an ideal space for childhood, where the future generation of communists would be nurtured. A formal architectural history of the Pioneer Palace is beyond the scope of this chapter, as is an extensive account of the activities it accommodated and enabled. My aim is, rather, to explore the secondary, connotative functions and symbolic meanings it held for its contemporaries.

Childhood embodies the collective future a society envisages for itself. It was particularly overdetermined in such a future-oriented society as the Soviet Union.[6] The Pioneer Palace presents a specially interesting case in the context of a study of the meanings of space under socialism and of how space shaped socialist identities. For the guiding trope for its transferred meanings was a spatial allegory, or homology. It was conceived as a homologue, or spatial counterpart, to the informal, multifunctional canvas village of a Pioneer camp. Crucial to this conception was the idea that children required their own, special space, segregated from, yet, at the same time, embedded in the wider, adult world. As the architects explained: 'The Pioneer Palace is a parkland complex; it is drawn back into the depths of the plot and situated in a green meadow far away from the noisy city thoroughfares. This treatment emerged from the theme itself – a children's complex which reflects the character of a camp.'[7]

The camp was *the* fundamental site for Pioneer ritual and symbolic meaning, just as it was for their bourgeois counterpart in the West, the Scouts.[8] It was the base for outward-bound activities, expeditions and adventure, which were not only important within the educational programme of the organization, but were also central to its symbolism and metaphorical language. Thus, outward movement or mobilization was the leitmotif of the Pioneer oath (cited in the epigraph), where it was imbued with ideological purposefulness in the service of the Party. Camps were to 'inculcate discipline, to improve the health of Pioneers and to accustom them to the life of soldiers in the field'.[9] Through exposure to nature and rigorous regimes, young people's bodies and wills were tempered.[10] As in a camp, the Moscow palace combined the apparently contradictory functions of protection with exposure; nurturing of the individual with physical and mental tempering; freedom of discovery with military-style discipline and ritual; and promotion of self-reliance with the tight bonding of a collective. These dichotomies were central to the design and reception of the palace.

Camps and Pioneer houses shared the same purposes: to bring up future citizens of communism, fit in mind and body; to nurture the all-round talents of the child; and develop political consciousness, patriotism and team spirit. While Pioneer houses and palaces tended to be in the vicinity of the children's homes, camps had a particular advantage for shaping children of impressionable age and building strong community bonds: they involved a journey, the children's physical removal from their quotidian environment. The transformative role, both physical and mental, of a sojourn at a camp was emphasized in press accounts that described children returning home tanned, fit, and yearning for the collective.[11] Far from home and parental influence, amidst beautiful natural surroundings, the routines of family life were replaced by the Pioneers' own routines, amongst which parades and campfires took central place. Around the campfire, under the stars, songs were sung and stories told that mingled romanticism and adventure with morals about self-dedication to the collective.[12] The actual distance travelled mattered less than the preparation and dislocation from normal routine it entailed.[13] What was most important was that children should have their own, segregated space.

Segregated Spaces of Childhood

Spatial models structure both Russian and Western discourses of childhood in the modern period. From the early kindergarten movement of the nineteenth century through to post-Soviet Russian popular psychology, child-rearing theories and practices assume that children's development requires a degree of physical and psychological autonomy, with a corresponding degree of spatial segregation from adults. Separation from the adult world is a necessary precondition for the child's self-realization and the formation of a mature, harmonious relationship with the material and social world before integration into adult society. It is fundamental, for example, to psychoanalytic and linguistic or semiotic conceptions of identity formation. The dialectics of separation and integration on a higher level of self-awareness and social maturity is explained by social historian E. Anthony Rotundo in regard to nineteenth-century America: 'boy culture' represented an escape from maternal constraints and was framed as oppositional to adults. Yet it prepared them for their future roles and adult masculine identities.[14] Adult practices of segregating spaces for children's upbringing draw, according to Russian psychologist Mariia Osorina, on children's own, spontaneous culture. Children seek out and construct their own secret worlds, whether in physical spaces such as attics, dumps or cellars, or by means of secret languages and codes that set off initiates from the outside world. The magic for children of a den or headquarters derives from its being secluded, hidden on the margins of the adult world, or in some way hard to get to.[15]

The myth of a special realm accessible only to children is thematized in popular children's fiction, whether it is the Secret Garden, Narnia or Never Never Land. For children in the postwar Soviet Union, the best known cultural embodiment of a distinct children's realm was in Arkadii Gaidar's highly popular children's story *Timur i ego kommanda* (*Timur and his Team*), written in 1941. *Timur* centred on the notion of a secret place, the headquarters of a self-regulating group of children led by a boy, Timur, who together observed a self-imposed code of conduct and engaged in adventures and good deeds in the wider, adult community. *Timur* shaped notions of childhood adventure for decades and was still potent during the Thaw.[16] The dialectics of going away and returning to the social body were also the defining chronotope of the youth novel, a variation on the *Bildungsroman* that became the leading genre during the Thaw. In Katerina Clark's analysis of the stock plot, the young hero's recuperation into the social body after sowing wild oats was achieved through an initial flight away from the centre of Soviet civilization, a journey to another, wilder place, 'far from Moscow'.[17]

The ability to demarcate childhood and provide it with its own, separate space had been a cultural marker of distinction since the Enlightenment, in Russia as in the West.[18] If in pre-revolutionary Russia and contemporary capitalist society the capacity to create a distinct realm of childhood signified individual privilege or upward mobility, under socialism it was an index of how life was getting better for the entire country. According to Lenin, children were to be the only 'privileged class' in the Soviet Union. Universal access to the elite privilege of happy childhood was part of the wellbeing and abundance that, Khrushchev promised, was the precondition for the imminent transition to communism. The demarcation of childhood and its culture as an idyllic realm with its own specific norms and forms was reinvigorated in the 1950s as part of the legitimation of the Khrushchev regime.[19] Moreover, in the global, Cold War conditions of 'peaceful competition', happy Soviet childhood proved to the world the socialist system's superior capacity to provide a high standard of living for all.

The ideology of childhood – beliefs concerning the accepted place of children in the larger world and what sets childhood apart from other phases of development – determines the nature of the special world adults create for children, and the choice of particular styles and forms of child-rearing artefacts and environments.[20] The modern constitution of childhood as a specially privileged and protected stage of individual development, has, from its emergence, found expression in material culture and the organization of built space; for example, floor plans of dwellings physically segregated children's space.[21] In Khrushchev's Soviet Union, much was invested in the creation of a separate world for happy childhood. Household advice manuals and magazines counselled that in the home, even if it consisted of a single room, 'a child should have his own corner in which he feels himself to be master'.[22] The children's corner should be an enclave of perfect cleanliness, brightness and joy, a segregated space set off for the child in the brightest and best part of the room, demarcated both through physical barriers such as a low shelving unit, and by a brighter colour scheme. Here children might enjoy a degree of independence and freedom not allowed them elsewhere. While such contingent independence was vital for their psychological and physical development, at the same time they were contained and safe. Moreover, allocated the most visually prominent corner of the room, they were under constant display and observation.[23]

Segregation of children, as the material premise of rational, communist upbringing, also shaped the more utopian housing designs of the 1960s, some of which even assigned separate wings for twenty-four hour communal childcare where children would live together apart from adult society.[24] Meanwhile, the Khrushchev regime's far-reaching reforms of the education system, beginning in 1956, engendered a need not only for more schools to be built faster and more cheaply, but for entirely new types of educational space. The ideal material environment for the education of future communists became a matter for lively debate in the context of the wholesale reorientation of Soviet architecture that began in 1954.[25] Design of a new system of boarding schools, one of Khrushchev's pet projects, was a particularly pertinent context for the Pioneer Palace. They, too, were to be self-contained, well-equipped, multifunctional complexes, model institutions for the all-round upbringing of young communists. They were to be built in picturesque, suburban localities so that children might benefit from the health-giving, aesthetic and moral influences of proximity to nature and remoteness from the city.[26]

The same principle of communal segregation determined the attention paid to Pioneer camps, which were also undergoing expansion and renovation in the Khrushchev period. Camps were not necessarily temporary canvas structures. Some, such as Artek on the beautiful southern coast of Crimea, were year-round children's health resorts with permanent constructions. They were dedicated to building children's physical robustness, resourcefulness and team spirit through exercise and exposure to the elements. Artek was the most directly relevant reference point in the construction of the Pioneer Palace. As the premier Pioneer camp under the jurisdiction of the All-Union Komsomol Central Committee, it shared the same All-Union status as the palace. Two new compounds were constructed at Artek at the same time as the Pioneer Palace was under construction in Moscow: the Togliatti Camp (1960–1) and the Pribrezhnyi Pioneer Camp (1960–4), by architects Anatolii Polianskii and D. S. Vitukhin.

These segregated children's spaces were, in a sense, utopias: they were enclaves of perfection and joy, '"sacred" and distinct realms of transcendent futurity',[27] set in the present day. Indeed, spatial segregation is a necessary condition of utopias, whose existence depends on their being hedged off from actual experience by a variety of techniques of border creation.[28] The design of the Pioneer Palace and Artek was governed by the utopian premise that a rational, harmoniously designed physical environment, close to nature, would shape the new person who was the building block of the perfect, communist society of the future. Although ideologues continued to repudiate any tendency to confuse the building of communism with utopianism, Khrushchev acknowledged the positive contribution of Tommaso Campanella, Fourier, More, Owen and other utopian socialists.[29] The Marxist materialist thesis that mentality is shaped by objective conditions of existence was also reinvigorated in this period and was invoked in support of the importance of developing good, rational, Soviet design. Every aspect of the material environment – from the organization of public space to the most trivial objects of daily use – played a part in 'organizing the psyche of the masses'.[30] It must, therefore, be consciously deployed to shape children's behaviour and beliefs. Regarding the Pioneer Palace, *Komsomol'skaia pravda* observed, 'the behaviour of children, as of grown-ups, depends very much on their circumstances', and, it concluded, 'In this house the walls will teach.'[31]

Shaping the Space of Childhood

The limitations of this study should be stated before going any further. What we are looking at is the design of children's world by adults. It tells us more about the meaning adults invest in childhood than about children's own material culture. Although young Pioneers themselves were invited to put forward ideas and designs for the Pioneer Palace by means of a competition in 1958, there is no record of how their wishes shaped the design process.[32] In the absence of any sociological or ethnographic data regarding the children-users' responses in the 1960s, the meanings to be discussed here are those invested in the palace by the client, designers and contemporary commentators – primarily pro-modernizing art and architecture professionals – in the name of children.

Construction of the Pioneer Palace was initiated and funded by the Party's organization for young people aged fourteen to twenty-eight, the All-Union Lenin Communist Youth League, or Komsomol.[33] What did the Komsomol, as client, want from the Pioneer Palace project? The answer has to be understood in light of the Youth League's ambivalent role in the Thaw: it was at once the progressive force of 'youth', representing the rejuvenation of the socialist project; and a force for order, containment and social control. Beginning with the Revolution, the communist future was personified by young people. Real young individuals did not always match the ideal, however. Youth behaviour was a source of growing social anxieties since the war. The Komsomol was charged with monitoring and combating the spread of westernized youth culture, disaffection and political apathy, antisocial behaviour and even delinquency. It adopted a dual approach to this task, providing sanctioned entertainment, leisure facilities and constructive activities for children and young people, while, at the same time, intensifying ideological intervention.[34] Transformed since the war from a small, elite vanguard of youth into a mass organization, the Komsomol took increasing responsibility for young people's educational achievement, ideological conviction and 'rational' use of their free time, becoming an instrument for the social control of youth by young people themselves.[35]

The Pioneer Organization, whose headquarters the palace was to be, was the Komsomol's instrument for socializing children and adolescents from ten to fifteen years old. A subsection, the Octobrists (*Oktiabriata*), recruited children aged seven to nine.[36] Beginning in 1957, the Pioneers' role was separated from that of school education, greater emphasis being given to the 'all-round, harmonious development' of the individual, which, Khrushchev promised, was a prerequisite for the transition to communism.[37] It was to develop children's initiative, self-reliance and mutual help, and cultivate their creative talents. At the same time it was to instil communist consciousness, social participation, duty and loyalty to the collective. To build identification with both the Pioneer Organization and the political system as a whole, extensive use was made of invented traditions and military-style rituals – reveilles, formal roll-calls, salutes, and parades with drums and bugles – as well as of symbolic attributes such as flags, music, emblems, mottoes, uniforms and badges. Nadezhda Krupskaia, whose pedagogical theories shaped the organization in the 1920s, had insisted that, with their elements of colourfulness, solemnity and play, rituals and symbols were a vital means to effect children's subjective, emotional appropriation of ideological truths. By working on children's emotions, they enabled 'moral norms to become inner convictions', to be *felt* rather than merely known.[38] Thus, for example, the initiation rite children underwent on joining the Pioneers helped them to internalize the meaning of their pledge to be an example to other children and be 'ever prepared'. Music played an important part in these rituals, as a means to organize children into collective action and emotion. So, too, did the built space and the monumental art which, by visually marking key axes and surfaces, articulated it.

Rituals remained fundamental to Pioneer practice in the Khrushchev period and were the focus of renewed attention; new forms were developed and their place in ideological education was defined. At the same time, constructive recreation and cultural enlightenment increasingly took precedence over direct political indoctrination. The Pioneer Organization became closely involved in the provision of sanctioned leisure facilities, including after-school and vacation activities based in Pioneer Houses and summer camps.[39] This by no means represented a de-ideologization of its role. On the contrary, the provision of camps and palaces was part of a pervasive campaign under Khrushchev in which the Komsomol took the lead. The aim was to entice young people away from spaces of unsanctioned and unproductive leisure, such as the street or the *dvor* (courtyard) by providing attractive, supervised alternatives; and, at the same time, to penetrate the supposedly 'private' spheres of leisure and the home with ideological significance.[40] The expansion of Pioneer facilities was one of a number of measures – also including the new boarding schools – which aimed at increasing the involvement of state and party organizations in the socialization of children and promoting the gradual withering away of the bourgeois atavism of the nuclear family. Parents could not be entirely entrusted with their children's upbringing, it was argued, for some continued to inculcate patriarchal values. Moreover, no child should remain outside a well-organized collective: only within the collective could the individual fully develop.[41]

In addition to the palace's internal function of educating its young participants and bonding them into a cohesive collective, it was also to exert an outward-reaching, inspirational influence, or 'Pioneer Effect': as an enclave of the communist future, its good example was actively to irradiate the wider adult society within which it was embedded. It would thereby catalyse the eventual transition of the whole of Soviet society to full communism.[42] 'Pioneer Action Zones' were designated around schools and clubs, within which the beneficial 'Pioneer Effect' was exerted both directly, through environmental and social work, and indirectly, through shining example.[43] The notion of Action Zones was an innovation of this period, and will help us to understand the way the spatial effect of the Pioneer Palace was conceived. As the All-Union headquarters of the Pioneer Organization, the Pioneer Palace in the Lenin Hills was to exercise a particularly pervasive and potent 'Pioneer Effect' which, transcending the local, was amplified to a nationwide resonance. For, as the Komsomol newspaper *Komsomol'skaia pravda*, put it: 'The Pioneer Action Zone of the new Palace is, of course, not only Moscow. It is the whole country.'[44]

A Prime Site: the Lenin Hills

Far more than an after-school facility for local children, the Moscow Pioneer Palace was to be an exemplary institution of national and, indeed, international importance. It was the hub of a growing network of children's clubs and camps offering a range of educational, creative and recreational activities that complemented the school curriculum. It was to incubate model practices, lead the rest of the country, and demonstrate to foreign delegations the socialist system's solicitousness for children's happiness and individual development. As a report in the architectural press crowed, 'The Pioneer Palace in the Lenin Hills is a glimpse into the future life of the Pioneer Organization of all our cities, of the entire country. It is to become the prototype for the development of other, similar mass complexes. Here, new forms of education and recreation for Pioneers will be tested.'[45]

Plans were already in place under the 1935 General Plan for the Reconstruction of Moscow to build a new Pioneer Palace in the Lenin Hills. These were shelved, however (according to Khrushchev because the country was not yet rich enough), and since 1936 Moscow's Pioneer activities had been housed in a wonderfully refurbished but nonetheless cramped nineteenth-century mansion in the city centre.[46] With the expansion of the membership and role of the Party youth organizations in the 1950s, and the requirement for their activities to keep abreast of modern science, technology and space exploration, the provision of spacious, purpose-built accommodation became pressing. In January 1958 the Komsomol Central Committee officially endorsed plans to build a brand new Pioneer Palace.[47] It was required to accommodate extremely diverse, even contradictory demands. It was to provide purpose-built accommodation for the numerous activities of the Pioneers, including club rooms, studios, workshops and laboratories for technology, photography and film production, aircraft modelling, homecraft, art, performing arts, local studies, science and technology, and indoor and outdoor sports. To tap the spontaneous enthusiasm aroused by Sputnik, a state-of-the-art Planetarium and Young Cosmonauts' club would teach patriotic pride along with astronomy. The palace had also to provide spaces for its other central functions: those of ritual, display and performance. To accommodate the militaristic ritual central to the internal life of the organization – and to enable its display to the outside world – there was to be a parade ground for 5,000 Pioneers and 3,000 guests, in addition to a theatre, concert hall, auditorium, exhibition spaces and international-level sports facilities.[48]

A plot was assigned, and the foundation stone was laid on 29 October 1958 to mark the fortieth anniversary of the Komsomol. Fifty-four hectares of thickly wooded park, just a short walk from the new Lenin Hills Metro station in one direction, and from the new building of Moscow State University (MGU) in the other, the site combined convenience with great natural beauty (see Figure 8.2). It was delimited by leafy Vorob'evskoe Shosse running parallel with the river below; and Vernadskii

Figure 8.2 Pioneer Palace, Moscow, 1962. Architects Viktor Egerev, Vladimir Kubasov, Feliks Novikov, Igor' Pokrovskii, Boris Palui and Mikhail Khazhakian; Engineer Iurii Ionov. Axonometric plan

Prospekt, which, continuing as Komsomol'skii Prospekt across the river, linked the south-west quarter of the city in a straight line to the very centre. At the opposite end, the territory abutted Universitetskii Prospekt. The fourth boundary was defined by natural features: a steep valley, full of lush vegetation, with a stream and ponds. Here, as in a nature reserve or a real camp, children could explore the relatively wild terrain, have imaginary adventures, and learn about nature. At the same time, as in a children's corner, they were contained in the safety of a demarcated space.

In a society where built space was at a premium, and where real estate lay wholly in the hands of the State and its agents, the allocation or withholding of physical space was a powerful means of social and cultural control.[49] Space was also an important currency for communication and was subject to hierarchical ordering. The symbolic significance of space was rooted in Russian religious culture's tradition of sacred topography, whereby a landscape was articulated and given meaning homologously, that is, in structural relation to another, remote holy site.[50] Since the 1930s, spatial hierarchy had been fundamental to Stalinist popular culture, which located Moscow 'on top' of the Soviet Union as a whole. Within the metropolis, meanwhile, some spaces were more prestigious and significant than others, above all the ancient centre of the city, the Kremlin and Red Square.[51] This centralized hierarchy was enshrined in the 1935 reconstruction plan for Moscow. Since the war, however, Moscow had begun a process of rapid growth, and between 1960 and 1961 the basic principles of a new, twenty-year plan for the expansion of the capital were developed. To alleviate the problems of metropolitan complexity on the vast scale of Moscow's projected growth, the ancient, monocentric structure based on arteries radiating out from the central hub of the Kremlin and Red Square, which Stalinist planning had taken over on a magnified scale from the medieval city, was to be abandoned in favour of eight planning areas.[52] Thereby, the centripetal, centralized hierarchy of Stalinist planning and mythology was exploded in favour of a centrifugal or broad-based principle premised on equality of parts. While dictated by real needs, this shift from a vertical to a horizontal model was also symbolic, providing spatial embodiment for Khrushchev's repudiation of privilege in favour of populism or 'democratism'.[53]

The spread of the city since the war, accelerating in the late 1950s, created a growing need to decentralize amenities, including leisure and entertainment facilities. As Mikhail Ladur (a designer of mass festivals since the 1920s, and advocate of organized public recreation in the 1960s) challenged in 1966, 'Let's face it, comrades, it is boring in the evenings in our capital. Look at the map of Moscow and try to mark the geography of our metropolitan entertainment facilities. Almost all are in the centre. So hundreds of thousands of people live here who in practice have no possibility even to go to the theatre because of the long journey.'[54] The building of the Pioneer Palace began the process of decentralizing the city's entertainment facilities and dispersing its ideological and ritual foci.

The Lenin Hills, where the Pioneer Palace was to be built, were a pleasant, semi-rural, wooded crescent formed by a loop in the River Moskva which washed its steep oak-, lime- and birch-clad cliffs. Located near what had, until recently, been the south-west perimeter of the city, the area was in the spotlight of planners' attention in this period. Even in the Stalinist spatial hierarchy it had been perhaps second only to the centre of power; at once invested with significance through actual and symbolic links with the centre, and set apart from it, it as if held up a mirror to the Kremlin. It was home to the power elite; many top party officials had their residences in this quiet, exclusive section of town. Plans to develop the area under the 1935 General Plan represented it as a gift bestowed on the people by the government as a token of its loving care.[55] It also had rich historical associations. For centuries the Sparrow Hills, as they were then known, had been a prized location over which State and people struggled for possession, being one of the nearest spots where one could escape the city, and reputedly the most beautiful place in Central Russia. The Tsars built their summer residence here in the sixteenth century. They later became the most popular suburban leisure resort for Muscovites. By the beginning of the twentieth century the human traffic was so great that the hills were the destination of one of the first tram lines. One of their attractions was the panorama from the promontory above the river, from which tourists could 'get to know Moscow in its entirety'.[56] A visit to the Sparrow Hills was a 'must' for every visitor to Moscow, along with the Kremlin and Red Square. Thus, long before they became the ceremonial axis of Stalin's imperial city, a direct link was already established between the centre of power and the Sparrow Hills by the tourist itinerary.

The cognitive advantages of the Sparrow Hills combined with opportunities for more corporeal and unregulated delights. While the commanding heights of the river buff allowed surveillance of the city, their wooded slopes provided a haven for unregulated and unedifying popular pleasures, and were frequented by young people seeking to escape the monitoring of behaviour, cramped quarters and lack of privacy. The hills were also historically identified with other freedoms: freedom of thought and the struggle for political freedom from autocracy. When Stalin decreed in 1948 that Moscow State University (MGU) should have a new home in the Lenin Hills, the chosen site was the very spot where, in the summer of 1827, inspired by bucolic nature, as the last rays of the setting sun glinted on the cupolas of the city's churches across the river, the youthful Alexander Herzen and Nikolai Ogarev swore to dedicate their lives to the revolutionary cause. Occupying this site, the university appropriated the romantic, revolutionary tradition of youthful idealism to its own legitimation.[57] At the same time, as an institution for the education of leading party youth, the grandiose new building (1949–53, Lev Rudnev and associates) was a stake claiming the territory for the Komsomol: it imposed its discipline and centripetal spatial order on this unruly area. Its great tower – one of the ring of seven pinnacled 'high buildings' erected around the city in Stalin's dotage – commanded the panorama across the river and privileged axis to the heart of the city and State, the Kremlin. This direct sight-line was paralleled below ground by the prestigious red line of the Metro and above ground by Komsomol'skii Prospekt, which linked it to the centre. With the building of MGU, a historical aspiration of both the tsarist and Stalinist regimes had at last come to fruition: to site a great tower in the Sparrow Hills as a triumphal assertion of power.[58]

In the early 1950s the Lenin Hills became almost synonymous with the university.[59] After Stalin's death, however, the expansion of the city, accelerating with Khrushchev's housing campaign and the new city plan, opened the region and its meanings to reconfiguration. The Lenin Hills were the crux of plans to develop the entire south-west quarter as a kind of alternative, modern capital. A new, two-level road-rail bridge was thrown across the River Moskva, a wonder of modern technology that set the tone of the area. Here was to be built a whole new government centre, conceived after the Twentieth Party Congress to symbolize the fresh start on the path to communism.[60] While maintaining the associations with communist education and youth established by MGU, major efforts were invested to distance the area from Stalinist authoritarianism and historicism, and to rebrand it in terms of the new, forward-looking, people-oriented and technologically progressive values of Khrushchevism: socialist democracy, modernity and scientific-technological progress.

The south-west of the city became a laboratory for experimental new forms of urban planning and housing construction, which put into practice Khrushchev's 1954 edict that the architectural profession must abandon the bombast and excesses of the late Stalinist 'triumphal style', develop cost-effective, standardized building types, and utilize the most contemporary construction technology and materials.[61] It was here that the most visible and widely publicized efforts to develop a modern or 'contemporary style' of Soviet architecture were undertaken. The never-completed project for a Palace of the Soviets – on which hopes for the emergence of a distinct Soviet style had been pinned in the 1930s – was resurrected. It was now to be built in the shadow of Moscow University, as the lynchpin of the new government quarter. Two rounds of competitions between 1957 and 1959 for this major public edifice established the parameters of the contemporary style. Based on the imperatives of simplicity, clarity and truth to function, it was to make efficient use of contemporary materials and technology. At the same time, New Cheremushki and other parts of the south-west region were the location of experimental prototypes of mass housing and urban layout. Widely represented in the popular press, these developments were written into a process of redefinition of the area as a realm of modernity, rationalism, socialist 'democratism', and the rejuvenation of the communist project. In contemporary discourse the south-west quarter figured as a kind of *tabula rasa* on which a modern, socialist city was rising. It was a place where, to paraphrase a central principle of Socialist Realism, one could 'catch a glimpse of tomorrow being prepared in the present day'.[62] Here, 'Moscow of the 1960s is especially visible.'[63] When the Pioneer Palace opened, commentators emphasized the significance of its location in the Lenin Hills in terms of the region's separateness from the old centre and its modernity. Set apart from the city by the river, it was like a distinct new town, somewhere between the countryside and the city. To travel there across the new bridge, to walk along its broad, tree-lined streets surrounded by the new architecture, was to shake off the trace of the past, inescapable in the centre, and enter the brave new world.[64]

The Palace of the Soviets project was dropped once more. Its role as a flagship of architectural 'contemporaneity' was taken over, however, by the children's palace. The insertion of the Pioneer Palace into this region was an important element in its reconfiguration as the harbinger of the communist future. Although contemporary accounts represented the area as one free from the footprint of the past, the continued presence of that great monument of Stalinism, MGU, reasserted itself daily in people's lived experience. MGU proved to be an insurmountable problem for would-be designers of the Palace of the Soviets. Try as they might to avoid entering into competition with it on its own terms, they only succeeded in reaffirming its dominance.[65] What was to be done with it? To pull it down was not feasible: apart from the waste of resources, this would constitute a more categorical repudiation of the Stalinist legacy than the Khrushchev regime was up to. But if it could not be erased from the picture, then MGU, built as it was to further the cause of Soviet science and education, must be recuperated for the narrative of modernity by incorporating it into the image of the Lenin Hills as the realm of scientific and social progress, of youth and the future. In a photomontage by A. Sorokin in *Uchitel'skaia gazeta* (Teachers' Gazette) of 1 February 1958, illustrating an article entitled 'Raise the new person, the constructor of communism', MGU towers behind a female teacher and her pupils. It stands for the paternal state's role in upbringing and the opportunities it afforded to young people. The construction of the Pioneer Palace on its doorstep was, similarly, to contribute to the realignment of the 'Palace of Science'. Whereas the symbolic headquarters of the all-people's government, the Palace of the Soviets, could not have allowed itself to be dwarfed by Stalin's tower, a children's institution had no need to enter a contest for power on terms set by the past.

Destalinizing the 'Palatial'

The Lenin Hills were to become a 'Land of Palaces'.[66] Even children were to have a palace of their own there. Palaces occupy a special role in children's culture: they are the enchanted space of fairy tales, where miraculous transformations take place and nothing is quite as it seems. The design of a socialist 'people's palace' had been a central task of Soviet architecture from the start. In the early 1920s, discussions around the Palace of Labour focused on the need to appropriate the 'palatial' for the people and transform it from a symbol of their oppression into one of the triumph of the new, 'people-oriented' social order. New palaces designed under Stalin, however, reinstated many of the signs of power and order that had signified 'palaceness' in the past, including verticality, imposing scale, rich ornamentation, sumptuously finished interiors, symmetry, classical orders, colonnades and neoclassical porticos marking grand entrances.[67] The first Pioneer Houses were remodelled palaces of the tsarist aristocracy, including, alongside the 1936 Moscow palace conversion, the Leningrad Pioneer Palace which was housed in the former Anichkov Palace (converted by Aleksandr Gegello and David Krichevskii, 1937). When new Pioneer palaces began to be constructed in the mid-1930s they, too, emulated palace architecture of the past. But in light of Khrushchev's denunciation of the historicism and 'excesses' of Stalinist architecture and his promises of a new 'democratism', the democratization and modernization of the 'palatial' became one of the central questions in defining the plan and style of the Pioneer Palace.

On the grounds that the Pioneer Palace was a crucial element within the composition of the burgeoning south-west region of the city, its design was opened up to competition in 1958. The competition brief, defined by representatives of the Central Committee and Moscow Party Committee of the Komsomol in consultation with pedagogues, doctors and other specialists, stressed that the buildings had to be thoroughly multifunctional, and that everything must be interesting and instructive, convenient and beautiful. For, according to the reinvigorated principle of environmental determinism, the architecture and the spatial organization were to contribute directly to the education of the new person. The four competing solutions cannot be analysed in detail here; space only permits us to draw out the criteria on which the expert commission judged them.[68] These emerge most clearly from what it rejected: above all the project by the studio of the neo-Palladianist doyen of the Stalinist architectural establishment, Ivan Zholtovskii. It was altogether too rigid and conventional in its interpretation of the idea of 'palaceness'. Placing a grand, neoclassical façade along the main road, Vorob'evskoe Shosse, looking out over the River Moskva towards the Kremlin, as if imitating MGU, its plan took the site 'abstractly', ignoring the natural relief of the plot. The park was subordinated to the building, and laid out with geometric regularity and imposing symmetry that took account neither of the natural contours nor of the diverse functions it was to accommodate. Access was through a large courtyard enclosed by wings extending from the main four-storey block, a spatial organization the commission found too 'official' for a children's institution.

The commission clearly prioritized truth to the palace's multiple functions, and to the specificity of its children users, over any *a priori* conception of what a palace should be. It was also concerned that, like a camp, the complex should work with, rather than against, the natural features of the site. The most successful project was that of a group of unknown young architects from the construction institute Mosproekt, led by Igor' Pokrovskii and including Viktor Egerev, Vladimir Kubasov and Feliks Novikov. Rather than locate the main building along the perimeter road, they embedded it in the midst of the park. Eschewing the symmetrical monumentality of Stalinist palaces and Zholtovskii's design, they treated the plan freely on the basis of the contours of the plot. Thus they proposed a single, unified complex in a finger plan comprised of a main block of two adjoined buildings, with four wings arranged perpendicular to the enfilade. Pokrovskii's project was applauded for its freshness, expressiveness and responsiveness to both the nature of the site and the purpose of the complex, and, above all, to the specific needs, scale and character of its children users. It was adopted as the basis for further work to be undertaken by a brigade consisting of Egerev, Kubasov, Novikov and Pokrovskii, with the addition of Boris Palui and Mikhail Khazhakian. They were instructed to make use of progressive construction methods and new materials, and to observe economic constraints.

Susan E. Reid

The Children's Republic

The palace opened on the International Day of Protection of Children, 1 June 1962. The inauguration ceremony was the culmination of two weeks of national celebrations for the fortieth anniversary of the 1922 foundation of the Pioneer Organization. Through association with the founding historical event, the palace was consecrated and enabled to transcend the profane space of everyday life.[69] Its extraordinary status was underlined by the fact that Khrushchev himself cut the ribbon and launched the first goldfish into an indoor pond, just as, twenty-six years earlier, he had opened the first Moscow House of Pioneers – a connection the press did not fail to point out. Conducted by the architects Pokrovskii and Khazhakian, the leader toured the whole complex and surrounding terrain by mini-railway, viewed the exhibition '40 Years of the Pioneer Organization', and witnessed a ceremonial parade. In his opening speech, he pronounced the palace 'a fine example of good taste', and expressly welcomed the way the architects had used the natural relief of the plot, freely deploying the buildings in the heart of the park. 'I like your palace', he declared. 'I am giving you my opinion.'[70]

The First Secretary's pronouncement was an important endorsement of one of the most innovative and controversial aspects of the design: the architects' decision to tuck the main building into the downward slope of the site, well away from the main city thoroughfares. Although this solution was affirmed at the competition stage, it had to be defended tenaciously in the subsequent course of planning. In face of scepticism – 'Is this really a palace?' – the architects argued that a palace for children should not even try to compete with MGU and dominate the city. On the contrary, its representative functions should be subordinated to its purpose as a space for children's development. Thus, 'It was most appropriate to subordinate the architecture to the "microclimate" of the site, to create an "inner environment" that made no claim on any direct compositional connection with the city.' Just like a camp settlement, it should be a 'picturesque' ensemble integrated with its natural environment, accommodating rather than suppressing the irregular contours and natural features of the plot.[71] This was not merely a matter of rhetoric: the building's asymmetries and irregularities were dictated, in part, by efforts to preserve mature trees, which also determined the organization of construction work even at the expense of efficiency.[72] The end result 'as if dissolves into nature. The parade ground and greenery become an inseparable part of the building, and the building looks like an organic element of the surrounding landscape.'[73]

Contemporary accounts set great store by the openness and accessibility of the palace, which like the Pioneer Organization itself was to be open to all children. It could be accessed from a number of directions rather than being dominated by a single main façade and 'parade entrance'. Since both the linear medium of a text and bodily movement through space must begin somewhere, however, we shall start our brief tour from what was the preferred approach and the chosen viewpoint for press photographs: the corner of the site nearest the river, just opposite the Metro station where one would arrive from the centre (see Figure 8.2). The first impression is of a picturesque, lushly wooded park in whose midst various low buildings are informally distributed without symmetry or apparent order. On arrival, we are separated from the main building by a great, green, open space. We have to cross first an open meadow and then the parade ground, where we are immediately introduced into the symbolic world of the Pioneers, passing on our right a statue of a bugling Pioneer and the flagpole and, on the left, an emblematic campfire – its flames set permanently in stone and overlaid by a large red star – with a place for a real fire on a platform above (Figure 8.3). The locus of the collective-building rituals, which were at the heart of the Pioneer way of life, the

Figure 8.3 Emblematic stone campfire in the grounds of the Pioneer Palace, overlaid with the red star, with the flagpole and the spire of Moscow University rising behind. Photo: Georgii Arzamasov, 2001

parade ground forms the compositional and social-functional centre of the whole complex. Its surface is laid with two superimposed patterns, which relate to its dual function as parade ground and approach. A grid maps the orderly formation of the parade; meanwhile, cutting diagonally across this, two converging paths of white stone direct one's steps to an entrance that is sheltered and emphasized by a porch. The humble simplicity of the porch belies its symbolic, ritual importance, a matter to which we shall return below. It is set asymmetrically in a low, picturesque construction of continuous glazing and reinforced concrete, which is strung out in an irregular line along the parade ground, stepping now forward, now back to accommodate a group of trees. This is the main activity block of the palace, housing a large foyer, cloakrooms, a winter garden, exhibition halls, a 'Lenin Hall' (for important assemblies and indoor parades) and a room for 'noisy games'. All these spaces could be joined together by the removal of partitions for large-scale events to foster the self-recognition of the Pioneers as a cohesive mass. On the far left, above a steep incline, two adjacent, curved volumes, like a three-dimensional semicolon, mark a provisional pause before one passes on round to the other side of the building perched over the valley. They consist of a parabolic block – whose unusual external form reflected its internal function as an auditorium – and the catenary dome of the planetarium, rising slightly over the long, flat roof of the building.

Gone without trace are the formal rigidity and verticality of a traditional palace. Everything emphasizes an easy-going horizontality and responsiveness to its surroundings. Both the elevation and the roofline undulate freely. Two storeys of equal height are divided by a broad horizontal band marking the first-floor level, and surmounted by a simple cornice beneath the flat roof. These parallel bands unify the façade, and their flowing horizontality is underscored by purely decorative, broken lines scattered irregularly across the otherwise transparent wall. Still viewing the complex across the expanse of the parade ground, the visitor might allow her eye to be carried by these horizontals along the low, fluid line of the building to the 300-seat Pioneer theatre in the far right-hand corner. Adjoined to this at right angles by a gallery at first-floor level is a high, glazed volume housing a concert hall. Together with the main building it forms an 'L' that encloses the parade ground on two sides. On the other two sides the parade ground is left wide open to the surrounding region, divided from Vernadskii Prospekt above only by a wide lawn and long, stepped rampart. No walls, fences or gates enclose the territory. The perspective is closed off visually, however. Whether one's eye traces the shifting line of the palace buildings or gazes directly across the parade ground, it is irresistibly drawn to the great tower of MGU, a fact that was recorded, not denied, in contemporary photographs (see Figure 8.3). Indeed, a deliberate visual and semantic relationship is established with it by the fifty-five metre stainless steel flagpole in the parade ground. Raised during the night before Khrushchev's visit so that the Red Flag could be ceremonially hoisted, it was a stake in the ground, establishing the camp and the territorial claim of the yet uncompleted palace. Thus, MGU, far from being effaced or outdone, becomes the crux of the Pioneer Palace's visual effect: it completes the field of vision, closes off the open space, and counterpoises its horizontality. At the same time, MGU is assimilated into a thoroughly modern composition of horizontals and verticals that conformed to the new architectural aesthetics.[74]

The concert hall itself was staggeringly modern for its day, even compared with other recent icons of architectural modernity such as the Rossiia Cinema on Pushkin Square or the Czechoslovak Pavilion at the Brussels 1958 World Fair, which may have inspired it. Great walls of glass soar high above the visitor. A low, broad flight of steps leads up to its entrance, placed off-centre under a heavy, cantilevered lintel. The lintel bears a deep, monochrome relief, designed by sculptors Iu. Aleksandrov, I. Aleksandrova and T. Sokolova, and monumental painters Andrei Vasnetsov and Viktor El'konin (Figure 8.4). The insistent weightiness and

Figure 8.4 Pioneer Palace. *Music* frieze over concert hall entrance. Andrei Vasnetsov, Viktor El'konin, Iu. Aleksandrov, I. Aleksandrova and T. Sokolova. Photo: Susan E. Reid, 1994

materiality of this incised block of rough, raw concrete emphasizes, by contrast, the apparent immateriality of the transparent wall. It is perceived against a ground of coloured murals of children dancing and playing, painted on the internal wall of the concert hall foyer, which can be seen through the veil of the great windows (by Grigorii Derviz, Irina Lavrova-Derviz, Igor' Pchel'nikov, E. Ablin and A. Gubarev).

Like a signboard announcing the function of the building, the concert hall relief takes music as its theme. But, where a naturalistic or allegorical illustration would have been obligatory less than a decade earlier (and was still demanded by art-world Jeremiahs), it represents music in emblematic, decorative and abstract terms. Abstracted, fragmented motifs of musical instruments and other attributes of music are combined in a tightly knit composition that, through the interplay of the long, horizontal lines of bugles with repeated, jagged diagonals, and the counterpoint of light and shade, expresses the idea of polyphony and vigorous rhythm in visual and spatial terms. As a participant in a professional discussion of the palace commented, 'There is nothing there, yet at the same time it is beautiful'.[75] It breathed new life into a key symbol of Pioneer life and emblem of the Pioneer Palace, the bugle, which had become a notorious cliché of Stalinist urban space.[76]

The bugle not only pointed to the theme of music appropriate to the concert hall, but to the ritual role of music in the life of the Pioneers. The bugle's call was the signal that organized movement and announced the transition from one phase of a Pioneer ceremony to another.[77] The musical motifs of the frieze refer to both the aesthetic and the ritual-spatial functions of music in Pioneer life, which in turn correspond to the pediment's dual function: not only does it mark the entrance to the concert hall; it is also a tribune overlooking the parade ground, the point to which marching Pioneers would turn to acknowledge leaders and honoured guests. Walking past the frieze one is almost compelled to fall into step.

Anathema against abstract art continued unabated in official discourse. However, by the early 1960s modernizers in the art world were emboldened to argue that abstraction had legitimate uses in the context of architecture and decoration, and that abstract form could convey meaning and emotion. They attributed the capacity of the material and visual environment to organize and transform people's minds and bodies precisely to abstract characteristics such as proportion, rhythm, tonal and colour relations, and the articulation of space. Monumental painting and sculpture could organize movement within, around and through the spaces they subtend, in a similar way to music. If the plan and architectural features eschewed rigid hierarchy, symmetry, physical control and inhibition of access and passage, a strong organizational role was played by pictorial decoration.[78] As the architects put it, 'In the building of the palace, freely laid out in the park, in which every façade is important, its spatiality [*prostranstvennost'*] is emphasized by monumental painting.' The palace was to be cognized in movement, which was organized and directed as much through visual cues as through actual, physical barriers and openings.[79]

The modernizers championed the palace as a flagship of the synthesis of the spatial arts of monumental art and architecture. Already in the context of the Palace of the Soviets competition, the seventeenth-century utopia of Tommaso Campanella (which had earlier inspired Lenin's Plan for Monumental Propaganda in 1918) was invoked to support the inclusion of monumental art in rationalist, contemporary style structures. Campanella emphasized the direct educational efficacy of visual aids. In his utopia, the City of the Sun, children imbibed their lessons from the images that decorated the walls, learning as they played in their midst, without even being conscious of it.[80] One of the most vocal apologists of synthesis, Vladimir Favorskii (prominent as a printmaker, monumental artist and theorist in the 1920s and early 1930s, and highly influential once again in the 1950s) argued in 1958: 'monumental art, along with architecture, organizes space, and organizes us. It can be compared here to music: how, for example a march influences us . . . With our whole body, our whole being, we feel its influence on us, whether sad or lively and happy. So, too, monumental art has the capacity to make us live in a particular rhythm.'[81] Or as sculptor Ernst Neizvestnyi (originally intended to design the bugling Pioneer for the palace's main approach) argued, the function of monumental art within an architectural ensemble was to organize 'a particular ritual (I am not afraid of this word) which creates a requisite emotional mood. We know how the church used this . . . I don't mean we must use their devices, but we must set against them our own principles: for example, a monumental work, "Pioneers", allows the possibility of conducting a Pioneer parade, while a monument "To Victims of Fascism" might give the possibility of kneeling before an eternal flame.'[82]

The experience and space of the hypothetical viewer attracted much theoretical attention in this period. As leading reformist theoretician Nina Dmitrieva put it, unlike easel painting, monumental art could affect the viewer 'even if he does not specifically concentrate on looking but simply finds himself inside a harmonious ensemble. He involuntarily experiences the influence on him of the "force field" radiating from it.'[83] For Dmitrieva, Favorskii and others, the success of a work of monumental art or architecture depended on its effectiveness in creating what they referred to as a 'force field' or 'zone of action' around it. Like the children playing amidst the frescos in Campanella's City of the Sun, anyone located within this force field came under the beneficial influence of the monumental art.

How was a 'force field' achieved here? The frieze of musical emblems was to draw visitors arriving for a concert straight across the parade ground to the concert hall as well as to beat out the rhythm of the march on ceremonial occasions. For the palace's everyday users, meanwhile – children arriving regularly to participate in its various activities – the most important entrance was diagonally across from it, under the porch that projects from the long façade on the left. The porch shelters a large, brilliant orange and ultramarine mosaic on the theme of *Young Leninists* (Figure 8.5). The mosaic is executed in a mixture of coloured, shining ceramics and *smalto* (sections of coloured glass rods) in saturated, complementary colours, which contrast both with incised areas of raw, matt cement, and with the grey ground of the concrete and continuous glazing to either side. The mosaic reads, from a distance, as a large, vividly coloured panel that ceremonially accents the main entrance to the building: in the language of the time, it 'organizes the façade', gathering it into a coherent visual composition with a main focus.[84] The intensely coloured, recessed mosaic and the monochrome, abstracted, cantilevered *Music*

Figure 8.5 Pioneer Palace. *Young Leninists* mosaic marking the entrance to the main block. Irina Lavrova-Derviz, Grigorii Derviz, Igor' Pchel'nikov, E. Ablin, and A. Gubarev. Photo: Georgii Arzamasov, 2001

relief constitute two contrasting visual accents that compete for attention across the parade ground. Thereby they charge the intervening space with a dynamic tension, creating, in other words, a 'force field' between them.[85]

The *Young Leninists* mosaic surrounding the main everyday entrance plays a central role in the spatial and ritual effect of the palace. Its iconography also represents the key emblems and rituals of the Pioneers. The doorway is flanked by large janissary figures, incised in profile and superimposed on each other in a shallow, frieze-like space. On the left, occupying the full height of the panel, giant Pioneers play a fanfare, their bugles silhouetted against a bright solar disk. On the right, somewhat smaller figures represent the Communist Party and Komsomol – the Pioneers' mentors and their future adulthood. The large-scale fanfare image, combined with the intense colour of the mosaic, summons children from afar. But it is only as they come closer that smaller images over the doors become clearly visible, drawing them into the more hermetic aspects of the Pioneers' world and the intimate, bonding moments of the collective. A crimson banner bearing Lenin's profile billows above a group of children who are being initiated into the organization. Meanwhile, somewhat separated from the surrounding images in an incised cartouche of cement directly above the doors, a group of Pioneers of different races kneels around a campfire. This campfire motif, the focus of the mosaic and of the parade-ground façade as a whole, points to the significance of the *Young Leninists* panel in the process of a child's appropriation of the identity of a Pioneer. The campfire was the most effective and memorable ritual of Pioneer life; it played a crucial role in the child's emotional identification with the organization. As *Komsomol'skaia pravda* recounted, 'The day begins with military ceremony – the raising of the flag, roll call – and ends with discussions around the campfire.'[86] If this were a real camp, the campfire would be located in the common area onto which the tents opened. Engaged in their rituals of initiation and bonding around the campfire, the mosaic Pioneers look out from the shelter of the porch as if from under a canopy or entrance of a tent. From its protected space they are able to check out visitors as they approach across the parade ground.

The flat porch, supported on slender, cylindrical piers, appears a thin and flimsy covering. Contemporary accounts referred to it as a *'kozyrek'*, the term for a canopy or temporary shelter, which aptly conveyed its apparent flimsiness and impermanence. In form it resembles the flap of a tent propped up on poles to allow access. Contemporary accounts set great store by the openness of the palace, both its physical permeability and its visual transparency. 'How many doors are there in the new

Susan E. Reid

palace? You can't count them. And all suddenly flung open!', *Komsom-ol'skaia pravda* enthused.[87] The application of contemporary materials and technology allowed continuous glazing of a light frame structure, such that 'The external walls made entirely of glass give children the total illusion of a space under the open sky among greenery.'[88] As a result, even in the depths of winter, when the children had to be cooped up indoors, they could relive the camp experience in a space that was at once visually open to the outside world and protected from the elements. The free interaction of interior and exterior, together with the absence of a single, dominant façade were central principles of international modernism. But they were invested with specific ideological meanings in the Soviet context of destalinization and the rejuvenation of the socialist project. They represented the antithesis of the monumental impregnability of Stalinist palaces. At MGU, for example, narrow, guarded gates admitted only the chosen to the privileged space inside, thereby asserting control and hierarchy. By contrast, the Pioneer Palace's openness of access was 'democratic' and 'people-oriented', just as the ideals of Khrushchevism claimed to be.[89]

The great expanses of glass advertised to the outside world the joyful life to be found within. As in the children's corner, children were on display to interested adults.[90] Meanwhile, the transparent walls revealed their activities enticingly to other children. As Larissa Zhadova enthused, 'This architecture hospitably opens itself to children, it invites them to come in, and actively interests them in the most varied activities and things.'[91] *Komsomol'skaia pravda* described the initial encounter with the complex in terms of the spatial experience of a young body moving through it, rather than of instantaneous visual comprehension. Coming into the new palace, even an adult became like an excited child: 'You, too, suddenly feel like a little boy and want to run around and see everything at once.'[92] According to art historians Viktoriia and Valentin Lebedev, it was precisely the dynamic interpenetration of inside and outside that enabled the palace to exercise the external influence on society – or Pioneer Effect – with which it was charged. 'The palace easily interacts with its surroundings. Space seems to pour into the building through huge vitrines. The interiors, in turn, seem accessible to observation by a person standing outside. Thereby, the sphere of real spatial existence of the architectural complex turns out to be incomparably wider than the area defined by the contours of its plan.'[93] The great windows connect the interior spaces of the palace with the wider social world. Thus, while contained and protected, the children were at the same time prepared for reinsertion into the wider society as fully integrated, mature social beings. As Zhadova put it:

'Moscow enters through the great windows . . . In such architecture children feel themselves to be a part of the great life of society, in the world of the most important and serious affairs.'[94]

Yet, notwithstanding the actual and rhetorical emphasis on openness, access was not automatic and uninhibited. As the title of Elem Klimov's 1964 film about a Pioneer Camp announced: 'Welcome, or No Trespassing'. Invitation coexists with exclusion; the identity of the Pioneer collective is affirmed by its limits. The paradox is most explicit at the main entrance embellished by the *Young Leninists* mosaic, as two architects observed:

> The basis of the spatial composition of the palace is the opening up of the interiors into the surrounding space. The city is as if brought into the interior of the edifice, whereby its social essence is architecturally predetermined; it is hospitably open for all little citizens, for all young Leninists. Welcome! *And suddenly at the main entrance the reception turns out to be destroyed – before you stands a wall.* It is all the more strange because the whole remaining façade is open and already from afar one can see many interesting things [inside] . . . Enormous glazing rising almost from the very ground invites one to enter the building, but just where one can [actually] do so a wall appears, which, even if it is artistically decorated, in effect turns the main entrance into a narrow passage.[95]

The commentators dismissed this paradox as absurd. However, if we consider the function of the threshold mosaic in relation to Pioneer ritual and to the palace's purpose as a space for incubating the future communist society, not only does it make sense; it unlocks the spatial conception of the palace as a whole.

The *Young Leninists* mosaic hovers in front of the entrance to the main block, marking the threshold to the palace. It is a liminal plane, passing through which one leaves the outside world and is initiated into the inner domain of the Pioneers with its symbols and rituals. It is also the portal from which the serried ranks of Pioneers will issue onto the parade ground when, in fulfilment of their oath, they are summoned forth in the name of the Party. As a boundary between one realm and another, it both separates and unites. Mikhail Bakhtin identified the threshold as the 'chronotope of *crisis* and *break* in a life', highly charged with emotion and value and connected with life-changing decisions and beginnings.[96] In the Pioneer Palace, the threshold mosaic marks the place where the child takes the life-changing step of entering the Pioneer collective. Art historian Dmitrii Sarab'ianov likened it to the frontispiece of a children's book: it is a visual image at the interface between the everyday world about to be left behind, and the world of wonder about to be entered. Like a frontispiece, its role is to engage children's imagination and disengage them from surrounding realities, to entice them in, set the tone and encapsulate the world of images which will then accompany them throughout their time in the palace.[97]

The *Young Leninists* mosaic marked the everyday entrance for palace users. They were to come freely to the palace. But, familiarity and universal access should not breed contempt; an everyday occurrence should not become unthinking, meaningless routine. Just as a frontispiece makes one pause momentarily before immersion in the hermetic world of a book, so, too, the mosaic wall was a delaying mechanism. It was to make the Pioneer stop a moment, straighten her red kerchief, put herself in the appropriate frame of mind, remember what it meant to be a Pioneer . . . and only then pass on in. Or, to take a liturgical metaphor, like an iconostasis it is at once a passage through to the blessed realm and a barrier that blocks profane access to that sacred space.

The dialectics of contingent separation and ultimate integration that are played out in the *Young Leninists* mosaic are also expressed in the palace's location in the Lenin Hills and its treatment as a camp. Of course, the palace could not remove its participants so thoroughly as a camp. But its designers aimed at least to dislocate them: the journey to maturity and integration into the body of adult Soviet society was to be facilitated by a contingent removal from quotidian surroundings and sojourn in a purposefully designed physical space. In children's imagination the journey there across the Moskva River could take on the proportions of an expedition, invested with an element of adventure and independence. Separate from the city, far from everything, it had to be reached by public transport. It was precisely to create a separate world, like a camp or a children's enclave – 'an inner environment' with its own microclimate, 'commensurate with the little person, its future master' – that the architects had taken the radical decision to turn it inward, away from the road. 'We decided that it should be a children's republic, an organism in itself.'[98] To go there was to enter a different world, to make a 'journey into the land of Pioneriia', to the 'Land of Romantics' or Pioneer Wonderland (*chudesnaia pionerskaia strana*). It was a sovereign enclave within the larger social space, a putatively adult-free zone, operating according to its own Lilliputian scale, its own laws, customs and conventions: a 'Pioneer Republic' where children were the masters.[99]

Notes

1. Compare Alfred Roth, *The New School* (Zurich, 1950). This trilingual publication may have been known to the architects. I am indebted to Catherine Cooke for incisive comments on an earlier version of this chapter.

2. 'Spravka o Moskovskom dvortse pionerov', 1962, Pioneer Palace Archive (henceforth PPA), Moscow; Russian State Archive of Literature and Art (henceforth RGALI) f. 2943, op. 2, ed. khr. 82 (Discussion of Pioneer Palace, 7 June 1962); Viktoriia and Valentin Lebedevy, 'Novoe v oformlenii obshchestvennykh zdanii', *Iskusstvo*, no. 9 (1962), pp. 27–34; L. Zhadova, 'Probuzhdat' khudozhnikov', *Dekorativnoe iskusstvo SSSR* (hereafter *DI*), no. 4 (1964), p. 7; K. Barykin, 'Pionerskaia respublika', *Sovetskaia Rossiia*, 4 June 1959; V. Lebedeva and V. Lebedev, 'Gorod schast'ia', *Sovetskaia kul'tura*, 8 April 1962; S. Soloveichik and E. Bruskova, 'Kliuch ot strany romantikov', *Komsomol'skaia pravda*, 2 June 1962, pp. 1–2; S. Soloveichik, 'Eto Vam, schastlivye!', *Komsomol'skaia pravda,* 1 June 1962, p. 4; I. Svadkovskii, 'Vospitanie dlia schastia', *Uchitel'skaia gazeta,* 19 December 1961.

3. V. Egerev *et al., Moskovskii dvorets pionerov* (Moscow: Stroizdat, 1963).

4. Nikita S. Khrushchev, *O shirokom vnedrenii industrial'nykh metodov, uluchshenii kachestva i snizhenii stoimosti stroitel'stva* (Moscow: Gospolitizdat, 1955), p. 20; A. Vlasov, 'Stil' nashei arkhitektury', *Izvestiia*, 25 November 1959; Catherine Cooke, 'Beauty as the Path to the "Radiant Future"' , *Journal of Design History*, 10, no. 2 (1997), pp. 138–9.

5. For a concise account of Khrushchevism see Ronald Hill, 'State and Ideology', in M. McCauley, ed., *Khrushchev and Khrushchevism* (London: Macmillan, 1987), pp. 46–61.

6. 'In the Soviet Union, spokesmen for the regime are fond of the ritual reference to younger generations as "our future".' Allen Kassof, *The Soviet Youth Program* (Cambridge, MA: Harvard University Press, 1965), p. 2; V. Buchli and G. Lucas, 'Children, Gender and the Material Culture of Domestic Abandonment in the Late Twentieth Century', in J. S. Derevens—ki, ed., *Children and Material Culture* (London: Routledge, 2000), pp. 131–8. A society's views of age, and specifically of youth, are an important reflection of its perception and definition of self. Philip Abrams, 'Rites de Passage: The Conflict of Generations in Industrial Society', *Journal of Contemporary History*, 5, no. 1

Susan E. Reid

(1970), p. 178; Anne E. Gorsuch, *Youth in Revolutionary Russia. Enthusiasts, Bohemians, Delinquents* (Bloomington: Indiana University Press, 2000), p. 12.

7. Egerev, *Moskovskii dvorets*, p. 6.

8. Nadezhda Krupskaia had argued in the 1920s that the Pioneers must critically assimilate the most effective aspects of Scout rituals, symbols and practices. See V. T. Kabush, *Pionerskie simvoly, ritualy, traditsii,* 2nd edn (Minsk: Narodnaia asveta, 1985), pp. 23–5.

9. Ralph Talcott Fisher, Jr., *Pattern for Soviet Youth. A Study of the Congresses of the Komsomol, 1918–1954* (New York: Columbia University Press, 1959), p. 239.

10. Khrushchev emphasized that to 'temper' (*zakaliat'*) was an aim of the Pioneers when he opened the palace. 'Vystuplenie N. S. Khrushcheva,' *Komsomol'skaia pravda,* 2 June 1962. On the educative role of Pioneer camps and expeditions in developing initiative, organizational skills, collectivism and endurance, as well as a knowledge of the natural world, see Y. Broditskaya and I. Golovan, *This Palace Belongs to the Children,* trans. M. Wettlin (Moscow: Foreign Languages Publishing House, 1962), pp. 182–95; K. Bardin, 'Pesnia u kostra', *Sem'ia i shkola,* no. 7 (1962), pp. 44–5; D. Latyshina, 'Razvivaite samodeiatel'nost' pionerov', *Sem'ia i shkola,* no. 6 (1961), pp. 13–14.

11. 'Za obraztsovuiu rabotu kazhdogo pionerskogo lageria', *Komsomol'skaia pravda,* 3 July 1952, p. 1; Broditskaya, *This Palace,* pp. 182–95.

12. Bardin, 'Pesnia u kostra', pp. 44–5; V. Kaspina, 'Ne tol'ko otdykh, no i . . .', *Sem'ia i shkola,* no. 8 (1959), pp. 7–8.

13. The same applied to the related ritual of the *pokhod* or expedition – another Pioneer practice appropriated from the Scouts as well as from children's spontaneous culture. A. Inkeles and K. Geiger, *Soviet Society* (London: Constable & Co., 1961), p. 451; A. Gaidar, 'Pokhod' (1940), in *Arkadii Gaidar. Sobranie sochinenii,* vol. 3 (Moscow: Detskaia literatura, 1964), pp. 80–1; Kabush, *Pionerskie simvoly,* pp. 59–61.

14. E. Anthony Rotundo, 'Boy Culture', in Henry Jenkins, ed., *The Children's Culture Reader* (New York University Press, 1998), pp. 337–62. Compare Mark Dudek, *Kindergarten Architecture: Space for the Imagination* (London: E. & F. N. Spon, 1996).

15. M. V. Osorina, *Sekretnyi mir detei v prostranstve mira vzroslykh* (St Petersburg: Piter, 2000), pp. 148–9 and *passim.*

16. Arkadii Gaidar, 'Timur i ego komanda', in *Arkadii Gaidar. Sobranie sochinenii,* vol . 3, p. 86. 'Timur' was so much a part of the cultural baggage of the generation that grew up in the 1940s and 1950s that it may reasonably be assumed to have figured in the memories of childhood that the young architects, as well as their client, the Komsomol leadership, brought to the conception of an ideal space of childhood. See I. I. Rozanov, *Tvorchestvo A.P. Gaidara* (Minsk: BGU (Belorussian State University), 1979), pp. 116–17.

17. Katerina Clark, *The Soviet Novel* (Chicago: University of Chicago Press, 2nd edn, 1985), pp. 228–9.

18. Although not, of course, without biological foundation, childhood is a cultural construct that has to be analysed in historical and social terms, as Karl Mannheim argued in his 1928 essay, 'Das Problem der Generationen'. See Paolo Capuzzo, 'Youth Cultures and Consumption in Contemporary Europe', *Contemporary European History*, 10, no. 1 (March 2001), p. 156; and Philippe Ariès's seminal text *Centuries of Childhood*, trans. Robert Baldick (New York: Vintage Books, 1962). On childhood as a myth see Henry Jenkins, 'Introduction: Childhood Innocence and Other Modern Myths', in Jenkins, *Children's Culture Reader,* p. 15.

19. Catriona Kelly, e-mail, 8 February 2001. I am indebted to Catriona Kelly for allowing me to see part of the manuscript of her forthcoming study on Russian children's culture. One of the architects of the Pioneer Palace, Igor' Pokrovskii, recalled: '"happy childhood in our country" was the central theme of children's literature'. Igor' Pokrovskii, interview with the author, Zelenograd, 6 November 1994. See also Mikhail Yampolsky, 'In the Shadow of Monuments. Notes on Iconoclasm and Time', in N. Condée, ed., *Soviet Hieroglyphics* (Bloomington: Indiana University Press, 1995), pp. 93–111, n. 5. The myth of childhood as a distinct and specially happy time was canonized in nineteenth-century Russian literature, beginning with Tolstoy's *Childhood*. Andrew B. Wachtel, *The Battle for Childhood: Creation of a Russian Myth* (Stanford: Stanford University Press, 1990). 'Happy Childhood' was a pervasive aspect of Stalinist propaganda in the 1930s. However, by the postwar period, the dogmatic insistence on a unified set of norms across all forms of cultural expression, regardless of their medium or their audience, had erased any significant differentiation of cultural production for (or even by) children. E. Z. Gankina, *Russkie khudozhniki detskoi knigi* (Moscow: Sovetskii khudozhnik, 1963), p. 204.

20. See Karin Calvert, 'Children in the House: The Material Culture of Early Childhood', in Jenkins, *Children's Culture Reader,* p. 69; and Derevenski, *Children and Material Culture.* The ideal of childhood and the corresponding environment fashioned for children by adults is not necessarily the same thing as children's spontaneous popular culture or subculture, although it is the framework that both enables and constrains the latter. On children's popular culture see E. K. Zelensky, 'Popular Children's Culture in Post-Perestroika Russia', in A. M. Barker, ed., *Consuming Russia* (Durham, USA: Duke University Press, 1999), pp. 138–60; and Osorina, *Sekretnyi mir detei.*

21. Derevenski, *Children and Material Culture*, esp. Introduction, and Buchli and Lucas, 'Children', pp. 131–8; Calvert, 'Children,' pp. 67–80.

22. 'Malysh i ego ugolok', in I. Abramenko and L. Tormozova, eds, *Besedy o domashnem khoziaistve* (Moscow: Molodaia gvardiia, 1959), pp. 40–4; I. Gil'ter, 'Ugolok rebenka', *Ogonek,* no. 24, June 1960; O. Baiar and R. Blashkevich, *Kvartira i ego ubranstvo* (Moscow, 1962); and Victor Buchli, *An Archaeology of Socialism* (Oxford: Berg, 1999), p. 143. In the 1920s the inability to create a special environment for children was regarded as a sign of deprivation. Gorsuch, *Youth*, p. 31. In present-day Russia, to aspire to the means to create a fairytale world for one's children is a hallmark of the new middle class. Zelensky, 'Popular Children's Culture', pp. 139–40; and C. Creuziger, *Childhood in Russia. Representation and Reality* (Langham, MD: University Press of America, 1996), p. xii.

23. Buchli, *Archaeology*, p. 143.

24. S. G. Strumilin, 'Kommunizm i rabochii byt', *Novyi mir,* no. 7 (1960), p. 212.

25. T. Agafonova, 'Novye zdaniia dlia novoi shkoly', *Komsomol'skaia pravda,* 18 January 1959, p. 2; G. Nidekker, 'Proektirovanie internatov pri shkolakh', *Arkhitektura SSSR*, no. 12 (1958), pp. 36–7; K. Frenkel' and G. Madera, 'Eksperimental'nyi proekt shkoly na 1000 uchashchikhsia', *Arkhitektura SSSR*, no. 5 (1959), pp. 32–5; S. Zmeul, 'O printsipakh proektirovaniia sovmeshchennykh detskikh uchrezhdenii', *Arkhitektura SSSR*, no. 9 (1959), pp. 8–12; I. Fedorova and V. Stepanov, 'Neobkhodimy novye tipy shkol-internatov', *Arkhitektura SSSR*, no. 9 (1959), pp. 3–7. Numerous articles were also devoted to the issue of school buildings in *Uchitel'skaia gazeta* between 1958 and 1962. At the same time, Komsomol 'raids' sought out 'reserves' of under-used space to requisition for education. Interview with N. K. Korol'kov, 'Komsomol'tsy Moskovskoi oblasti vyshli v reid', *Uchitel'skaia gazeta,* 26 May 1959.

26. N. Sementsov and Iu. L'vovskii, 'Takimi budut doma pionerov', *Uchitel'skaia gazeta*, 19 December 1959; T. Mal'kovskaia, 'Formirovaniie lichnosti v komsomol'skom kollektive', *Uchitel'skaia gazeta*, 12 April 1958; 'Vospityvat' ideinuiu molodezh", *Uchitel'skaia gazeta*, 8 October 1959, p. 1; John Dunstan, 'Soviet Boarding Education: its Rise and Progress', in J. Brine, M. Perrie and A. Sutton, eds, *Home, School and Leisure in the Soviet Union* (London: George Allen & Unwin, 1980), pp. 110–41; and Judith Harwin, *Children of the Russian State 1917–95* (Aldershot: Avebury/Ashgate 1996), pp. 27–9.

27. The phrase is borrowed from Buchli and Lucas, 'Children, Gender', p. 135.

28. Michael Holquist, 'How to Play Utopia: Some Brief Notes on the Distinctiveness of Utopian Fiction', in M. Rose, ed., *Science Fiction* (Englewood Cliffs, NJ: Prentice Hall, 1976), pp. 136–8.

29. Jerome M. Gilison, *The Soviet Image of Utopia* (Baltimore: Johns Hopkins University Press, 1975), p. 24.

30. Ibid., pp. 165–6; RGALI, f. 2943, op. 2, ed. khr. 82; N. Dmitrieva, *O prekrasnom* (Moscow: Iskusstvo, 1960), p. 65; Vlasov, 'Stil"; I. Matsa, 'Mozhet li mashina byt' proizvedeniem iskusstva?', *DI*, no. 3 (1961), pp. 14–16; K. Iogansen, 'Rol' veshchi v esteticheskom vospitanii', *DI*, no. 5 (1961), p. 2; S. Kh. Rappoport, *Tvorit' mir po zakonam krasoty* (Moscow: Sovetskii kompozitor, 1962).

31. Soloveichik, 'Kliuch', p. 2.

32. Izrail Gol'dberg (leader of photography studio since opening of the Pioneer Palace) interview with the author, Moscow, 18 January 1998; Pioneer competition announcement, 'Kakim dolzhen byt' dvorets pionerov?', PPA. I have been unable to locate the children's responses.

33. All-Union Pioneer Organization Resolution: 'O rabote v sviazi so stroitel'stvom Dvortsa pionerov v g. Moskve ot 31.1.1958' (draft), and Postanovlenie Sekretariata TsK VLKSM, protokol no. 67, 4.9.61: 'O stroitel'stve Mos. gorodskogo dvortsa pionerov', PPA; Egerev, *Moskovskii dvorets*, p. 101; and Igor' Pokrovskii, interview with the author, Zelenograd, 6 November 1994.

34. On youth problems, delinquency and alienation in the postwar period see Merle Fainsod, *How Russia is Ruled* (Cambridge, MA: Harvard University Press, 1956), pp. 255–61; and Dunstan, 'Soviet Boarding Education,' pp. 110–41. The problem arose frequently in *Komsomol'skaia pravda*, in the 1950s, for example: 'Zabota o byte i dosuge molodezhi', *Komsomol'skaia pravda*, 2 August 1952; 'Vospityvat' ideinuiu molodezh", *Komsomol'skaia pravda*, 8 October 1959.

35. Fisher, *Pattern,* p. 251; Hilary Pilkington, '"The Future is Ours": Youth Culture', in C. Kelly and D. Shepherd, eds, *Russian Cultural Studies* (Oxford: Oxford University Press, 1998), pp. 370–1.

36. The Pioneers were founded in 1922, four years after the Komsomol. Age limits, rituals and other aspects of the Pioneers varied in the course of their history.

37. Resolution of Eighth Plenum of VLKSM Central Committee, 1957: 'On measures for improving the work of the Lenin Pioneer Organization'. See A. Kutsenko and S. A. Furin, 'Lenin All-Union Pioneer Organization', *Great Soviet Encyclopedia*, vol. 5 (trans. of 3rd edn, Moscow, 1970; London and New York: Macmillan, 1974), pp. 242–6.

38. Kabush, *Pionerskie simvoly,* pp. 18–30; Svadkovskii, 'Vospitanie'; V. Strunin, 'V odnom stroiu', 1960 (typescript article for *Uchitel'skaia gazeta),* PPA; Kutsenko, 'Lenin All-Union Pioneer Organization', p. 244; Friedrich Kuebart, 'The Political Socialisation of School Children', in J. Riordan, ed., *Soviet Youth Culture* (London: Macmillan, 1989), pp. 111–12; Fisher, *Pattern,* p. 239.

39. Izrail Gol'dberg, interview with the author, Moscow, 18 January 1998. Numerous articles on the need for vacation activities for children appeared in *Uchitel'skaia gazeta* in summer 1958.

40. See for example, 'Vospityvat' ideinuiu molodezh', *Uchitel'skaia gazeta,* 8 October 1959; and Kutsenko, 'Lenin All-Union Pioneer Organization', pp. 242–6.

41. Svadkovskii, 'Vospitanie'; Mal'kovskaia, 'Formirovaniie lichnosti'; Urie Bronfenbrenner, 'The Changing Soviet Family', in D. Brown, ed., *The Role and Status of Women in the Soviet Union* (New York: Teachers' College, Columbia University, 1968), pp. 98–124; Urie Bronfenbrenner, *Two Worlds of Childhood: U.S. and U.S.S.R.* (London: George Allen & Unwin, 1971), chap. 2; Strumilin, 'Kommunizm', pp. 214–19.

42. Kabush, *Pionerskie simvoly,* p. 26; Kutsenko, 'Lenin All-Union Pioneer Organization', p. 244.

43. Kutsenko, 'Lenin All-Union Pioneer Organization', p. 244.

44. Soloveichik, 'Kliuch', p. 2.

45. E. Dzhavelidze, A. Riabushin and M. Fedorov, 'Dvorets pionerov na Leninskikh gorakh', *Stroitel'stvo i arkhitektura Moskvy,* no. 7 (1962), p. 17. One was built in Kiev in 1966, but on a different design.

46. 'Moskovskii dom pionerov i oktiabriat', *Arkhitektura SSSR,* no. 10 (1936), pp. 1–18; S. Borisov, *Iugo-zapad Moskvy* (Moscow: Moskovskii rabochii, 1937), p. 100.

47. The idea was conceived in 1957 by Vadim Strunin, director of the Moscow City House of Pioneers. Draft Resolution of All-Union Pioneer Organization: 'O rabote v sviazi so stroitel'stvom Dvortsa pionerov v g. Moskve', 31 January 1958, PPA; and Postanovlenie Sekretariata TsK VLKSM. Protokol no. 67, 4.9. 61: 'O stroitel'stve Mos. gorodskogo dvortsa pionerov', PPA.

48. 'Dlia iunykh lenintsev', *Pravda,* 30 October 1958; 'Spravka o Moskovskom dvortse pionerov', 1962, PPA.

49. Susan Costanzo, 'A Theatre of Their Own: the Cultural Spaces of Moscow and Leningrad Amateur Studios, 1957–1986', *Canadian Slavonic Papers*, 36, nos. 3–4 (1994), pp. 333–47. On the objective and subjective dimensions of 'living space' see Vladimir Papernyi, 'Men, Women and Living Space', and Stephen Kotkin, 'Shelter and Subjectivity in the Stalin Period', both in W. C. Brumfield and B. A. Ruble, eds, *Russian Housing in the Modern Age* (Cambridge: Cambridge University Press, 1993), pp. 149–70 and 171–210.

50. At the seventeenth-century monastery of Novyi Ierusalim at Istra near Moscow the topographical features and their spatial interrelations were reshaped and renamed as a homologue for the real Jerusalem. For this and other Russian examples of symbolic landscape, including the Lenin Hills, see Robin Milner-Gulland, *The Russians* (Oxford: Blackwell Publishers, 1997), pp. 208–26. On the way spaces become meaningful through repetition of celestial archetypes compare Mircea Eliade, *The Myth of the Eternal Return*, trans. Willard R. Trask (New York: Pantheon Books, 1954), pp. 6–21.

51. See James von Geldern, 'The Centre and the Periphery: Cultural and Social Geography in the Mass Culture of the 1930s', in S. White, ed., *New Directions in Soviet History* (Cambridge: Cambridge University Press: 1992), pp. 62–80; Evgenii Dobrenko, '"Iazyk prostranstva, szhatogo do tochki" ili estetika sotsial'noi klaustrofobii', *Iskusstvo kino*, 2 parts: no. 9 (Sept. 1996), pp. 108–17; and no. 11 (Nov. 1996), pp. 120–9.

52. B. M. Frolic, 'The New Moscow City Plan', in M. F. Hamm, ed., *The City in Russian History* (Lexington: University Press of Kentucky, 1976), pp. 276–88.

53. On spatial dichotomies in Russian and Soviet culturology see V. Papernyi, *Kul'tura dva* (Ann Arbor: Ardis, 1985); Dobrenko, 'Iazyk prostranstva'; R. Stites, 'Crowded on the Edge of Vastness', in J. Smith, ed., *Beyond the Limits: The Concept of Space in Russian History and Culture* (Helsinki: Studia Historica 62, 1999), pp. 259–69; and Stephen Lovell's chapter in this volume.

54. M. F. Ladur, 'Iskusstvo radosti', *Sovetskaia kul'tura,* 1 May 1966, reprinted in M. F. Ladur, *Iskusstvo dlia millionov* (Moscow: Sovetskii khudozhnik, 1983), p. 105.

55. Borisov, *Iugo-zapad Moskvy,* pp. 30, 100.

56. I. Zykov, 'Dvorets nauki', *Novyi mir,* no. 1 (1953), pp. 158–9.

57. Ibid., p. 158; A. Herzen, *Childhood, Youth and Exile,* trans. J. Duff (Oxford: Oxford University Press, 1980), pp. 63-4.

58. This had been the chosen location for the Russian government's first project for the Cathedral of Christ the Saviour in 1817 by Aleksandr Vitberg, to commemorate the 1812 victory over Napoleon. Herzen, *Childhood,* pp. 242–53; Zykov, 'Dvorets', p. 160; Elke Pistorius, 'Der Wettbewerb um den Sowjetpalast', in Gabriele Gorzka, ed., *Kultur im Stalinismus. Sowjetische Kultur und Kunst der 1930er bis 50er Jahre* (Bremen: Edition Temmen, 1994), p. 153; and Milner-Gulland, *The Russians,* p. 225.

59. Reports on construction of MGU in 1952 simply referred to the Lenin Hills, e.g. N. Frolov, 'Na Leninskikh gorakh', *Komsomol'skaia pravda,* 3 July 1952, p. 1.

60. E. N. Sil'versan, *Dvorets Sovetov. Materialy konkursa 1957–1959* (Moscow, 1961). I am indebted to Sona Hoisington for bringing this competition to my attention.

61. Khrushchev, *O shirokom vnedrenii,* p. 20; Vlasov, 'Stil''; S. O. Khan-Magomedov, 'Novatorstvo i konservatizm v tvorchestve arkhitektora', *Voprosy sovremennoi arkhitektury,* no. 1 (1962), pp. 31–48.

62. D. Sarab'ianov, 'Real'nye plody sinteza', *Tvorchestvo,* no. 9 (1962), p. 1; I. Loveiko, 'Khorosheet nasha Moskva!', *Ogonek,* no. 1 (Jan. 1958). See also Iurii Gerchuk, 'The Aesthetics of Everyday Life in the Khrushchev Thaw in the USSR (1954-64)', in Susan E. Reid and David Crowley, eds, *Style and Socialism: Modernity and Material Culture in Post-War Eastern Europe* (Oxford: Berg, 2000), pp. 82–9.

63. Zhadova, 'Probuzhdat' khudozhnikov', p. 8.

64. Ibid.; Sarab'ianov, 'Real'nye plody', p. 1.

65. Sil'versan, *Dvorets Sovetov,* pp. 103–4 and *passim.*

66. Iu. Kotler, 'Strana krasnykh galstukov', *Sem'ia i shkola,* no. 1 (1959), p. 28.

67. A. V. Ikonnikov, *Tysiacha let russkoi arkhitektury* (Moscow: Iskusstvo, 1990), p. 359; E. Val'dman, 'Stal'noi i stekol'nyi rabochii dvorets', *DI,* no. 6 (1963), pp. 1–4.

68. This section is based on: 'Dvorets moskovskikh pionerov. S zasedaniia arkhitekturno-stroitel'nogo soveta', *Arkhitektura i stroitel'stvo Moskvy,* no. 8 (1958), pp. 9–14.

69. 'K trudu i bor'be gotovy!', *Komsomol'skaia pravda,* 20 May 1962, pp. 1, 4; 'Bud'te vsegda gotovy k bor'be', *Komsomol'skaia pravda,* 19 May 1962; Z. Khromova *et al.,* 'Bol'shoi, radostnyi prazdnik iunykh moskvichei', *Uchitel'skaia gazeta,* 2 June 1962; Soloveichik, 'Eto Vam'; Soloveichik, 'Kliuch'. Compare Clark, *Soviet Novel,* pp. 39–40; and Eliade, *Myth of the Eternal Return,* pp. 34–48.

70. Text of Khrushchev's opening speech, 1 June 1962, PPA; and 'Vystuplenie N. S. Khrushcheva', *Komsomol'skaia pravda,* 2 June 1962, pp. 1–2; Egerev, *Moskovskii dvorets,* pp. 5–6.

71. Egerev, *Moskovskii dvorets,* p. 6; RGALI, f. 2943, op. 2, ed. khr. 82, l. 52 (Pokrovskii); F. Novikov, *Formula arkhitektury* (Moscow: Detskaia literatura, 1984), p. 105.

72. Igor' Pokrovskii, interview with the author, Zelenograd, 6 November 1994; Egerev, *Moskovskii dvorets,* p. 6.

73. Dzhavelidze, 'Dvorets', p. 17.

74. G. Borisovsky, 'Architecture and Technical Progress', *The Soviet Review,* 3, no. 2 (February 1962), p. 18, translated from *Novyi mir,* no. 5 (1961); Egerev, *Moskovskii dvorets,* p. 30. The spire of MGU is also assimilated into the regenerative meaning of the palace by the stone campfire. In contemporary press photographs it appears to rise directly out of the flames. See the photograph by S. Kosyrev in *Komsomol'skaia pravda,* 17 May 1962. The effect in the photograph was clearly not accidental, since it required the use of a telephoto lens as well as careful alignment.

75. RGALI, f. 2943, op. 2, ed. khr. 82, l. 47.

76. Eternally bugling boys, mass-produced from concrete, were ubiquitous in public spaces, and were replaced as fast as they disintegrated. S. M. Orlov, 'Skul'ptura v gorode', *Iskusstvo,* no. 4 (1958).

77. Kabush, *Pionerskie simvoly,* pp. 161–2.

78. Egerev, *Moskovskii dvorets,* p. 48; and, for example, V. Favorskii, 'Mysli o monumental'nom iskusstve', *Moskovskii khudozhnik,* 15 April 1958 (written March 1958) in E. Murina, compiler, *V.A. Favorskii* (Moscow: Sovetskii khudozhnik, 1988), pp. 423–5.

79. Sarab'ianov, 'Real'nye plody', pp. 1–4.

80. Sil'versan, *Dvorets Sovetov,* p. 33; Tommaso Campanella, *The City of the Sun: A Poetical Dialogue,* trans. Daniel J. Donno (Berkeley: University of California Press, 1981), pp. 33–7.

81. Favorskii, 'Mysli', p. 424.

82. Ernst Neizvestnyi, Minutes of Ideological Commission of Central Committee of CPSU, 15 May, in *Ideologicheskie komissii TsK KPSS, 1958–1964. Dokumenty* (Moscow: Rospen, 1998), p. 490; E. Neizvestnyi,

'Otkryvat' novoe!', *Iskusstvo*, no. 10 (1962), p. 11; A. Khalturin, 'Novye skul'pturnye pamiatniki', *Iskusstvo*, no. 11 (1960), pp. 15–20.

83. N. Dmitrieva, 'Stankovizm i monumental'noe iskusstvo', *DI*, no. 1 (1961), pp. 1–3; and Favorskii, 'Mysli', p. 424. Compare discussion of monumental sculpture's 'space of effect' by N. Voronov, 'Sovetskaia monumental'naia skul'ptura 1960–1980 (Moscow: Iskusstvo, 1984), pp. 181–91; and of the 'sacral zone' created by monuments by Mikhail Yampolsky, 'In the Shadow of Monuments', pp. 93–112.

84. Lebedevy, 'Novoe', p. 31.

85. Sarab'ianov, 'Real'nye plody', p. 3; Egerev, *Moskovskii dvorets*, p. 30.

86. 'Za obraztsovuiu rabotu kazhdogo pionerskogo lageria', *Komsomol'skaia pravda*, 3 July 1952; Bardin, 'Pesnia u kostra', pp. 44–5.

87. Soloveichik, 'Kliuch'.

88. Sarab'ianov, 'Real'nye plody', p. 4

89. Zhadova, 'Probuzhdat' khudozhnikov', p. 7. On the 'parade entrance mentality' see Stites, 'Crowded', p. 263. The contrast also expressed the difference between the Pioneer organization and the Komsomol. Where the Pioneers were a mass organization whose membership embraced the majority of school children, entry to the Komsomol was more selective, and followed a programme of preparation and a ritual of admission.

90. Intourist ran special tours and buses to bring foreigners to the palace. Stowers Johnson, *The Two Faces of Russia* (London: Robert Hale, 1969), p. 39.

91. Zhadova, 'Probuzhdat' khudozhnikov', p. 7.

92. Soloveichik, 'Eto Vam', p. 4.

93. Lebedevy, 'Novoe', p. 29.

94. Zhadova, 'Probuzhdat' khudozhnikov', p. 7.

95. I. Bebiakov and Iu. Driashin, 'Eshche raz o sinteze', *Tvorchestvo*, no. 11 (1962), p. 16. Emphasis added.

96. Mikhail Bakhtin, 'Forms of Time and of the Chronotope in the Novel', in M. Holquist, ed., *The Dialogic Imagination* (Austin: University of Texas Press, 1981), p. 248; Deborah Haynes, *Bakhtin and the Visual Arts* (Cambridge), p. xiii. In Iurii Lotman's terms, it is 'the hottest spot for semioticizing processes'. Yuri M. Lotman, 'The Notion of Boundary', in *The Universe of the Mind* (London: I. B. Tauris, 1990), pp. 131–62. On Pioneer initiation rituals see Christel Lane, *The Rites of Rulers: Ritual in Industrial Society* (Cambridge: Cambridge University Press, 1981), pp. 90–4.

97. Sarab'ianov, 'Real'nye plody', p. 3. 98.

98. Igor' Pokrovskii, interview with the author, Zelenograd, 1994; RGALI, f. 2943, op. 2, ed. khr. 82, l. 52; Egerev, *Moskovskii dvorets*, p. 30.

99. E. Koridalina, 'Oni zdes' khoziaeva', *Sem'ia i shkola*, no. 4 (1962), pp. 9–10; 'Kliuch ot strany romantikov', *Komsomol'skaia pravda*, 2 June 1962; Zolotoi kliuchik'; Soloveichik, 'Kliuch'; L. Fedorov, 'Puteshestvie v stranu "Pioneriiu"', *Uchitel'skaia gazeta*, 17 May 1962; V. Kuskov, 'Zdes' budet "strana Pioneriia"', *Sovetskaia Rossiia*, 22 October 1960; Barykin, 'Pionerskaia respublika'; Kotler, 'Strana', 28–9; and Broditskaya, 'This Palace'. The idea of a segregated space where the child was master was also a topos in discussions of children's corners and of Pioneer camps. In Elem Klimov's 1964 film set in a Pioneer camp, *Welcome, or No Trespassing,* a banner proclaims 'Children – you are the masters of the camp!' Josephine Woll, *Real Images: Soviet Cinema and the Thaw* (London: I. B. Tauris, 2000), p. 175.

–9–

Warsaw Interiors: The Public Life of Private Spaces, 1949–65

David Crowley

> Fourier, the dreamer, charmingly foretold that lemonade would flow in the seas. Does it flow? They drink water from the sea, crying: 'lemonade!' returning home secretly to vomit.
>
> Adam Ważyk, 'Poemat dla dorosłych', 1955

Warsaw, as the capital of the People's Republic of Poland, was perpetually in crisis. Perhaps the gravest problem facing the city was a constant shortage of living space. Wartime devastation of the housing stock, which had never been adequate, followed by an exceptionally dynamic pattern of urbanization in the 1950s and 1960s, produced a prolonged housing crisis.[1] Whilst the situation was critical throughout the country, Warsaw was always recognized as rather a special case: unlike other cities, for instance, the ownership of all land within the city boundaries passed to the control of the municipal authorities in 1945, and in 1949 all existing housing was taken under state control or 'communalized', bar small, single-family homes. Ten years later housing policy was subject to a degree of liberalization to take pressure off the city's resources. New cooperatives – usually responsible for large, modern estates – drew people's savings in return for a shorter wait on the housing list. Housing in the city was a matter of great political sensitivity, not least because it was in this field, perhaps more than in any other, that achievement would be measured by the very people the Party claimed to support. Each successive administration damned the failures of their predecessors and proclaimed cause for renewed optimism. Such pronouncements, at least in the early years of the new state, revealed a kind of faith in environmental determinism, i.e. the notion that in reshaping the spaces of socialist Warsaw, new kinds of cultured citizens of the city would be fashioned. The capital of the future, for instance, was invariably to be a city of libraries, cultural centres, schools and theatres: 'factories of culture' that would produce new kinds of Poles. This vision of the metropolis, characteristic of the Eastern Bloc, has a long and rich history. It represents what James Donald has described as the 'overweening dream of Enlightenment rationalism; to get the city right, and so to produce the right citizens'.[2]

If the 'public' spaces of the socialist city were more or less clearly articulated in official plans and architectural schemes, the 'private' socialist home remained a rather more ambiguous concept. Whilst official rhetoric proclaimed a great investment into the 'new collective life of the masses', the communist authorities in Poland, following the lead set by the Soviet Union in the 1930s, were committed to older 'bourgeois' social forms, not least that of the family. Consequently, the 'standard' dwelling provided by the State and the housing cooperatives that acted on its behalf was the single-family apartment. Meanwhile, the provision of other common residences like the 'barracks' that still housed Warsaw citizens into the 1960s and might have been claimed as a model of collective life, was a matter of contingency rather than doctrine. In this essay I explore the public and private character of such family apartments in the 1950s and 1960s. In what ways did the socialist project, initiated in Poland in the late 1940s and then modulated during the period of the Thaw, shape public discussion of new Warsaw homes?

Contrary to the Party's rhetoric, an economy of spatial shortage dominated everyday life for all but the privileged few. In the 1950s, many squatting in the ruins planned their escape from insanitary and uncertain lodgings, while others dreamed of leaving the cramped communal billet. Even when modern flats became more widely available in the 1960s, other compromises had to be made. Like sardines in a tin, families were raised in small, one- or two-room apartments in which the living room often doubled up as a bedroom for more than one generation and the 'blind' kitchen was a windowless galley. The fact that priority on the waiting list for such flats was given to families encouraged early and sometimes ill-suited marriages. In this context of shortage, it comes as no surprise that Warsaw citizens watched their city rise from the ruins with more than just polite interest or civic pride. As Leopold Tyrmand remarked in his novel *Zly*, 'In the 'fifties everyone in Warsaw knew a little about architecture, just as everyone in the Yukon knew something about gold.'[3] After Gomułka took power and the Party began to address the needs of the Poles as consumers in a more self-conscious manner, magazines like *Ty i Ja (You and I)* attracted large readerships by dealing with matters relating to the home like shopping, cooking and furnishing. Such 'popular' representations, produced 'under licence' from the State, provide rich material with which to explore both the evolving public image of the 'socialist home' and changing conceptions of the notion of privacy, in a period of political and material change. The Bierut years make an ideal starting point for this survey.

Inside Outside

The home was sketched in little more than broad outline by the Party leadership as part of its blueprint for the new society after they consolidated their power in Poland in 1949. One can identify important statements of policy, a significant example of which was *Sześcioletni plan odbudowy Warszawy* (Six-Year Plan for the Reconstruction of Warsaw) credited to the authorship of party leader Bolesław Bierut.[4] Such announcements tell us little however about the particular qualities of the 'socialist home'. His summary of the principal characteristics of the city's new apartments – that they should be 'comfortable, sunny, dry, aesthetic and adequately heated' – was hardly shot through with ideological elixir. At the same time, he mapped abstract spatial dimensions with obsessive precision: 'the Five-Year Plan foresees the construction of 120,000 new homes of a total capacity of 12,000,000 cubic metres'.[5] Not only did these calculations accord with the narrow terms of the command economy, as numeric mantras they also suggested the dizzying scale of the projects undertaken by socialism.

This kind of statistical representation recurs in all such official statements about housing in the People's Republic. At a macroeconomic level, it seemed that every metre of the new city could be accounted for: at a microeconomic level, 'sanitary norms' measuring spatial 'allowances' suggested social justice. In this vein, *Sześcioletni plan odbudowy Warszawy* was typical. It promised to end privileged possession of, and access to space. Bierut expressed the ideological significance of the new housing in terms of its potential to redress historic wrongs. No longer was the centre of the city to be the domain of the bourgeoisie: the 'workers' capital' was to be reclaimed in a great programme of social engineering. As if in opposition to the pattern of suburban drift found in the West, Stalinist planning claimed to encourage the return of the workers to the centre of the city to enjoy cultured lives.[6] In a very literal manner, the five- and six-storey elevations of apartment buildings dressed with classical cornices, lintels and miniature porticos – the preferred taste of the haute bourgeoisie in 1900 – were replaced by ostensibly similar new buildings for 'the workers' in the 1950s. The tasks of architects were prescribed by the formulas of Socialist Realism, a Soviet import that placed great emphasis on the political effects of architecture.[7]

The much-vaunted urban schemes planned and built in the capital in the early 1950s were crucial symbols in the Party's claims on authority in a very literal sense. Of course the new flats that rose from the rubble in the city centre were actual, material spaces inhabited by actual Varsovians (often Party officials, prominent figures in Polish society and leading workers, recipients of awards for their feats of productivity). But they were also representations of ideal spaces. Flats in prominent schemes like the *Marszałkowska Dzielnica Mieszkaniowa* (Marszałkowska Housing District/MDM) were made into images for the attention of the public, primarily the readers of popular magazines and other publications in which new interiors were often reproduced textually and photographically. Roland Barthes once described this phenomenon as the 'publicity of the private'.[8] What he had in mind was 'the explosion of the public into the private' that began with the advent of photography in the nineteenth century and led to the modern condition of 'celebrity'. However, his suggestion that publicity has compromised the notion of 'the private' as 'the absolutely precious, inalienable site where [one's] image is free' has, as I will show, particular resonance in Poland in the 1950s.

These flats in new housing schemes were subordinate to the public's gaze in a second sense. In the most prestigious Warsaw schemes, they were characterized by awkward spatial planning with high ceilings and parsimonious allocation of floor-space; rooms opened into one another without a corridor or hallway that might have afforded some kind of privacy to inhabitants; and load-bearing columns often disturbed domestic spaces and the distribution of light. As interior spaces, these flats were compromised by their relation to the monumental form of the building. For instance, many of the earliest housing schemes such as MDM and the Muranów district built on the ruins of the Ghetto were dressed in the retro style of Socialist Realism. Typically, for instance, the allotment of balconies, a popular and useful feature, bore little or no relation to the needs of the residents. Their distribution was determined by such aesthetic imperatives as 'the harmony of the façade'.

The emphasis on visuality in architecture was recognized and criticized by a number of contemporary observers, often sharing a kind of phenomenological interest in space, across Europe in the 1950s. I will discuss the Polish voices below. However, it is useful to refer to the thinking of the French Marxist philosopher and sociologist, Henri Lefebvre, for his critical analysis of spatial politics could be vented with greater freedom than was available to commentators in Poland. The central themes of his writings from the 1940s, emphasizing the need for creativity and spontaneity to combat the bureaucratization of modern life, had taken their impetus from the development of dismal and anonymous suburban housing developments on the fringes of French cities from the 1950s. For Lefebvre the possibility of resistance to this architecture, albeit fleetingly, could be found in 'the appropriation of space, in the activity of the body and the activitation of desire'.[9]

In his book, *The Production of Space* (*Production de l'espace*, 1974), Lefebvre expressed an antipathy to what he saw as the shallow conceptions of space held by architects and planners ('bureaucrats') and, ultimately, by authority. He rejected the perspective of architects and their patrons as being too fixed, or in his terms, subject to an 'immobile perceptual field'. What he saw as a prevailing obsession with the vista and the façade, abstracted space at the expense of those who inhabit it:

> The tendency to make reductions of this kind – reductions to parcels, to images, to facades that are made to be seen and to be seen from (thus rein-forcing 'pure' visual space) – is a tendency that degrades space. The facade (to see and to be seen) was always a measure of social standing and prestige.[10]

A fetishistic concern with the vista characterized many aspects of city planning during the Stalin period in Poland, from precise optical calc-ulations about the visibility of prominent buildings on the distant horizon to the aesthetic effects of the façade. Contemporary commentators often compared the self-interest of those who erected buildings in the 'era of capitalist economy' in the second half of the nineteenth century (with their lack of regard for the aesthetics of the street and the city vista) with the vision of city planners in the 'age of socialism'. Edward Muszalski, for instance, argued that uncoordinated development before 1939 had 'spoiled' Warsaw's appearance.[11] It was as if the chimera of the collective city could be achieved by demanding its harmonious appearance.

Within a few years, critics would argue, in a moment of relatively free speech during the Thaw, that the city and its buildings had been dimin-ished during the Stalin years, reduced to a series of controlled theatrical sets and staged vistas. Leopold Tyrmand, a novelist, put it most succinctly in 1954 when he wrote: 'the city is not a picture' (*'miasto to nie obraz'*).[12] He understood that in the Soviet-styled city, space was subordinate to images and effects, and, by the same system, interiors were inferior to the exterior forms that produced them. Space was impoverished by the political imperative to create a particular form of 'representational architecture', the term that Lefebvre employed to describe the dominance of the visual effects over space. Warsaw humourists had already anticipated this theme: washing clothes in her kitchen in a cartoon published in *Świat*, a housewife (an archetypal figure in the productive economy) is concerned that her shabby laundry will spoil 'the aesthetic effect of the city' (Figure 9.1). The precise location is suggested by the profile of overbearing street light seen through her window: she lives in Constitution Square in Warsaw, the model of Stalinist city planning that was opened with great pomp in 1952. Signs of a private imperfection, it seems, risked disfiguring the order of the public realm. (What is less clear, however, is whether the architect or the housewife is the butt of this joke.) In an economical manner, the cartoonist contrasts the untidiness of life with the desire for social order expressed by architects, planners and their client, the State.

Private Sanctuaries?

In a context in which the State had nationalized the housing stock and was the sole builder of new schemes, in what ways might homes be conceived as private spaces? Is it possible to characterize the ordinary, 'private' homes in the new Warsaw housing schemes of the 1950s and 1960s as sites of

Figure 9.1 Cartoon published in *Świat*, 1953

opposition? In the discussion below, I will contrast the understanding of the home as a site of sanctuary with Henri Lefebvre's dichotomous conception of private space as a site of conflict with the public realm. With Warsaw in mind, it is not difficult to conceive the private space of the home as a place of escape from a cheerless environment and from ethical compromises. This has been a persistent theme in descriptions of life under socialism. Czesław Miłosz in his classic early account of Stalinism in Poland, *The Captive Mind*, produced a typology of loyalty. Describing the practice of deception for reasons of self-preservation, he wrote:

> A man of taste cannot approve the results of official pressure in the realm of culture no matter how much he applauds the latest verses, how many flattering reviews he writes of cultural art expositions, nor how studiously he pretends that the gloomy new buildings coincide with his personal preferences in architecture. He changes completely within the four walls of his home. There one finds (if he is a well situated intellectual) reproductions of works of art officially condemned as bourgeois, records of modern music, and a rich collection of ancient authors in various languages. This luxury of splendid isolation is pardoned him so long as his creative work is effectively propaganda. *To protect his position and his apartment (which he has by the grace of the State), the intellectual is prepared to make any sacrifice or compromise; for the value of privacy in a society that affords little if any isolation is greater than the saying 'my home is my castle' can lead one to surmise.*[13]

In other words, public acts of faith secured private freedoms. In this vein, the 'private' home – even if publicly owned – was understood as being the limit of intrusions from the public sphere. The home was claimed as a sanctuary, private in the sense of being a hidden or inaccessible realm.

However, Lefebvre suggests a different conception of the private realm: one in which the inhabitation of space is made up of acts of appropriation and even struggle against order. He wrote: 'When compared with the abstract space of the experts (architects, urbanists, planners), the space of everyday activities of users is a concrete one, which is to say, subjective. . . . It is in this space that the "private" realm asserts itself, albeit more or less vigorously, and always in a conflictual way, against the public one.'[14] From his perspective, the private realm might be viewed not as an escape from the public one but its opponent. It is clear that the 'threat' of the private was recognized by authority in Poland in the early 1950s: one can find many examples of 'top-down' strategies to influence behaviour. The State sought to exercise its influence over life behind 'closed doors'. In apartment blocks, residents' committees (*komitety blokowe*) – a Soviet import described in its original setting by Katerina Gerasimova in this book – not only policed the residence but also sought to promote the self-improvement of householders by, for instance, requisitioning books for a collective library.[15] Even the extent of privacy was to be parsed. The meagre proportions and limited facilities of the single-family apartment – the main unit of all new housing provision – were sometimes explained in terms of the new society being constructed in Poland. Leisure was no longer to be appropriated from the commonweal for private enjoyment, but was to be appointed outside the home for the collective good. Olgierd Szlekys, a prominent furniture designer, explained in 1955: '[In socialist Poland] we have changed the forms of our life. We have moved part of private life to the houses of culture, to clubs and cafes which are places to meet comrades replacing, we say, the old salons.'[16]

To characterize socialist spaces in terms of the containment of the private would hardly be a new avenue of intellectual enquiry. However, what Lefebvre's assertion does demand is investigation into ways of living that persisted in spite of ideological prohibition. In this, we may even be able to explore how people made homes in ways that confuted the idealized image of the new socialist habitat. I do not mean to emphasize by this the practice of turning the home into a site of dissidence by, for instance, making the apartment into a theatre for the performance of new and sometimes prohibited plays as the poet Miron Białoszewski did in Warsaw in the late 1950s.[17] Such homes were the exception: their significance lies in the ways that they were transformed into sites of production and in their relation to a circumscribed order of the public sphere – the 'parallel society' later associated with *Solidarność* – rather than in their home-like qualities.[18]

Can, therefore, ordinary, 'private' homes in the new Warsaw housing schemes of the 1950s and 1960s be understood as sites of opposition? Given the State's monopoly over public expression – whether in the form of the press or via the activities of 'licensed' voluntary organizations with an interest in domestic matters like *Liga Kobiet* (Women's League) – few if any unguarded and articulate statements of opposition could be vented in Poland during the period. Despite this, the frequency of campaigns designed to model particular aspects of life can be taken as signs of persistence and perhaps even resistance on the part of those who were their targets.[19] In thinking about the oppositional meanings that might be lent to the home – either by occupants or subsequent analysis by others – the problem of evidence is further underscored by the relatively unselfconscious ways in which domestic spaces and ordinary things are generally consumed in the course of everyday life. Consumption, as various commentators have noted, is rarely an act of enunciation.[20] It is rather in the discourses around and about things and spaces that meanings are established and often negotiated. Furthermore, the 'private' location of the home does not necessarily inhibit the cultivation of what Jan Kubik has called 'counterhegemonic' attitudes and practices but, as he remarks, 'only when those attitudes and beliefs become public is the established order threatened'.[21] In order to refute the 'socialist home', private values and practices had to be demonstrated in public. In Poland in the 1950s and 1960s the richest source of such material, with the widest band of opinion (though I stress this has to be seen in relative terms) on the home, were the popular weekly magazines such as *Przekrój* (*Cross-section*) and *Kobieta i Życie* (*Woman and Home*), largely produced for women readers. Articles published in this medium represented not only the State's interest in disciplining the home but also, as I will suggest, attempts to speak for the private – a particular form of the 'publicity of the private'.

Ideal Homes

The steady stream of statistical hyperbole issuing from the lips of party functionaries reveals little of the design or, more significantly, what might be called the 'ideological character' of the new socialist home. In this vacuum, popular magazines constituted an important medium for communicating official views of domesticity to a readership who were to be its beneficiaries. Women's magazines contained guidance on home furnishing and domestic economy as well as discussions of the aims and achievements of the reconstruction programme. Like all publications in the People's Republics, they were subject to censorship and so spoke with an official voice on all matters.[22] However, as I will show, they were not as single-minded as they might appear. Although the party line was clearly drawn for censors, editors and journalists when addressing self-evidently political subjects like the death of Stalin, they were less certain when dealing with articles on home decoration. Although it would be an exaggeration to describe discussion of the domestic realm as pluralistic, some articles contained a good deal more reflection than condemnation. Even when articles reviewed domestic arrangements in the West, although writers were compelled to expose the social injustices obscured by great luxury or avant-garde taste, the accompanying images offered tantalizing images of prohibited lifestyles. As minor and incidental products of socialism, these magazines reflected some of the ambiguities that surrounded the concept of 'the socialist home'.

In the early years of the 1950s the home, perhaps not unsurprisingly, was typically represented in all sectors of the press by *new* residences from the Warsaw reconstruction programme, i.e. public housing in common ownership and, as such, a measure of achievement in the present and a metonym for a future Poland. Old flats partitioned into cramped homes inhabited by two or more families, and frequently the dingy basements that had been colonized by the homeless, remained largely unrepresented until the Thaw (only appearing as a notional baseline from which new achievements would be measured). Moreover, in official ideology during the Stalin period, the domestic realm was reconceived as a place where practical needs could be met. A utilitarian attitude to the home was encouraged. The value of a 'functional kitchen' was, for instance, emphasized to resonate with the mood of asceticism that the Party sought to promote:

> The new, bright and comfortable flats are not only a place of rest for the working man. They are also a place where one can work on self-improvement, a place where one may work out many of the ideas about efficiency that present themselves in the course of professional work.[23]

New homes, in other words, were sites for the reproduction of the new socialist citizen. The visual clichés used to illustrate these reports included images of boys and girls reading and women sewing. In a public discourse that valued production, the new home was not to be a site of consumption where commonplace things were appropriated into personal, interior 'spaces' of memory and association. The socialist home was presented as another site of production alongside the factory and the office, where the material environment was disposed and actively designed to assist in the manufacture of a new self. Although the home was conceded as 'private' in the narrow sense of being the domain of an individual and her family, it bore no traces of what might be described as 'personality'.[24] Few unruly details entered into the frame to disturb the emphasis on the collective and conventionalizing virtues associated with good *character*, namely self-control and good conduct. Populated by generic social types ('everywoman') rather than named or identified individuals, these interiors inhibited any reflection on the part of the reader on the individual idiosyncrasies, personal needs and interests of their inhabitants. These new 'ideal homes' were not 'private' in Barthes's sense of being the 'absolutely precious, inalienable site where [one's] image is free'.[25]

The emphasis on good character underscored a series of practically minded articles entitled 'How to furnish the new apartment?' which

appeared in 1953 in *Stolica* (Capital City), a fortnightly that was dedicated to reporting Warsaw's reconstruction. Most authors writing in this
series accepted the notion of the standard flat as a solution to the pressing
requirements of postwar economy and, ideologically, the material expression of social justice.[26] Their reflections focused on the problem of how
to furnish such apartments, for the prewar possessions which most families
brought to their new homes were traditional in character and excessive in
ornament. Whilst these articles invariably emphasized utility and economy,
they gave few practical clues to the eager designer let alone the householder as to the character of 'socialist furniture' (not least because demotic
'Functionalist' design associated with the prewar Modern Movement was
under Soviet-led prohibition). The ontological possibility of 'socialist
things' – implicit in the materialist conception of progress – remained a
matter of rhetoric rather than reality. Nevertheless, the furnishing practices represented in these articles suggest ways that the new flat might be
considered a site of conflict where the State asserted its 'right' to organize
life.

In one of these articles in March 1953 Stanislaw Komornicki, for
instance, alluded to two 'conflicts' over interior space in the new Warsaw
home. Staying well within the class terms of political orthodoxy, he
focused his criticisms on the peasantry and the middle classes. Peasants
had been welcomed into Warsaw as part of a symbolic occupation of the
capital by the people: *'Socjalistyczna stolica – miastem każdego obywatela,
– robotnika, chłopa i pracujácego inteligenta'* ('The socialist capital city
for every citizen: worker, peasant and intellectual'). Yet in their small
flats, according to Komornicki, these new metropolitans reproduced the
social spaces of the peasant home. The small, often meanly proportioned,
kitchen was used like the traditional *czarna izba* (black chamber) in the
peasant home, a multi functional room organized around the fireplace
where household labour was conducted and meals consumed. In trans-
position, this 'disposition' in the new Warsaw apartment left the much-
trumpeted collective services like the communal laundry unused. The
other, *biała izba* (white chamber), which in rural lives had been used as
a site of display and for the reception of guests, was preserved as a space
of display rather than of virtuous production or utility. The small, new flat,
which typically accommodated a family in two or three multi-purpose
rooms, was designed according to principles of utility. In effect, the
design of the apartment was disregarded by its inhabitants. In the view of
this apologist for the new Warsaw, this trace of the peasant disposition in
new socialist spaces 'was an unfortunate memory of long-past, unhappy
times'.[27] What Komornicki had in mind was not the 'private' time of

biography but the epochal conception of historical materialism in which life was regulated by the metre of progress: in this teleology, peasant life was destined for extinction. Ideologically correct, his article sought to raise a consciousness that would speed its disappearance.

To view the difference between the kind of ideal lifestyles projected by the housing schemes and the kinds of peasant household practices reported by Komornicki as a 'conflict' would, however, be to aggrandize ordinary life. Given the great difficulties associated with finding and furnishing a flat in the miserable conditions of postwar reconstruction, it is probably more appropriate to view the mismatch between dwellers and dwellings as a mismatch between habitus and environment. In sociologist Pierre Bourdieu's conception of this term, habitus is understood as 'durable but transposable dispositions' that integrate past experiences and shape perceptions, appreciations and actions in the present.[28] Habitus is supra-personal in that it can be transposed across settings and is common. In short, in being shaped by a 'home culture', common to a social group or class, all are equipped with a habitus. Yet, at the same time, habitus is embodied: inscribed in behaviour, and what is sometimes called 'body language', as well as in the ways that space is occupied. Rejecting the notion of cultural conditioning, Bourdieu suggests a more subtle relationship of individual, society and environment: habitus, he argues, enables an agent's collusion with the society of which he or she is a member: 'agents merely need to let themselves follow their own social "nature", that is, what history has made of them, to be as it were, "naturally" adjusted to the historical world they are up against'.[29] Individuals are not, therefore, subject to the unassailable logic of a dominant habitus like the spatial order of the new Warsaw. The use of the kitchen as a *czarna izba* indicates that whilst the inhabitant of the flat may have been the subject of attempts to discipline behaviour, in the home, and perhaps in other settings too, untrained 'dispositions' persisted.

At Home During the Thaw

One consequence of destalinization in the mid-1950s was that the discourse about the home changed, with new and more diverse voices being heard. Marek Hłasko's Social Realist novels and short stories of the period, for instance, represented the cheek-by-jowl existence in communal apartments and dank basements as a kind of urban pathology. His controversial 1956 novel, *Osmy Dzien Tygodnia* (Eighth Day of the Week) – much celebrated as a classic example of Thaw writing – tells the story of a couple's despondent search for private space in which to make love.[30] In the overcrowded city, only the filthy and rubble-strewn ruins offer the space for them to satisfy their desire. Hlasko's candour was rare and, in fact, soon quashed; his novel was banned in 1958, charged with decadence. Whilst the moral void at the heart of his novel was certainly controversial, it was perhaps Hlasko's refusal to identify its causes that alarmed the Party ideologues. Ultimately, his reader was left to reflect on the social effects produced by the desolate environment that he described so vividly. His was an interpretation of Warsaw homes that, whilst holding with environmental determinism, shared none of the Party's optimism.

The politics of the Thaw encouraged new kinds of thinking about housing, if not necessarily the home. This episode in the political history of the Soviet Bloc has been interpreted by various writers, most often as an ideological retreat in which Polish communists moderated their commitment to Marxism-Leninism in order to hold onto power. Post-Stalinist authority sought to lower the ideological temperature by deferring to the technologically driven and efficient force of 'Progress'. By attaching its programme to highly visible symbols of modernization, the Party cast itself as a technocratic influence over Polish life. At the same time, its 'leading role' – and claim on legitimacy – was built on promises to improve the living standards of ordinary Poles. Asceticism, which had characterized much discussion of personal consumption in the first half of the 1950s, was abandoned. Numerous new homes were promised (though somewhat fewer built) in Gomułka's Poland for a frustrated population who required more living space and better conditions. The new Five-Year Plan for Housing announced in 1960, for instance, promised the construction of over 75,000 new flats in the city.[31] New districts on the city's fringes like Grochów appeared. With a population of 24,000 people, this was the first of a series of new estates designed to house large numbers. These new estates had a significant effect on housing density, when measured in terms of room occupation, bringing it back down to prewar levels.

Gomułka's new regime made a particular investment in modern building types. In the late 1950s Polish cities began a process of transformation that resulted in a new urban fabric, formed from the numerous panel built, high-rise blocks for which the Eastern Bloc became notorious.[32] The tall block became an important symbol of socialist futurology, endorsed both by regime and architects as the triumph of pragmatism over ideology.[33] At the same time, the State flashed its technocratic credentials, promising to use the resources of the command economy to produce high quality mass housing. Bolesław Szmidt, a high-profile architect, charted a new relationship between architects and the State as well as the criteria used to judge new buildings, when describing designs for new twelve- and fourteen-storey blocks of flats:

> This work is mostly based on a 1960 decree of the Council of Ministers advocating the design and erection of prototype blocks of standardized apartments, intended for prefabrication and mass production. If a prototype building is found by a commission of experts to be progressive technically and economical in exploitation, then it is recognized as a 'type' and passed for mass production.[34]

In other words the architectural profession was licensed to experiment within a narrowly defined field of technical competence. Architects responded positively to the oft-repeated challenge to design buildings that could be built 'cheaply and quickly'.[35] The emphasis on efficiency enlarged the interest of architects in some aspects of the interior. In 1961–2 Maria and Kazimierz Piechotka, for instance, presented a typical scheme in which prefabrication was not only applied to constructional elements of the building but also to parts of the interiors. Designs and specifications were drawn up for standard kitchen and bathroom fittings that could be industrially produced and used in all new homes. And whilst encouragement was given to such invention, the 'guiding' principles of sanitary norms, albeit based on an expanded per capita 'allowance' of space, and the requirement of family occupation, checked any radical social visions on the part of architects.

The Party's claim to be engaged in the modernization of the socialist project was paralleled by a symbolic modernization of other aspects of the home. Numerous exhibitions promoted modern domestic design produced by state agencies like the Institute of Industrial Design (Instytut Wzornictwo Przemysłowego) and semi-private cooperatives like Ład.[36] The interior schemes displayed at the 1957 Second All-Poland Exhibition of Interior Design in Warsaw and the 1958 'Exhibition of Contemporary Furniture' in Cracow, for instance, followed the proportions of housing association apartments. These interiors were furnished with prototypes that could be put into production by the small-scale workshops (that the economic reforms of the period sought to revitalize). These objects included brightly coloured, modular storage schemes; ratan-seated chairs on spidery metal frames; and abstractly patterned curtain fabrics; each demonstrating their designer's awareness of the latest trends in the West. These designs not only suited the new flats in their modest proportions, but corresponded with the patterns of life that they were to accommodate. Beds that could be folded into chairs or storage units that could be used to partition space were well suited to rooms that had to serve different functions and different users during the course of a day. Whilst the new apartments were not 'open-plan' in the spatially fluid sense suggested by the Modern Movement in the 1920s, or in the ostentatious fashion advanced by American designers like Ray and Charles Eames in the 1950s, they nevertheless broke with the tradition of the inwardly focused, functionally segregated home.

In their promotion of contemporary style aesthetics, the 1957 and 1958 exhibitions of furniture and applied arts were typical of many such displays at this time. Modern design was vigorously promoted. Its merits were usually advanced by designers in narrow terms of utility and economy. But what of its relation to ideology? Were homes in the new style more or less 'socialist'? A direct parallel, for instance, might be drawn with the renewal of a modernist aesthetic in the Soviet Union during the Khrushchev era (and, in fact, there is some evidence that Polish modern design was considered strikingly bold there[37]). Party ideologues sought to find a new legitimacy during the Thaw by turning 'back to Lenin', i.e. to the roots of the Revolution to rediscover principles that had been abandoned by Stalin. This was coincidental with a renewal of interest in the social and aesthetic vision of the Constructivists, the avant-garde of the 1920s. Back on track, Soviet socialism, it was claimed, would draw closer to the collective life predicted in full communism. Domesticity, defined as private life and private possessions, would become irrelevant. The promotion of modern design with its emphasis on utility and technology, and with roots in avant-garde thinking, might be seen, therefore, not only as a refutation of attitudes to domesticity that had been encouraged during Stalinism, but as a step closer to the communist paradise.[38] Advice literature and articles in women's magazines as well as the housing committees run by Party activists promoted reform of the single family flat and the communal apartment. Practically, this meant stripping ornamental features from old-fashioned furniture and eliminating 'knick-knacks' from the home; adopting centripetal interior schemes that diminished the significance of fixed features like the traditional hearth or the centrally placed dining table; and developing new types of transformable furniture that could perform two or more functions.

In Poland, whilst the aesthetics of modernization in the home were similar, the ideological shift that they represented was somewhat different. Unlike the Soviet Union where a specialist design press aligned the contemporary style with neo-productivist discourse, in Poland the aesthetic was promoted without reference to any socialist principles (bar the compulsory reference to economic prudence). In the popular press it was usually placed within what might be 'proto-consumerist' discourses of individual taste and fashion. Interiors could, for instance, be described as 'fashionable' and 'colourful', suggesting not just design characteristics but, in their association with variety, social values too. In such exhibitions, the modernization of the home was not a 'project' in the sense that it carried an ideological imprimatur: it was far closer to what has been described as 'Refrigerator Socialism', the redirection of the economy to improve the supply of consumer goods that occurred under Gomułka.

'The Individual in Great Number'

For the most part, as I have stressed, the architectural profession appears to have accepted its newly appointed role as a technocracy with alacrity. The combination of decorative excess and the ideological load that buildings had been forced to bear during the period of Socialist Realism

Figure 9.2 Cover of *Dookołaświata* (12 May 1957) representing Oskar and Zofia Hansen's scheme for *Ogólnopolskiej Wystawa Architekturej Wnętrz* (National Exhibition of Interior Design) held in Warsaw in that year

left most architects keen to adopt the positivistic rhetoric of late modernism, avoiding theory or ideology. However, there were some exceptions. Perhaps the most innovative architectural thinker of the Thaw was Oskar Hansen, who elaborated a theory of *Otwarta Form* (Open Form). Formulated at the height of the Thaw, Hansen first published his ideas in *Przegląd Kulturalny*, a publication described as 'one of the journals that lit the fires of the dramatic liberalization of 1956'.[39] and illustrated in the following year in interior schemes at the Second All-Poland Exhibition of Interior Design described above (Figure 9.2). In both theory and practice, Hansen sought to encourage new ways of making space private.

Hansen's purpose – as it developed in the course of the 1950s and 1960s – was to release the creative capacities of the majority. Buildings designed as 'open forms' would be positively 'incomplete', leaving opportunities for occupants to shape their domestic environment in meaningful ways. He argued that his 'system' would change the content of architecture by exploiting not only the resources of the community but also those of the individual. Unusually for an architect, Hansen positioned the structures and technology of modern architecture – which he regarded as the 'domain of the community' – *against* the interests of the individual in moulding his or her environment. Hitherto, the 'Greater Number' had been treated as passive and, in the words of one commentator, 'faceless numerals' who were to be merely accommodated in the most narrow, utilitarian sense of the term.[40] Hansen was later to detect traces of his system in the practice of some young Polish architects: for instance, in the early 1960s he applauded Grebecka and Kobylański's design for a housing estate in Płock in which the architects had adopted an 'open-plan system where only the main construction walls and sanitary equipment were mass produced' and the 'inhabitants were easily able to lay out and erect pre-fabricated partitions [to] allow for future change'.[41] The theory of 'open form' was not merely a rhetorical indictment: it was a practical design method 'against the dull uniformity of housing design' and the suppression of 'personality in the community' in Gomułka's Poland.

Hansen's ideas were particularly well received in the West, where commentators like Charles Jencks located them in a general vein of architectural thinking that eschewed dogma along the lines of Karl Popper's influential critique of historicism and teleological ideologies.[42] Jencks suggested that in some general sense Hansen's 'Open Form' correlated with Popper's 'Open Society'. Whilst Hansen's ideas had international currency (as well as precursors in the investment made in the free-plan by Le Corbusier and others in the 1920s), they had a particular relationship to the reshaping of the domestic environment in Poland in the second half of the 1950s. Hansen's theory of Open Form was, in effect, a challenge to the two-dimensional conception of space that had been evident in architectural thinking during the Stalin years. Not only had the interior been subordinate to the visual effects of the exterior (what Hansen neatly described as 'the aesthetics of the Closed Form'), but domestic space had been measured in sanitary norms, the narrow economic terms of the command economy. Moreover, through the period, apartments had been conceived by architects working under the direction of Socialist Realism, and later as modernists, in terms of 'parcels' of space – as standard and fixed allotments. Hansen described this 'problem' in archetypal terms: '[as] how to shape space in the form of innumerable cells, each of them containing, not – as those of a honeycomb – a bee, but a human individual'. The solution lay, he argued, in conceiving space in terms of movement, whether in terms of a synchronic potential to be reorganized by those who occupy it, or in its diachronic capacity to change over time. Hansen's thinking also suggested the possibility of a new, more pluralist conception of private space, at least within the context of state socialism. The interior was to be private in the sense that it marked the point at which the architect, an agent of the State, should limit his or her interest. Ultimately, this put Hansen at odds with the massive building programme that was being orchestrated by a state committed to controlling and effectively constraining the use of resources.[43]

Some parallels can be drawn here with Lefebvre's thinking. However, the French social theorist's ideas also indicate the limits of Hansen's project. Lefebvre's highly influential writings on architecture in the 1960s celebrated the 'imaginary' in terms not dissimilar to Hansen's conception of creativity, 'as the appropriation of space, of physiological activity and of desire'. Like Hansen, Lefebvre reflected on the private, accentuated the dynamic qualities of lived space: 'Any mobilisation of "private" life would be accompanied by a restoration of the body, and the contradictions of space would have to be brought out into the open. Inasmuch as the resulting space would be inhabited by subjects, it might legitimately be deemed "situational" or "relational" – but these definitions or determinants would refer to sociological content rather than any intrinsic properties of space as such.'[44] And again like the Polish architect, Lefebvre held the view that the architecture measured its achievements prematurely. Of 'lived space', the French social theorist wrote: 'As a space of 'subjects' rather than of calculations . . . it has an origin and that origin is childhood, with its hardships, its achievements and its lacks. Lived space bears the stamp of the conflict between an inevitable, if long and difficult, maturation process and a failure to mature that leaves particular resources and reserves untouched.' Despite their kinship, Lefebvre's observations ultimately suggest the limits of Hansen's project, for the 'privatisation' of space required the exercise of subjective capacities beyond the sphere of the professional architect. As Lefebvre suggests in his allusion to childhood and the laying down of subjective experience, private space is closely connected to what has been called the unfolding of 'private time'.[45] To find traces of this phenomenon we need to look elsewhere.

Speaking for the private

Hansen's theories were widely reported in Poland in the late 1950s and 1960s. The fact that his ideas were vented in the popular press testifies both to the interest in new thinking about building at a time of great housing shortage and, more significantly, to their correspondence with a desire on the part of inhabitants to assert control over domestic spaces. In 1963 he was interviewed by a journalist from the popular magazine *Ty i Ja*.[46] It is not surprising that this magazine gave space to Hansen to rehearse his ideas, not least because its editors had been sponsoring similar, if less theorized, ways of understanding domestic space.

First published in 1960, *Ty i Ja* was a remarkable publication for many reasons, not least because it attracted a large readership for its synthesis of high-brow culture from both the East and West with discussions of the material culture of modern life.[47] A typical issue might include a long article on the life and poetry of the Russian modernist poet, Mayakovsky, between an analysis of the erotic in traditional Indian sculpture and a striking fashion collage plucked by the magazine's designer from the pages of *Vogue* and *Elle*. What was conspicuously absent from its pages was any discussion of the social or cultural merits of living in a socialist state. Like the Pop Art aesthetic that informed its celebrated graphic design, the magazine seemed to eschew strict cultural hierarchies. Each issue included a regular feature entitled 'Moje mieszkanie to hobby' ('My Flat is My Hobby') in which readers were invited into the homes of well-known writers, artists and actors. These features were striking for many reasons, but I will reflect on two key interrelated themes: the 'personalization' of the standard flat and the celebration of 'personality'.

These articles tended to dwell on one issue above all others, that of how to domesticate and privatize the modern flat. The relative 'placelessness' of the new tower block may have been beyond the influence of its residents, but the indeterminate, anonymity of the interior was not. As a journalist writing about one of the interiors in the series put it:

David Crowley

May I boldly announce: 'Finally'. Finally I have an opportunity to present an authentic modern solution to the functional interior and this type of regular urban flat of a standard size.[48]

The 'problem' was so evident to the readers of the magazine that it did not need to be articulated: it was how to maximize and personalize the monotonous, meanly proportioned and badly lit M2 and M3 flats, the basic units of all new housing schemes, within limited material resources (limits that tended to reflect as much the failings of Polish industry as the pockets of the householder). The answer lay in clever organization of screens, imaginative lighting, multi-purpose furniture and so on. If the notion that the homes of others could provide inspiration for the creative occupation of the standard flat could be made any clearer, it was when the editors launched a readers' competition in 1964. Prizes of money and consumer durables were awarded to the winners who furnished their flats with greatest invention.[49] While in his theory of the 'Open Form', Hansen had suggested a tactical incompleteness should be a feature of the design of new homes to stimulate imaginative inhabitation, in practice it was the practical limitations of the command economy that had produced this creative resourcefulness. The invention and hand-making skills required to improve the standard flat were hardly powerful symbols of the socialist economy.

Figure 9.3 'My Home is My Hobby', a spread from *Ty i Ja* (November 1965)

Not only providing explicit information about the use and construction of things unavailable in the command economy, the 'Moje mieszkanie to hobby' articles reflected on values that had hitherto been suppressed (Figure 9.3). The title included a provocative anglicism, 'hobby', suggesting the home as a site of leisure and as an expression of an individuated taste and identity. These were the homes of actual people, even if they belonged to the ambiguous social category of 'celebrity'. Hitherto, in the People's Republic, this mark had been attached to figures in the public settings of political life or the workplace (even if that employment was in the entertainment industry). By contrast, these *Ty i Ja* reports offered a more intimate construction of celebrity than that which had been produced in the Eastern Bloc before. Whilst many of inhabitants of the flats were stellar figures from Polish culture like Andrzej Wajda, the filmmaker, or the painter, Tadeusz Kulisiewicz, the emphasis was on their activities as consumers rather than as producers of culture. Each piece took as its focus the material organization of their homes. In most features, old furniture, 'exotic' souvenirs and *staroci* (bibelots) were used to broadcast personal narratives: to tell of journeys abroad and family histories. Month by month, *Ty i Ja's* investigation of the interior suggested the currency of differing and relative values and ultimately a conception of private life that had been contained during the Stalin years. In 1965, for instance, *Ty i Ja's* readers were invited into the home of Stefan Flukowski, a poet and novelist. The opening passage sets the scene:

> Here . . . more than in any other example we can reveal the harmonic and peaceful background of family life. The banal architecture of MDM – the two-room apartment – does not particularly mar the individual atmosphere of the Flukowski family home; a congenial atmosphere despite the design of the flat.[50]

In this account of an MDM interior that a little over ten years earlier could only be discussed in terms of public achievements, could be described in terms of a disavowal of the public realm. The tour of Flukowski's home allowed the magazine to sermonize: 'the best flat must be an individual one'. The flat was an extension of the inhabitant: in other words it was an index of personality rather than of 'good character', the virtue so frequently praised in the Bierut years.

In bringing these homes into the public realm, the editors of *Ty i Ja* publicly 'spoke for' the private. Neither sanctuary for escape from the compromises of everyday life nor sites for the reproduction of good comrades, these private homes were made public to assert individual histories over collective futures. First 'licensed' by reform sensibility of the late 1950s, they continued to be published despite the ideological retrenchment that took place in Poland in the 1960s. The fact that these articles could appear was a sign of the fact that the private (in the sense of that which is individual, had been sanctioned by the post-Stalinist regime). Not only was the private home legitimate but, importantly, this fact could be asserted publicly.

Conclusion

This essay has explored the representation of domestic space in Warsaw in the period between the Five-Year Plans announced in 1949 and in 1960. A parallel history could be written of the provision of actual spaces themselves, perhaps concentrating on more properly architectural matters such as the relation of common facilities like laundries and shops to the apartment block or competing ideas about the most economic use of space in the galley kitchen. However, I would suggest that this would be a rather level history without peaks of dramatic transformation or troughs of controversy. In fact, successive communist authorities were remarkably faithful to a rather conservative vision of the home, i.e. that of the family apartment. Whilst one 'generation' of architects was compelled by diktat to adhere to the doctrine of Socialist Realism and a later one was encouraged to adopt the formal principles of modernism, the flats that they designed were relatively alike when considered in terms of space. In fact, most housing schemes throughout the period viewed inhabitation within narrow, functional limits. Space was a resource to be apportioned like any other in the command economy. In practical terms of privacy, the flat in the Socialist Realist apartment block in the city centre was much like the flat in the high-rise tower on the outskirts (and in fact often preferred because of its location).

If the provision of actual Warsaw apartments might be characterized by such veins of continuity, it is clear that the representation of the home was not. In particular, the relative meanings attached to the notions of private and public – articulated through the everyday media like the weekly magazine – changed remarkably over the period: the public/publicity had been privileged over the private/privacy during the Bierut period of Stalinism, whereas during the Thaw it was subordinate. It would be a misunderstanding of the nature of socialism in Poland to claim that this was a victory of the private in some kind of ideal sense, as the sudden availability of a 'site' free from public and, as such, political concerns: the course of events in the 1970s and 1980s proved otherwise. In fact, the long inability of the socialist economy to provide housing was to become a recurrent theme of protest, a vein of criticism that judged the failures of the State on the terms of the socialist ideology it prescribed.

Notes

1. Juliusz Gorynski, 'Housing Policy in Poland', in Stanisław Ehrlich, ed., *Social and Political Transformations in Poland* (Warsaw: PWN, 1964), pp. 99–113.
2. James Donald, 'This, here, now. Imagining Modern Cities', in S. Westwood and J. Williams, eds, *Imagining Cities* (London: Routledge, 1997), p. 182.
3. Leopold Tyrmand, *Zly* (London: Michael Joseph, 1958), p. 157.
4. B. Bierut, *Sześcioletni plan odbudowy Warszawy*, 1949, published in English as *Six-Year Plan for the Reconstruction of Warsaw* (Warsaw: Książka i Wiedza, 1951).
5. Bierut, *Six-Year Plan*, p. 181.
6. The authoritative account of the principles of socialist city planning written to endorse Soviet practice was E. Goldzamt, *Architektura zespołów śródmiejskich i problemy dziedzictwa* (Warsaw: Państwowe Wydawnictwo Naukowe, 1956).
7. For discussion of the introduction and promotion of Socialist Realism in Poland see W. Włodarczyk, *Socrealizm* (Paris: Libella, 1986) and A. Åman, *Architecture and Ideology in Eastern Europe During the Stalin Era* (Cambridge, MA: MIT Press, 1992).
8. Roland Barthes, *Camera Lucida* (New York: Hill and Wang, 1981), p. 98.
9. Henri Lefebvre, *Critique de la Vie Quotidienne* (Paris: L'Arche Editeur, 1958), published in English as *Critique of Everyday Life* (London and New York: Verso, 1991); and *Le Droit à la Ville* (Paris: Editions Anthropos, 1968).
10. Henri Lefebvre, *The Production of Space* (Oxford: Blackwell, 1991), p. 361.
11. Edward Muszalski, 'O Popsutych Perspektywach', *Stolica* (30 May 1954), pp. 8–9.
12. Leopold Tyrmand, *Dziennik 1954* (Warsaw: Tenten, 1995), p. 233.

13. Czesław Miłosz, *The Captive Mind* (1953) (Harmondsworth: Penguin, 1985), p. 64–5 (my emphasis).
14. Lefebvre, *Production of Space*, p. 362.
15. See B-D, "Wędrówka po powiśle', *Stolica* (21 March 1954), p. 2.
16. Szeklys's comments were made in a round table discussion recorded in *Stolica* (3 February 1955), p. 2.
17. See Miron Bialoszewski, *Teatr Osobny, 1955–1963,* with an introduction by Artur Sandauer (Warsaw: Państwowy Instytut Wydawniczy, 1971).
18. On this see, for instance, *Reinventing Civil Society. Poland's Quiet Revolution, 1981–1986* (New York: Helsinki Watch, 1986); Sabrina Petra Ramet, *Social Currents in Eastern Europe* (Durham, NC: Duke, 1995), pp. 84–118.
19. This principle has been adopted by writers who have examined, for instance, the ideological crusade mounted against 'anti-social tendencies' like the fascination with American popular culture in the first half of the 1950s. See, for instance, R. P. Potocki, 'The Life and Times of Poland's "Bikini Boys"', *The Polish Review*, no. 3 (1994), pp. 259–90.
20. Colin Campbell, 'When the Meaning is Not a Message: A Critique of the Consumption as Communication Thesis', in Mica Nava, Andrew Blake, Iain MacRury and Barry Richards, eds, *Buy this Book. Studies in Advertising and Consumption* (London: Routledge, 1997), pp. 340–52.
21. Jan Kubik, *The Power of Symbols Against the Symbols of Power* (Boulder: Penn State Press, 1994), p. 265.
22. Although dealing with a later set of controls, Jane Leftwich Curry, ed., *The Black Book of Polish Censorship* (New York: Vintage Books, 1984) explains the censorship practices and mechanisms employed by the Polish state in great detail.
23. *Świat* (March 1953).
24. See Karen Hultannen's discussion of these terms in Simon J. Bronner, ed., *Consuming Visions: Accumulation and Display of Goods in America 1880–1920* (New York and London: W.W. Norton, 1989).
25. Barthes, *Camera Lucida*, p. 98
26. See for instance E. Tatarczyk's contribution under the title 'Standard Mieszkaniowy' *Stolica* (31 May 1953), p. 10.
27. Stanisław Komornicki, 'Jak Urządzić Nowe Mieszkanie. Artykuł dyskusyjny', *Stolica* (1 March 1953), p. 11
28. Pierre Bourdieu, *Outline of a Theory of Practice* (Cambridge: Cambridge University Press, 1997), pp. 79–87.

29. Pierre Bourdieu, *In Other Words: Essays Towards a Reflexive Sociology*, trans. Matthew Adamson (Stanford: Stanford University Press, 1990), p. 90.

30. Marek Hłasko, *The Eighth Day of the Week*, trans. Nobert Guterman (London: Secker and Warburg, 1991).

31. Adolf Ciborowski, *Warsaw. A City Destroyed and Rebuilt* (Warsaw: Polonia, 1964), pp. 176–81.

32. The greatest number of these schemes was built during the 1970s but the course had been set earlier by Gomułka's regime.

33. See Waldemar Baraniewski, 'Odwilżowe dylematy polskich architektów', in *Odwilż*, (Poznań: National Museum of Poznań, exh. cat., 1996), pp. 129–38.

34. Bolesław Szmidt, 'Modern Architecture in Poland', *Architectural Design* (October 1962), p. 496.

35. T. K., 'O mieszkaniach optymistycznie', *Stolica* (27 August 1961), p. 5.

36. On these design bodies see my '"Beauty, everyday and for all" – the social vision of design in Stalinist Poland', in J. Attfield, ed., *Utility Reassessed* (Manchester: MUP, 1999).

37. The Polish novelist Tadeusz Konwicki recalled a party one evening in Moscow in the 1960s at which his hosts placed a great deal of emphasis on the fact that their modern furniture was Polish. See *Moonrise, Moonset* (London: Faber and Faber, 1988), p. 180.

38. See Susan Reid, 'Destalinisation and Taste, 1953–1963', *Journal of Design History*, 10, no. 2 (1997), pp. 161–75 and V. Buchli, 'Khrushchev, Modernism and the Fight against *Petit-bourgeois* Consciousness in the Soviet Home', *Journal of Design History*, 10, no. 2 (1997), pp. 161–75.

39. Leftwich Curry, *Black Book of Polish Censorship*, p. 27.

40. Alina Moffatt, 'Oskar Hansen', *Architectural Design*, 2, (1967), p. 77.

41. Oskar Hansen, 'Open form and the Greater Number' in John Donat, ed., *World Architecture*, I (London: 1964), pp. 140–4.

42. Charles Jencks, *Modern Movements in Architecture* (Harmondsworth: Penguin Books, 1977), p. 332. With an impressive modernist 'pedigree', Hansen carried a particular authority in post-Stalinist Poland. He had worked with Pierre Jeanneret between 1948 and 1950 and was a participant at the last CIAM congress in Otterlo in 1959 where the influence of Team X gathered pace. See Oscar Newman, *CIAM '59 in Otterlo* (London: Alec Tiranti Ltd), pp. 190–7.

43. Working with his wife, Zofia, Hansen had two major opportunities to put his thinking into practice: the Lubelskiej Spółdzielni Mieszkaniowej estate in Lublin (1965) and the Przyczółek Grochowski estate in Warsaw (1963–9).

44. Lefebvre, *Production of Space*, p. 363.
45. Susan Stewart, *On Longing. Narratives of the Miniature, the Gigantic, the Souvenir, the Collection* (Durham, NC: Duke University Press, 1993), p. 139.
46. *Ty i Ja* (May 1963), p. 14
47. Accurate readership figures for publications of this period are difficult to ascertain. However, anecdotal evidence suggests that *Ty i Ja* was popular and disappeared quickly from Polish newsstands.
48. Felicja Uniechowska, 'Moje hobby to mieszkanie', *Ty i Ja* (January 1966), p. 36.
49. See 'Rozwiązanie konkursu Hobby-Mieszkanie', *Ty i Ja* (August 1964), pp. 33–7.
50. Felicja Unechowska, Moje hobby to Mieszkanie', *Ty i Ja* (November, 1965), p. 41.

10

Public Privacy in the Soviet Communal Apartment

Katerina Gerasimova

The communal apartment (*kommunalka*) was an important feature of every-day life in the Soviet Union as well as being a place that has attracted the attention of foreign scholars interested in the unique forms of Soviet society.[1] This type of housing, where several unrelated families were forced to live together sharing the bathroom, toilet, kitchen, hallways and telephone, has been the domestic habitat of several generations of Soviet citizens. It might seem that the inhabitants of communal apartments were unaware that they lacked privacy, but the concept of privacy has never been a feature of Russian and Soviet culture and, in fact, the term itself is hard to translate into Russian. Nevertheless, in recollecting their experiences, the inhabitants of communal apartments often talk of feelings of humiliation, discomfort and tension similar to those felt by people in the West when their privacy is violated. Since the boundary between private and public can be connoted in a metaphorical and a physical sense, the phenomenon of the communal apartment presents an important opportunity to explore the idea, experience and legacy of a Soviet version of privacy.

Although the terms 'private' and 'public' are vague, and their suitability in any analysis of socialist societies is debatable, they have frequently been used to indicate important relations between individuals, social groups, society in general, and the State. As a product of Western civilization and thought, this 'great dichotomy' encourages scholars to find equivalents in other cultures. The impossibility of direct translation of 'public' and 'private' into Slavonic languages has inspired a search for alternative terminology as well as reflections on the concepts themselves. During the course of the history of the Soviet Union a need emerged to speak about levels of privacy, as well as of hybrid spheres like the 'social'.[2] The Russian scholar Oleg Kharkhordin argues that the use of the dichotomy private/public in any analysis of Soviet society is misleading.[3]

Nevertheless, I have chosen to use these categories in this essay in order to compare and contrast them with the ways in which they are understood in the West and to establish the ground for further cross-cultural analysis.

The communal apartment hardly belongs to the social (*obshchestven-naia*) sphere. This type of housing cannot be defined as entirely private space either, even though the Western concept of home is intimately connected with one of privacy.[4] Life in the communal apartment cannot be described as purely domestic or simply personal as it includes social relations with those who are neither members of the household nor of the family, and everyday life is regulated from outside. One of the aims of my research, therefore, has been to reconstruct, from the emic categories used by ordinary people in the course of everyday life, analytical ones which accord with the concept of privacy.

This essay is based on research carried out in St Petersburg (formerly Leningrad) between 1996 and 1999; the research comprised thirty-eight interviews with former and current inhabitants of communal apartments, participant observation in three communal apartments, as well as analysis of official documents and archive materials.[5] Leningrad was infamous for having the highest percentage of communal housing among Soviet cities. In 1951 an average of 3.3 families lived in each apartment in the city.[6] According to the All-Russia National Census conducted in 1989, the percentage of communal apartment inhabitants in St Petersburg was still 23.8 % of the city's population and was 4.8 times higher than average in Russia and 2.6 times higher than in Moscow.[7]

Private and Public Spaces in Soviet Society

All cultures have their own specific types of private and public spaces, which are often woven into complex systems of values that encompass the open and closed, collective and individual, state and non-state, family and societal, inside and outside, etc. There are many ways of conceptualizing the public/private dichotomy but, as Jeff Weintraub maintains, at the deepest and more general level, and lying behind the different forms, there are two fundamental and analytically quite distinct kinds of imagery through which private can be contrasted with public:

   (i) What is hidden or withdrawn versus what is open, revealed, or accessible; and

  (ii) What is individual, or pertains only to an individual, versus what is collective, or affects the interests of a collectivity of individuals.[8]

I will employ this distinction to sketch in changes in the configurations of the private and public in the history of the Soviet Union as well as their spatial correlates in dominant housing types.

The establishment of the new social order in the Soviet Union made it necessary to redefine private/public boundaries socially and spatially.[9] The politics relating to the division of private and public spheres in the first post-revolutionary decade was encapsulated in the ambition 'to blow up the shell of private life (*chastnaia zhizn'*)'. Everything closed to and detached from the State or the collective was considered counter-revolutionary. The author of an article in 1919 entitled 'The House is a Soviet Fortress' stated: 'Everything physical is to be controlled by the State when the latter is under reconstruction.'[10] This particular configuration of private and public was predominately determined by the openness of the private sphere to the State and the collective. This could be called 'total publicity'.

Private ownership of housing was abolished. The home was conceived as part of the public sphere and, as such, open to any intrusion by the State. Accordingly, collective modes of housing, typically in the form of the house-commune, were promoted.[11] The house-commune was conceived as a large building containing a system of rooms for individuals or collective dormitories for men and women, with a common kitchen or canteen for all the tenants, shared toilets, showers and leisure rooms, a library, theatre hall, laundry etc.[12] The main idea of the commune was that each member should have equal living space, equal amounts of money for personal needs (or no money at all) as well as equal participation in the management of the commune and responsibility for housekeeping. Mutual control and discipline should serve to unify the collective. The actual construction of house-communes according to this blueprint was impossible because of the economic crisis that confronted the Soviet Union in the 1920s. Similarly, the organization of a commune in existing buildings also required the investment of scarce resources as well as the goodwill of tenants. As a result, a few communes were organized in large apartments (*bytovye kommuny*). Their members were usually young people, living together as a single household, who pooled and redistributed their earnings according to the needs of the collective.[13] However, it did not become a widespread practice.

The major change in the general course of Soviet policy in the 1930s has become known as 'the Great Retreat'. A new middle-class elite became firmly established in the social hierarchy, possessing forms of 'cultural capital' that were unavailable to the greater part of the population. These higher echelons of Soviet society 'became bourgeois' and wanted to lead a 'cultured way of life'.[14] A comfortable life – based on higher levels of domestic consumption, social protocols and proprieties – was important to the new elite. Accordingly, the frontier between public and private spheres changed. Personal life (*lichnaia zhizn'*) as individual or family was no longer under prohibition but private life (*chastnaia zhizn'*, literally 'particular life'), which was supposed to be closed and, in fact, challenged state control of its citizenry, was rejected. Personal life, however, was still open to the scrutiny of the State. Moreover, the State itself adopted many 'private' symbols, from the metaphorical slogan 'Stalin is our father' to the wider system of social security, children's upbringing, etc. In Weintraub's terms, the prevailing configuration of private and public during the Stalin period emphasized visibility as a characteristic of the public sphere and individuality as a characteristic of the private one. This configuration can be defined as 'public privacy' and it was realized (and found its spatial expression) in the form of the communal apartment.

When 'the Thaw' began in the second half of the 1950s, the configuration of private and public changed again. The process of symbolic privatization of domestic space accelerated in the 1960s. Vladimir Shlapentokh describes the following developments as signs of the privatization of life: mass construction of prefabricated blocks with apartments for separate families, increased ownership of private transport, and an increasing orientation towards circles of friends on the part of individuals that led to the rebirth of friendship.[15] The home was promoted as a site of withdrawal from the environment and, similarly, the family was claimed to offer protection from the consequences of urbanization (such as information redundancy, tension between different social roles, breakdown of the extended family, density of population).

Nevertheless, collective ideals remained strong and alternative public spheres based on friendship networks were formed at a time when the official public sphere was in crisis. Issues that should have been a matter of public concern such as the future development of society, matters of culture and political events were often debated in private places. Moreover, the informal (or 'Second') economy was mostly based on immediate social and family connections and was, in some sense, private. Public facilities and public goods were often used for private needs. These arrangements were controlled less by the State and took place on private or 'privatized' territories but were nevertheless collective in their form. We might define this configuration of private and public spheres that combined collectivity but were closed to the State as 'private publicity'.[16]

Since the late 1980s the extent of state control has decreased, but the public sphere, in the sense of civil society, remains relatively weak. At the same time, the private sphere has been strengthening considerably, supported by the privatization of property. Social differentiation has been accompanied by a strong drive to individualization and a desire to see the home as an expression of social status and identity. Whilst current developments in Russia show many signs of a return to domesticity, and an orientation to Western-type notions of private life (with the term privacy [*privatnost'*] gaining currency), the communal apartment – a pattern of domestic life shaped by the Soviet experience – has not disappeared.[17]

A Short History of the Soviet Communal Apartment

Before embarking on my analysis of the territory of the communal apartment, I will present a short history of this type of housing.[18] The communal apartment emerged during the period of housing redistribution (1917–21). After the Revolution all housing was expropriated by the State. The newly privileged were given the opportunity to improve their living conditions by occupying high-quality housing. A proportion of former householders was evicted from their apartments, while others were allowed to remain by sharing their former homes with less wealthy families resettled from poorer outskirts. As a considerable part of the housing stock in the centres of big cities consisted of spacious apartments, the Bolshevik authorities decided to solve the housing problem by reducing living space through the 'condensation' (*uplotnenie*) of apartments that belonged to the formerly well-to-do. As a rule, each family was allocated one room, with living space determined by sanitary norms. In 1919 the sanitary norm was established at 8.25m^2 per person but real figures were considerably lower. By 1931 the average living space per capita in Leningrad equalled 6.7m^2.[19] Immediately after the Second World War, the official sanitary norm was expanded by 3m^2, gradually increasing to 12m^2 by the 1990s. A family whose living space exceeded this norm was not permitted to enrol on the waiting list for state housing.

In the 1920s the communal apartment was envisaged as a temporary phenomenon that would be overcome in the near future. However, a constellation of different factors and circumstances allowed this type of housing to spread, becoming the typical form of housing in large cities. These factors included the failure of the ideological project of collective housing (house-commune), underinvestment in new housing construction, the rapid growth of the urban population, as well as the general adaptation of the population to the *kommunalki*. In the late 1920s and early 1930s the communal apartment became established as a social institution with its own rules, arrangements and hierarchical systems of power. For instance, the figure of the senior plenipotentiary in the apartment (*otvetstvennyi kvartupolnomochennyi*) was established. This official was responsible for maintaining the rules of registration and the sanitary rules necessary to maintain the apartment. NKVD-approved 'Rules of internal order in houses and apartments' regulated relations in the apartment.[20] Yard-keepers (*dvorniki*) were also key persons in the everyday life of the communal apartment. Apart from their direct duties, they took an interest in the different quarrels between tenants and collaborated with the security services. 'Misbehaviour' by a tenant could lead to prosecution in a comrades' court (*tovarishcheskii sud*), a disciplinary body orchestrated by the housing authorities. The State and Communist Party intruded into the domestic life of citizens by the imposition of rules as well as by inspections by their representatives and by neighbours. In such ways the communal apartment fitted perfectly into a system of social and political control. Further, in outward appearance this kind of housing seemed to realize ideas of collectivism and the much-vaunted 'withering away' of private property. While collective use of facilities and space do promote a kind of community, it is not one united by shared ideas, goals and a conscious commitment to the common good or social background. On the contrary it is shaped by hierarchical (vertical) and mutual (horizontal) control. Specific forms of spatial organization of the communal apartment were one of the key factors contributing to these kinds of subordination.

The spatial structure of the single-family or individual apartment is generally supposed to differ from that of public places, institutionalized semi-private spaces (like hospitals) and temporary housing (like dormitories or barracks). As planned space, the family apartment should conform with generally accepted cultural patterns.[21] In a 'homelike place', all family members have the right to use all or almost all of the rooms. The internal management of the home is practised by the inhabitants themselves. The private space of the home is relatively free from public control. Such private places aim at integration of the tenants. By contrast, regular and symmetrically placed rooms off long corridors occupied by isolated and separate inhabitants are characteristic of institution-like places. The spatial principle underlying such places seeks to partition and to effect control over their users. Michel Foucault calls this type of spatial structure 'cellular space'.[22] Space organized in this way has little chance of becoming a setting that might be called home.[23] The idea of home is associated with feelings of personal possession, physical, social and psychological safety as well as positive emotions born from recognition of the full control over a particular territory.[24]

Kommunalki were created in apartments that had belonged to middle-class and aristocratic families in pre-revolutionary Russia. (Figure 10.1) As a rule, these apartments were situated in city centres in tenements, constructed to individual blueprints. Typically, three or four rooms were organized for the private use of family members, two or three public rooms such as saloons or dining-rooms, two to three rooms for servants,

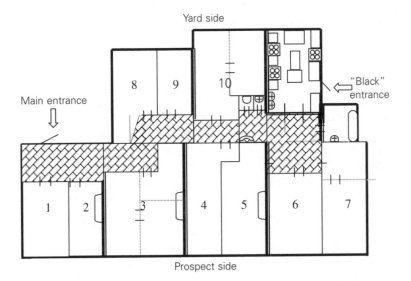

Figure 10.1 Plan of a typical St Petersburg communal apartment

a large kitchen, at least two toilets, a bathroom and two entrances (one for 'polite society' and the other for servants and tradesmen). The family lived in the so called 'master's part' (*gospodskaia chast'*). These rooms formed a suite along the façade side of the building and each had access to the main hallway. The servants' quarters were adjacent to the 'back' entrance and the facilities designed to service the home.[25] Form followed function, in that the design of the apartment corresponded with the cultural norms shared by the inhabitants at that time. Apartments for the less wealthy had fewer rooms dedicated to specialist functions, but still nevertheless displayed the principal characteristics of homelike space.

After 1917, the strategy of the Soviet authorities was to promote the opening up of private spaces to public and state intrusion. This strategy was connected to the redistribution of housing and the new calculations of 'living space'. In the 1920s, the practices of rationing housing according to sanitary norms, the practice of condensation, and an ideology of struggle against the 'old mode of life' (family life, conspicuous consumption as well as comfort and cosiness) led to the disappearance of the 'bourgeois' rooms with narrow specializations. Such spaces were characterized as luxuries and excesses that once belonged to the 'have-beens'.[26] All forms of excess were under prohibition and householders were obliged to divide their big rooms into smaller ones. After apartments had been condensed, doors between rooms were dismantled or simply closed. New, disciplinary spaces in which cells opened onto a common hallway were formed. Thus home was transformed into an institution-like space.

The institutionalization of the spatial structure brought about a system of horizontal control. In other words, everyone who happened to be in the hallway (or another common place) at any moment became an involuntary observer and controller. The importance of this supervisory mechanism in the creation of collectives and individuals in Soviet society has been analysed by Oleg Kharkhordin in his study of Soviet practices.[27] He argues that the process of individuation and individualization in the Soviet Union followed a different path from that taken in the West where the individual had emerged under disciplinary power. As Foucault showed, one of the key features of disciplinary power was hierarchical control. In Soviet civilization, the individual was formed simultaneously with the collective and as a result of collective practices of denunciation, the system of comrades' courts, purges and so on. Horizontal control seems, therefore, to have been a keystone of Soviet everyday routine. The ideal housing type of the early post-revolutionary years was the house-commune where the tasks of education and discipline were forms of horizontal control. The spatial structures of the communal apartment and house-commune appear to have been similar: the latter seemed to adopt the mechanisms of mutual discipline of the former. The communal apartment was a forced collective, united by shared space and equipment as well as mutual dependency. This kind of collectivism has been called 'communalism' by Stephen Kotkin.[28]

The Places of Common Use

The most important change imposed on the family apartment when remoulded into the *kommunalka* was the division of space into two kinds: places of common use (*mesta obshchego pol'zovaniia*) and rooms for families or individuals. Analytically, we can distinguish two types of common places according to the regime of use. The first type was used simultaneously by several tenants and included the kitchen and hallways. The second type was typically the bathroom and toilet, spaces that could only be used by one person at a time and had to be arranged to accommodate this type of use. The main social characteristic of the first type of common place was the inescapable and undesired company of others, while the most obvious feature of the second type was the queue.

Places of forced company: normalization of behaviour

Communal kitchens tended to contain a set of functions that differ from those exercised in a kitchen within a separate family apartment. In the communal kitchen, one seldom ate a meal, almost never received guests or watched television. On the other hand, the communal kitchen could be the site of the 'queue', the comrades' court, and simply a public place where one might encounter strangers. The kitchen was the major setting of the *kommunalka*. It was the central place because of its multifunctionality and open access. However, any purposeful common activity on the part of the tenants was an exception to day-to-day practice. The lack of any kind of joint activity might be compensated for by common talk or, otherwise, emphasized by silence.

The typical communal apartment had a long, narrow (up to one metre in width) and dark hallway. It was a necessary feature of the 'classical' communal apartment. One householder interviewed in St Petersburg recalled events from the early 1960s. Her family lived in a room with a through-passage (*prokhodnaia*) before the renewal she describes: 'When my first baby was born, I finally decided to have flat repairs done. We divided these two hallways and two connecting rooms. As a result we had a very long corridor, just like in a real communal apartment' (N. K., female, born 1929, living in a six-room apartment in the city centre).

Unlike the separate family apartment in which the hallway could be connected to the lobby and contain a coat-rack or hall-stand, shelves, places for shoes or a mirror, the function of the 'hall' in the communal apartment with its typical items of furniture and practices of use was often shared between the tenants' room and a part of the hallway adjacent to the room. Even shoes were sometimes kept inside residents' rooms if the hallway was too narrow or if their owners feared theft. One might have found, for instance, near the door to an individual room, a pile of old shoes and clothes that were no longer valued but awaited a 'second life' somewhere in the dacha. Such things were the specific decorations of the communal apartment. Let me illustrate this point with a quotation from an interview with a young doctor who described a visit to one of his patients' homes: 'Just imagine a communal apartment. Endless doors are along one wall – rooms, rooms, rooms, rooms. Along another wall are wardrobes, wardrobes, wardrobes, wardrobes, chest of drawers, wardrobes, dural-umin rails with curtains on them, plenty of garbage.' This commentator emphasized his feeling of the endlessness of the hallway, as well as its impersonality and sameness. When transformed into a communal hall-way, this space acquired new functions beyond the standard one, that is the connection of rooms with different specialist functions. The hallway was, in effect, the 'Broadway' of the communal apartment – the place where most of the unplanned, short, inevitable encounters and exchanges of views or greetings took place. Interaction during such encounters revealed the rules of everyday life as well as personal and power relations.

The places of social interaction or company in the communal apart-ment had the characteristics of both public as well as private places. On the one hand, these spaces contained activities that usually occurred within the private realm such as cooking, washing and conversations on the telephone. On the other, they presupposed the rituals associated with public encounters. Leaving his or her own room, a tenant came out in public (*na liudi*). In the course of everyday interactions, agents were in a zone of mutual visibility and therefore subject to 'corrective' controls. The spatial organization of the communal apartment contributed to the social control over and normalization of behaviour, i.e. it fulfilled one of the functions of public space. In the early 1930s the notion of 'discipline in everyday domestic life' (*bytovaia distsiplina*) emerged to regulate life behind the door of the communal apartment.[29]

Collective places for individual use: the communal queue

The toilet and bathroom are typically designed for closed, individual use. As collective facilities, they must be available to all. Typically, one lavatory in the 'bourgeois' apartment was adjacent to the bedrooms; another would have been in the more public part of the apartment and a toilet for servants would have been located near the kitchen. When an apartment was turned into a *kommunalka* no 'private' toilets could be saved. Since living space was in short supply, the toilet near the bedroom was usually dismantled. The servants' toilet was usually the most practical with regard to ease of access as well as spatial economy. As a result, it was not rare to find one toilet being shared by more than twenty people and located in the most public space. Whilst it should be acknowledged that after the Second World War the majority of these toilets were given doors that opened into the hallway, it remained impossible to use them without the attention of people in the kitchen. In some apartments the only sink was in the kitchen, whereas in others a sink was located on a wall in the hallway. Bearing in mind that some communal apartments did not benefit from a bathroom at all, the maintenance of bodily hygiene necessarily took place under the 'supervision' of the neighbours.

The queue is a typical form of distribution in the economy of shortage. It is a way of regulating access to goods and services according to principles of justice. In the communal apartment the main things in short supply were space and equipment. A queue would form to the single toilet in the morning and a schedule would often be drawn up to manage use of the bathroom. The queue and the schedule are forms of regulation appropriate to the public sphere. If one encounters schedules in the private sphere (for instance, in organizing the washing of dishes by family members) it is usually flexible and based more on the abilities of the individuals listed than on general justice. As one respondent recalled:

Q: Did you line up for the toilet?
A: Sure. Well, talking about toilets . . . People got used to it, they sometimes made a schedule, of washing and doing laundry. It is a must in big apartments. It was posted on the wall that, let's say, on Monday morning it is this person's turn to do laundry, in the evening someone's else turn, then on Tuesday . . . As for me, I am . . . always on a train that means getting up earlier, doing everything and going back to bed to be able to go out at the right time. Everyone left for work at the same time and I knew for sure that if I hadn't run into the loo . . . If you stayed there for more than five minutes . . . Forget about the toilet or shower even if there was hot

water! One bangs on the door because everyone wants to leave home on time. What can you do? So you do everything very quickly. As early as 4 am some kind of movements began in the apartment or you could use the bath at night (A. R., female, born 1951, has lived in communal apartments all her life. She is talking about a communal apartment with 20–22 tenants).

The interdependence of neighbours, objectified in the sharing of space and equipment, produced a common responsibility for shared space and equipment. Moreover, state ownership over and responsibility for the apartment produced a dependency on the State on the part of citizens. In the Soviet Union housing provision was supported by residence permits (*propiski*) and was part of a system of social incentives. The declaration of general equal rights to places and equipment, maintained by the State, led to what might be called 'parasitic attitudes'. Places in common use were perceived by tenants as belonging to the State, and equal rights and duties in relation to them often turned into general irresponsibility and reliance on the 'big neighbour' – the State. Concrete illustrations of these attitudes could be found in communal apartments when kitchen windows lacked curtains; or unshaded light-bulbs lit common spaces; or when fittings were broken. The abandonment, dirt and impersonality of these spaces was visible at a glance.

One's Own Spaces and Places

Personal life in the tenants' rooms

The most private spaces in the communal apartment were the tenants' rooms, although even here the character of this condition was not fully articulated. Individual rooms were not the private property of the tenants, though, by the system of secure rents, they could be fitted out to the taste of their occupants.

Patterns of behaviour inside the tenants' room (which was often called 'home') implied other sets of rules about communication. Intercourse in individual rooms, unlike that in the common places, was associated with good will and seen as a matter of choice. Most informants indicated that purposeful communication or even small-talk between different tenants in individual rooms was rare:

Nowadays all the socializing is mostly in the kitchen. We seldom go into each other's rooms . . . It is kind of inappropriate to go into rooms (V. I., female, born 1941, describing an eight-room apartment).

> As far as I remember we seldom entered neighbours' rooms. From time to time I came to see Lenia [a friend of the informant] or something like that. Usually we got together to chat in the kitchen (V. S., male, born 1938, who lived in nine-room apartment from 1950 to 1969).

However, these rooms were isolated only in relative terms. The boundary with areas of common space was marked by a threshold, but even behind closed doors a tenant could not be sure that his or her privacy would not be violated. There was no transitional space between the room and common space of the hallway. He or she always had to be ready to come on the communal stage (perhaps to answer a telephone call) and thereby to interact with neighbours. The triggers for interaction are many – from simple loneliness to a demand that a duty be fulfilled. And even if a tenant behind the door of their room was not visible, slim walls and partitions kept them within a zone of audibility.

When a 'home' was condensed to the space of a single room, it became necessary to create zones of relative privacy within that space. Light partitions, screens, curtains or wardrobes were used to mark boundaries:

> I got married and we found ourselves in the passage room. My brother lived in the next room, and one had to go to his room not straight but taking a detour [through the couple's room]. I started thinking what to do. I bought a screen. One day while we were sleeping a tall man came and his head was moving above the screen towards my brother's room . . . It was his very tall friend (N.k., female, born 1929, living in a six-room apartment in the city centre).

Different functional zones were signalled by the presence of furniture and other domestic equipment: a bed for a 'sleeping room', a desk for a 'study', a dinner table for a 'dining room', a children's bed and toys for a 'children's room'. In addition to what might be regarded as necessary features of any comfortable room such as lightness, individual rooms in the communal apartment were valued for their capacity to be divided into functional zones. Anyone accustomed to other forms of domestic spatial organization felt constant discomfort in rooms where life had been condensed in this way. A former aristocrat recalled:

> All of us lived in communal apartments. It was very difficult. Even without talking about the neighbours, who were all sorts of people, sometimes good, but more often strange and even alien to us, everyone had his own idea of what was good and what was bad. But even without neighbours it is very difficult to live with a large family in one room. Practically it means that the son-in-law is forced to take off his trousers in front of the mother-in-law, the children

listen to everything they should not hear and do their homework accompanied by the conversations of their grandmother with neighbours or relatives. The middle generation is in an awkward situation too. It is impossible to say anything sweet or reproachful, everybody hears everything . . .[30]

The personal or family life of the tenants took place in these rooms. 'Personal life' (*lichnaia zhizn'*) was understood to be closely connected with one's own family, friends and love/sexual relationships. Informants sometimes used the term 'intimate life' to describe sexual life and the maintenance of bodily hygiene. Lacking the possibility of isolation, people living in the spaces of the communal apartment complained that their personal life was lived 'in the sight of others' (*na vidu*) or 'in the presence of others' (*na liudiakh*):

It is ugly when your life is being constantly observed by others all the time, and you also [have to observe others' lives] . . . (A. I., female, born 1974, has lived in communal apartments since her birth).

As Vladimir Vysotskii sang, 'Don't get into my soul!' Of course, it is not what you want. And, in addition, living in communal apartments all of your personal life you are in sight of the others. They know who is coming, who is leaving . . . In general, of course I consider that this invention of Soviet power is such a humiliation of human dignity because personal life must not be in other people's sight. Personal life is your personal life, it is a secret! It is the same for everyone. That's it. (V. I., female, born 1941, has been living in an eight-room apartment since her birth).

It is not normal when you are an unintentional witness of your neighbours' matters that you have nothing to do with. And they are not interested in your business, but still . . . (E. M., female, born 1941, has lived in a communal apartment on the outskirts from 1945 to 1968).

All the informants considered the condition of being in the sight of others, as well as being in the position of an observer, as abnormal and lacking dignity. Bad soundproofing, the possibility of constant intrusion, having guests examined by one's neighbours as well as the absence of 'one's own corner' created the illusion of privacy rather than the condition of privacy.[31] All that might be considered to be personal was effectively open and controlled from outside. I should stress that the discomfort associated with openness in personal life emerged when social conventions or norms (such as the idea that personal life should be a secret) were contradicted by the real conditions of life. That is why the open/closed boundary became so particularly meaningful to citizens of the Soviet Union when, in the 1960s, a process of privatization of life began and the standard patterns of housing changed to the single-family apartment.[32]

One's Own Places Within Common Territory: Boundaries and Markers

In addition to their 'own' rooms, the inhabitants of communal apartments had their 'own' (*svoii*) places in the kitchen, bathroom, hallway or larder. In these common places the boundary of 'one's own'/ 'others" was crucial because of the absence of static physical markers. There were two basic boundaries in these common territories: one lay between the places of neighbours; the other marked one's own place within the common territory. The first boundary was strictly observed and its violation often caused significant disputes between neighbours. The second was more difficult to define and, as such, common places were always subject to intrusion.

One's own places in the common territory may have been under the control of a particular tenant but they did not have the essential characteristics of a private place, namely they were not capable of offering protection from external intrusion. In the same way as personal life in the communal apartment was not quite private, one's own places may have been personal/ familial but they were nevertheless open places. The boundary between common territory and one's own place was not strictly defined. The position of pieces of furniture (tables, shelves, cupboards) as well as utensils like pots and pans on the window-sill, dish-cloths on the common shelf over or above the sink, a glass containing toothbrushes were used as markers of one's own place, as well as the appropriation of common space.

Those who did not manage or did not want to stake a claim to any part of the common territory placed themselves low down in the communal hierarchy. Mastery of space meant power in the communal apartment. Without visible possession of their own tables, shelves or things in the kitchen or bathroom, tenants were considered to be mute on this stage and not active in communal life. Such figures were typically temporary residents living in the rooms of relatives and friends, those who had a residence permit but did not have tenancy in the apartment, or tenants who declared indifference to day-to-day domestic life (*byt*). Their opinions carried less weight and their claims on equal distribution of commonwealth were less strong than those who were represented spatially. In one communal apartment that featured in my research, a tenant's table was occupied by members of other families. This was a spatial projection of the power relations in the apartment. Disinherited spatially, this tenant was also disenfranchised and his opinion was not sought on common problems at all. By contrast, if a tenant introduced new or additional items into the kitchen (for example, a cupboard while the rest of the tenants have only tables and shelves), he or she declared – through this behaviour – a strategy in the apartment. In other words, common did not mean equal.[33]

Sometimes markers of one's own space were not used functionally but exclusively as markers of the claim that the place belonged to somebody. One encountered many empty wardrobes in the halls and shelves in bathrooms, as well as tables in kitchens that were not needed. When asked, people explained their presence as having a symbolic meaning. These things were once useful but at some time an element vital to their function had been stolen or the need to use them disappeared. However, these often numerous and broken things continued to occupy their place because in this way the tenants reminded each other of their presence and their rights.

We can see a similar logic in the way markers were established. A new tenant moved in to one of the communal apartments being observed. The former inhabitant of the room offered to buy a kitchen table because the newcomer did not have one. The new inhabitant refused because he was not planning to cook in the kitchen. As this discussion took place (in the kitchen), one of the neighbours broke into the conversation:

> How will you able to do without it? You need a table to place here to have your own place in the kitchen. So what that you aren't going to cook? You do need a place. Everybody ought to have it. Otherwise if you want one in the future it might be occupied. You won't be able to prove anything' (Sh. K., female, born 1931, has been living in an eleven-room apartment since 1954).

Whilst it might seem to be to everyone's benefit to have one less table in the kitchen, this was not clear to this 'adviser' who, having lived in the communal apartment for almost fifty years, had learned its rules by heart: a person without a kitchen table is an inferior member of this involuntary community. It became clear in interviews that when men and women gathered together in the kitchen to smoke or drink tea, they would sit at their own tables. It would seem that even where there was no need to protect 'one's own place' by the use of possessions as markers, these objects confirmed their owner's right to be in the common places of the communal apartment and to participate in its common activities.

Tensions of Public Privacy

Erving Goffman has argued that every person has their own spatial claims expressed in feelings about personal territory.[34] Possession and control over a territory and those things identified as 'one's own' are expressed in the notion of 'master' or 'householder' (*khoziain/khoziaika*). This designation carries with it the claim that a person or family has established rules for the use of things and patterns of appropriate behaviour that cannot be changed without permission. Possession of one's own place presents the opportunity to shape one's own strategy, while its absence requires adaptation or opposition to the strategies of others. Its lack makes one act tactically.[35] In the context of the communal life, the impossibility of controlling the entire domestic territory was associated with such conditions as 'dependency', 'necessity', 'discomfort', 'submission', that is with a weak, dominated position. This became especially clear when informants compared life in the communal apartment with that in the separate family apartment:

> Q: What was the main advantage of moving into the separate apartment?
> A: Probably when we had managed to arrange it all [furniture], to protect it all. The feeling that you are calm, that you are free (E. M., female, born 1941, lived in a communal apartment on the outskirts from 1945 to 1968).

> A: A separate apartment seemed to be the height of pleasure.
> Q: What was so special about it apart from a lot of living space?
> A: Because people wanted to have their own toilet. And do not want others in their bathroom! This was the point.
> Q: But still you say you had a pretty good communal apartment in terms of relationships? Did you want to have a separate apartment all the same?
> A: We wanted it, God! You think, my Lord, people do live so! And when I came in here [in the new apartment], I thought 'My God! This is all mine! The kitchen . . . everything! (N. K., female, born 1929, lived in a six-room communal apartment from 1929 to 1974).

> Q: What is going to be the best thing when you finally get a separate apartment?
> A: The most important thing is [to have] my own toilet! To sit down on one's own lavatory pan . . . Of course my own kitchen (V. I., female, born 1941, has been living in an eight-room apartment since her birth).

The possession of 'one's own space' opened up the possibility of leading a desirable life, whereas the communal apartment limited self-expression and the possibility of objectifying one's social status. An informant described the views of her daughter who lived with her parents and children in a communal apartment:

> She [daughter] dislikes living here. She does not feel comfortable here. She is almost fifty, but she does not have a separate apartment. She still isn't in charge of the space . . . Every family has its own organization of domestic life (*domostroi*). Maybe she would like to have her own *domostroi* . . . Her whole personal, family life has been broken (A. A., female, born 1923, has been living in communal apartments since 1927).

This informant viewed the organization of domestic life (*domostroi*) as the means to fulfil a lifelong ambition, in this case the possession of her own space. Anthropological studies dealing with dwelling as an expression of the inhabitants' identity are generally based on the notion that inhabiting one's living space and turning it into home is a means of self-expression.[36] In the communal apartment the habitat and identity of an inhabitant might appear not to correspond and even, in fact, to contradict each other. Communal living brought about the alienation of people from their habitat. In a key phrase, one of the informants encapsulated this feeling of alienation: 'Nothing is one's own here and nothing is for oneself.'

I have called the openness of personal life to public scrutiny and the location of everyday domestic activities in collectively controlled territory 'public privacy'. Tenants used different tactics to minimize the tension that accompanied this condition. The most obvious examples of this were efforts to protect privacy by the use of physical and symbolical boundaries. Curtains were sometimes added to the doorway to conceal the inner life of the room from the eyes of the neighbours when the door happened to be open. When tenants were strongly concerned to maintain their privacy, they preferred to keep all their intimate possessions in their room and adhere carefully to public-private boundaries.

Another tactic was the depersonalization of neighbours in which they were turned into mere 'elements' of the setting. This strategy had the effect of turning the whole apartment into private space. A young woman who had lived all her life in different communal apartments described this kind of attitude towards neighbours in the following way:

> You know, there are no good neighbours in the communal apartment. They are bad just because they are neighbours . . . For me they are nothing, they don't exist. For me, when you have lived your whole life in the communal apartment, neighbours don't exist any more . . . The attitude towards neighbours is similar to how, you know, when aristocrats could take off their clothes in the presence of the servants, and piss or defecate in front of them, did everything

they wanted. It's the same effect with neighbours. In principle, if I have some guests, or even if I live together with a boyfriend, I don't like to hang out my underpants for everyone to see, for instance. But I can hang them out in the bathroom without any problem to let my neighbours observe them. Nothing is wrong with that. My neighbour can do the same. She can walk around the apartment with hair-curlers. Neighbours are taken out of the frame of my perception (A. I., female, born 1974, has lived in communal apartments since her birth).

This kind of symbolic privatization of the apartment in which, by assuming an attitude of indifference, others are turned into things was not the only kind of social relationship that prevailed in the communal apartment. Brief mention should be made of the practice in which others were adopted as 'one's own' (*svoii*) and pseudo-familial relationships were established.[37] Unrelated neighbours might, for instance, be described as 'aunt' or 'uncle'. In this case, these relationships were based on a particular form of territoriality in which shared space was a prerequisite for community. Consequently, we can identify a range of different attitudes to space in the communal apartment from wholesale alienation in which one's own and common places are neglected, to 'domestication' in which the entire apartment is made cosy.

As we have seen, the emic categories of 'privacy' can be reconstructed from the use of concepts like 'one's own' (*svoi*), 'familial' / 'personal' (*semeinoe/lichnoe*) and 'closed' / 'hidden' (*zakrytoe/skrytoe*). Compounded together, these terms allow us, following the lead of the informants, to describe something (whether space, information or matter) as 'private'. Moreover, these terms, suggestive of an everyday conception of privacy, have spatial and symbolical dimensions: 'one's own' is an index of possession and control; 'family' / 'personal' suggests an acting and controlling subject; and 'closed' / 'hidden' refers to the spatial, communicative or psychological boundaries established by subjects. If the two latter categories are close to those differentiated by Weintraub, the category of 'one's own' does not fit his oppositions. As my discussion of the socio-spatial relations of the communal apartment shows, this notion would seem to be of crucial importance to the tenants of this particular form of Soviet housing in their attempts to master space.

Postscript

Housing privatization in Russia since 1991 has meant that the sanitary norms and other restrictions associated with the old housing system no longer apply. The opportunity to revive communal apartments as family housing now presents itself. Since 1998 tenants have only been allowed to privatize the entire apartment rather than the separate rooms within it. Consequently, today, only a tiny number of communal apartments have been privatized. Social differentiation and development of a property market has fuelled the demand for spacious apartments for the 'new rich'. Estate agents have encouraged tenants to privatize the apartment in order to sell it to a new owner for a good price and then buy better housing for themselves. In some cases the apartments undergo full reconstruction to something like the spatial arrangements of the pre-revolutionary period. Some new owners even try to reinstall fireplaces. Such apartments can be recognized easily today by their entrance doors: instead of numerous door bells each displaying the tenants' surnames or instructions (such as 'Ivanov – 3 rings'), these new family apartments greet the visitor with a steel door.

Most old apartment houses in St Petersburg combine communal apartments and newly privatized family ones. Houses in good condition and in attractive locations are likely to be turned into condominiums. Like those living in the communal apartment, householders in condominiums have some kind of responsibility for the common places but with quite different results. One can see flowers and rugs on the staircases behind the locked entrance and guarded yard. Unlike the public privacy of the communal apartments in which the tenants' rooms opened directly into the collective realm and state control, this new privacy is only connected to public space by numerous mediators. In such ways the symbolic and spatial divisions between the public and privates spheres are becoming more and more clear-cut, making these Western concepts more culturally 'translatable'.

Notes

The author thanks David Crowley for his work on editing the text and Andrei Khanzin for his help in the translation of the interview quotations.

1. S. Boym, *Common Places: Mythologies of Everyday Life in Russia* (Cambridge, MA: Harvard University Press, 1994); S. Fitzpatrick, *Everyday Stalinism: Ordinary Life in Extraordinary Times: Soviet Russia in the 1930s* (New York: Oxford University Press, 1999); S. Kotkin, *Magnetic Mountain. Stalinism as a Civilization* (Berkeley: University of California Press, 1995); P. Messana, *Kommunalka: Une*

histoire de l'Union Soviétique à travers l'appartement commun-autaire (Paris: J.-C. Lattes, 1995).
2. For example, see V. Shlapentokh, *Public and Private Life of the Soviet People. Changing Values in Post-Stalin Russia* (New York and Oxford: Oxford University Press, 1989), pp. 3–14.
3. M. Garcelon, 'Public and Private in Communist and Post-communist society' and O. Kharkhordin, 'Reveal and Dissimulate: A Genealogy of Private Life in Soviet Russia', in Jeff Weintraub and Krishan Kumar, eds, *Public and Private in Thought and Practice. Perspectives on a Grand Dichotomy* (Chicago and London: University of Chicago Press, 1997), pp. 303–65.
4. M. Perrot and R-H. Guerrand, 'Scenes and Places', in P. Ariès and G. Duby, eds, *A History of Private Life*, vol. IV (Cambridge, MA: Belknap Press of Harvard University Press, 1990), pp. 339–450.
5. The field research was supported by the Open Society Institute (RSS, # 971/1998).
6. B. Ruble, *Leningrad. Shaping a Soviet City* (Berkeley: University of California Press, 1990), p. 64.
7. K. Muzdybaev, *Dinamika urovnia zhizni v Peterburge* (SPb: SMART, 1995), p. 89.
8. J. Weintraub, 'The Theory and Practice of Public/Private Distinction', in Weintraub and Kumar, eds, *Public and Private in Thought and Practice*, pp. 1–43.
9. A similar process after the French Revolution is described in Ariès and Duby, *A History of Private Life*, vol. III.
10. 'Dom – sovetskaia krepost'', *Krasnaia gazeta* (4 December 1919), p. 4.
11. For a case study of a house-commune in Moscow and an outstanding analysis of Soviet domestic life (*byt*) see Victor Buchli, *An Archaeology of Socialism* (Oxford: Berg, 2000).
12. 'Obraztsovye doma', *Krasnaia gazeta* (3 June 1919), p. 3.
13. M. Bliznakov, 'Soviet Housing during the Experimental Years, 1918 to 1933', in William Brumfield and Blair Ruble, eds, *Russian Housing in the Modern Age: Design and Social History* (Cambridge: Cambridge University Press, 1993), pp. 85–148; K. Gerasimova, 'The Soviet Communal apartment', in Jeremy Smith, ed., *Beyond the Limits: The Concept of Space in Russian History and Culture* (Studia Historica 62. Helsinki: Finnish Historical Society, 1999) pp. 107–31; A. Kopp, *Town and Revolution: Soviet Architecture and City Planning, 1917–1935* (New York: G. Braziller, 1970); N. Lebina, *Povsednevnaia zhizn' sovetskogo goroda: normy i anomalii, 1920–30 gody*

(SPb: Neva, 1999), pp. 157–77; R. Stites, *Revolutionary Dreams: Utopian Visions and Experimental Life in the Russian Revolution* (New York: Oxford University Press, 1989).

14. N. Timasheff, *The Great Retreat: the Growth and Decline of Communism in Russia* (New York: Dutton & Co., 1946); V. Dunham, *In Stalin's Time: Middle-class Values of Soviet Fiction* (Durham, NC: Duke University Press, 1990); V. Volkov, 'The concept of *kul'turnost'*: notes on the Stalinist civilizing process', in S. Fitzpatrick, ed., *Stalinism: New Directions* (London and New York: Routledge, 2000), pp. 210–30.

15. Shlapentokh, *Public and Private Life of the Soviet People* pp. 153–64.

16. The Russian researchers V. Voronkov and E. Chikadze defined this sphere as 'private public' existing alongside the private and official public spheres. V. Voronkov and E. Chikadzhe, 'Leningrad Jews: Ethnicity and Context', in Victor Voronkov and Elena Zdravomyslova, eds, *Biographical Perspectives on Post-Socialist Societies* (CISR. Working paper 5. SPb: CISR, 1997), pp. 187–91.

17. For discussion of everyday life in contemporary large communal apartments in St Petersburg see I. Utekhin, *Ocherki kommunal'nogo byta* (Moscow: O.G.I., 2000).

18. For more discussion of the history of the communal apartment see Gerasimova, 'The Soviet Communal Apartment', and Lebina, *Povsednevnaia zhizn' sovetskogo goroda.*

19. Statisticheskii spravochnik po Leningradu i Leningradskoi oblasti (Leningrad: Izdatel'stvo Lenoblispolkoma i Lensoveta, 1932), p. 24.

20. 'Pravila vnutrennego rasporiadka v domakh i kvartirakh', *Zhilishchnoe delo*, no. 3 (1927), p. 13.

21. J. Robinson, 'Architecture as a Medium for Culture: Public Institution and Private House', in Setha M. Low and Erve Chambers, eds, *Housing Culture and Design: A Comparative Perspective* (Philadelphia: University of Pennsylvania Press, 1989), pp. 253–81.

22. M. Foucault, *Discipline and Punish: the Birth of the Prison* (Harmondsworth: Penguin Books, 1979), pp. 141–3.

23. The term 'setting' was used by E. Goffman in his analysis of the context of interactions, and used by anthropologist A. Rappoport to describe the spatial structure of the built environment. See E. Goffman, *The Presentation of Self In Everyday Life* (New York: Penguin Books, 1978), pp. 32–4; Amos Rappoport, 'Spatial Organization and the Built Environment', in Tim Ingold, ed., *Companion Encyclopaedia of Anthropology* (London and New York: Routledge, 1998), pp. 460–504.

24. K. Kumar, 'Home: The Promise and Predicament of Private Life at the end of the Twentieth Century', in Weintraub and Kumar, eds, *Public and Private in Thought and Practice*, pp. 204–33; A. Vysokovsky, 'Will Domesticity Return?', in Brumfield and Ruble, eds, *Russian Housing in the Modern Age,* pp. 271–309.

25. In a handbook on housing construction published in 1911, the following rooms were listed as standard elements of the family apartment: a lobby, a study, a hall and a reception room, a dining-room, bedrooms and a boudoir (closed off by drapery), a nursery, a governess's room, servants' rooms, a kitchen and larder. See A. Tilinskii, *Prakticheskaia stroitel'naia pamiatnaia knizhka. Posobie dlia stroitelei, domovladel'tsev i lits, prichastnykh k stroitel'nomu delu* (SPb: 1911), part II, pp. 25–6.

26. Julia Obertreis has identified a similarity between discourses on social space and housing space in the post-revolutionary era, namely a correspondence between a category of spatial excesses and that of the 'have-beens'. Both were expected to disappear in Soviet society. J. Obertreis, '"Byvshee" i "izlishnee": izmenenie sotsial'nykh norm v zhilishchnoi sfere v 1920–30-e gg. Na materialakh Leningrada', in T. Vihavainen, ed., *Normy i tsennosti povsednevnoi zhizni. Stanovlenie sotsialisticheskogo obraza zhizni v Rossii, 1920–30-e gody* (SPb: Neva, 2000), pp. 75–98.

27. O. Kharkhordin, *The Individual and the Collective in Russia. A Study of Practices* (Berkeley: University of California Press, 1999).

28. Kotkin, *Magnetic Mountain*, p. 160.

29. 'Obiazatel'nye pravila ukhoda za zhilishchem i vnutrennego rasporiadka v kvartirakh', *Zhilshchnaia kooperatsiia*, nos. 21–4 (1932), pp. 44–7.

30. N. F. Zvorykina, 'Zapiski' (unpublished family history) (Leningrad, 1984). The author would like to thank Sofia Tchuikina for making this material available (trans. Jacub Lopatko).

31. For discussion of privacy in communal apartments see also Boym, *Common Places*, pp. 121–50 and Kotkin, *Magnetic Mountain*, pp. 170–9.

32. Blair A. Ruble, 'From *khrushcheby* to *korobki*', in Brumfield and Ruble, eds, *Russian Housing in the Modern Age,* pp. 232–70; V. Shlapentokh and A. DiMaio, *Soviet Urban Housing: Problems and Policies* (New York: Praeger, 1974); A. Martiny, *Bauen und Wohnen in der Sowjetunion nach dem Zweiten Weltkrieg: Bauarbeiterschaft, Architektur und Wohnverhältnisse im sozialen Wandel* (Berlin: Berlin Verlag, 1983).

33. Similar distinctions of 'one's own' and 'others" apply to the maintenance of common territory or equipment. One respondent stated: 'I clean the whole cooker but my mother is a person who adheres to strict rules. She cleans only the place around her burner. She doesn't clean anyone else's even if it is creeping with worms. It is always so: their burner is clean, they cook on it but next to it could be anything, even cat's hair. This is an iron rule: if it is done not by you, don't touch it! It is a sacred rule. (A. R.)'

34. E. Goffman, *Relations in Public: Microstudies in the Public Order* (New York: Allen Lane, 1971), pp. 34–40.

35. On the characteristics of tactical and strategic actions see Michel de Certeau, *The Practice of Everyday Life*, (Berkeley: University of California Press, 1984), pp. XVII–XIX.

36. For example, see Janet Carsten and Stephen Hugh-Jones, eds, *About the House: Levi-Strauss and Beyond* (Cambridge: Cambridge University Press, 1995); Low and Chambers, *Housing Culture and Design*; James S. Duncan, ed., *Housing and Identity: Cross-cultural Perspectives* (London: Croom Helm, 1981).

37. E. Gerasimova, Sovetskaia kommunal'naia kvartira kak sotsial'nyi institut: istoriko-sotsiologicheskii analiz [The Soviet communal apartment as a social institution: a study in historical sociology] (Petrograd-Leningrad, 1917–1991) P.h.D. dissertation, St Petersburg: European University, 2000.

11

Curtains: Décor for the End of Empire
Mark Allen Svede

Within a polemic titled *Advertisements for Architecture*, Bernard Tschumi declared, 'Architecture only survives where it negates the form that society expects of it. Where it negates itself by transgressing the limits that history has set for it.'[1] Expectations of survival, however, are usually suspended from the outset when an architect is asked to design a structure for an international exposition, where the criterion of physical durability is collapsed into one season's serviceability, and where a pavilion's form, when it's not boorishly ethnographic, is often so unaccountable to expectation (or, more precisely, so beholden to expectations of exorbitant singularity) as to appear fatuous. What happens, though, when a pavilion, a deliberately temporary structure, survives the society that commissioned it? Or in an even more extreme scenario, what happens when this pavilion comes into being only after its society – by self-definition, the perfectible, perpetual sociopolitical system – has ceased to exist? Less than a year after the collapse of the Soviet Union, this very situation occurred at Expo92 in Seville. Appropriately, the transgressive architectural episode came courtesy of an ethnic minority whose own survival defied limits set by fifty years of the Kremlin's nationalities policy.

In September 1988, the State Architecture Committee of the USSR, the Architects' Union, and the House of Trade and Industry convened an architectural competition in Moscow to select a design for the Soviet pavilion at Expo92. Although a competition was standard procedure for projects of this magnitude and visibility, the progression and outcome of this competition would be anything but typical. Its design parameters, for example, were little more than a credo: 'Humanity discovers the world, and so achieves happiness', an uplifting sentiment in full accord with the official Expo92 theme, 'The Era of Discoveries', yet neatly sidestepping any of the postcolonial circumspection found in pavilion competitions elsewhere, particularly in nations already ambivalent about acknowledging the Columbian quincentennial. The competition further prescribed celebration of humankind's discovery of land, discovery of the cosmos, and self-discovery as evidenced by art, sports and science.[2] This troika of Soviet ideological warhorses also recalled highlights of the American pavilion at Expo70 in Osaka, which had contained a moon rock, folk art and Babe Ruth's uniform.[3] Although it was not stipulated that the Expo92 pavilion feature a model of the Mir space station, *matreoshki* or Olga Korbut's leotard, there was, with regard to the discovery of land, specific mention of Siberia, that object of manifest Russian destiny, to be treated within the design as a positive element of public memory. For the artist Ivars Mailītis and architects Juris Poga and Aigars Sparāns, however, Siberia held decidedly dystopian, Stalinist connotations, as it has for most Latvians.

Out of 164 entries amassed from throughout the Soviet Union, a proposal submitted anonymously by Mailītis, Poga and Sparāns was selected for the final round of competition. The team attributed their advancement to a highly detailed maquette and the conceptual clarity of their design (Figure 11.1). For instance, their tripartite interior could facilitate multimedia presentations about land, the cosmos and the achievements of *Homo sovieticus*; the seventy-five steps forming the façade

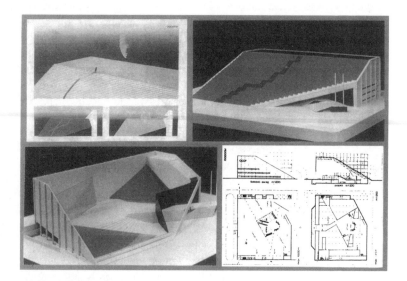

Figure 11.1 Sketches, plans and maquettes for the USSR pavilion at Expo92, Seville; 1988. The insolent identification code, 00000bі, is visible in the corners of the sketches and plans. Architects Juris Poga and Aigars Sparāns; artist Ivars Mailītis. Photo credit: Valts Kleins.

would correspond to the seventy-fifth jubilee of the USSR in 1992; and the front elevation, with its grid of computerized, rotating colour panels, would be read from afar as a dynamic banner.[4] Before a jury of nine, the Latvian proposal was then awarded six votes, with the other three finalists receiving one vote apiece.[5] When the designers of the winning entry were asked to present themselves to their assembled colleagues, nine elderly jurors were visibly shaken to learn that they had just awarded the prestigious commission to three very young and virtually unknown talents with conspicuously non-Russian names. Chief of the Architects' Union's creative division, A. Dubrovskii, would later divulge that the jury assumed the winners were members of the profession's Russian elite. Had the jurors pondered the winners' coded identity – a sequence consisting of five numerals plus one letter, required of all entrants – they might have suspected a less than reverent attitude toward the proceedings. By 'transliterating' zero into the letter *o*, the Latvian team's code of five zeros followed by the Cyrillic character *yery* (00000ы) would form a long, tired, exasperated *Oooooy*, more sighed than pronounced.

Moreover, had the jurors known the most recent work of Mailītis and his wife Inese Mailīte, they might have been less shocked by the project presentation given by the winning team. At the very least, they would have mistrusted the banner concept. Months before, a West Berlin museum had exhibited the Mailīši's installation of anthropomorphic fibre sculptures, titled *People as Flags*.[6] The spectral, bound figures, suspended from spears in a related performance alluded to the reality behind the shopworn political slogan 'Soviet man is the freest in the world.' These fibre forms were also hoisted above Riga's rooftops at the moment the flag of the pre-Soviet Latvian republic was being rehabilitated after a fifty-year ban. It was widely understood that these enshrouded, cocoon-like forms commemorated the mass graves of Latvians deported to Siberia in the 1940s.[7] In fact, a number of previous works by Ivars Mailītis had expressed his disgust with the Soviet system, at times turning its visual mythology against itself. For example, one year before the pavilion proposal, Mailītis was commissioned to design decor for the annual Komsomol celebration of the Great October Revolution. When this youth dance took place in Riga's Sports Maneže on 7 October, 1987, attendees were startled to find themselves within a work of performance art, cast as the Masses. This action, titled *Aurora and the Worm*, pitted a cardboard battleship *Aurora* against a monstrous black worm. They skirmished amid the dancing youths while the so-called Tsar Nicholas II Orchestra played on and the popular cartoon character Iskra – Spark (of the Revolution), actually a woman in costume – cavorted about the mayhem.

So, in much the same way that the Young Pioneers danced, heedless of their Revolution's demise, or Ivars and Inese Mailīši assumed a corporeal stake in their performances of *People as Flags*, visitors to Expo92 could physically enact the essence of Soviet history. Ascending seventy-five steps, their bodies swarming – or were they trampling? – the analogue banner, the masses would arrive at the top of this stairway to heaven to find that the mirrored surface of the roof inverted the sky's reflection into . . . an abyss (Figure 11.2a). But what about Siberia? Delivered in that Moscow auditorium, the artists' exegesis went on to insinuate that the simple trapezoidal geometry of the pavilion's exterior bore an interesting similarity to the *zarks*, a traditional Latvian peasant casket (Figure 11.2b). They neglected to add that anyone familiar with Baltic folk ways would also see a resemblance between sketches Mailītis had made of the pavilion elevation and a ubiquitous grave marker variant (Figure 11.2c), with the cruciform elements to be recuperated, if subliminally, in the finished structure by a multistorey, steel-grid exonarthex that would usher visitors

(a)   (b)

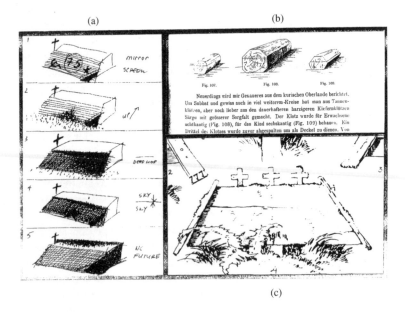

(c)

Figure 11.2(a) Conceptual sketches for the USSR pavilion. Ivars Mailītis. 1988. Author's archive; **(b)** Illustration of two traditional Latvian peasant caskets, from August Bielenstein, *Die Holzbauten und Holzgeräte der Letten. Ein Beitrag zur Ethnographie, Kulturgeschichte und Archaeologie der Völker Russlands im Westgebiet* (St Petersburg, 1907–1918); **(c)** Illustration of a traditional Latvian grave marker

into a cage-like entrance. Perhaps the most galling aspect of this subterfuge was the fact that these morphological antecedents had been prompted by ethnographic self-awareness, one of the few officially tolerated means of defining and expressing Latvian national identity under the Soviet regime (not to mention the source of countless anachronistic, propagandistic exposition displays sponsored in the past by central authorities).

The political ramifications of such symbolism were instantly obvious to most everyone in the auditorium. Earlier that year, in the spirit of *glasnost'*, the Soviet Latvian government had sanctioned the first public demonstration commemorating victims of the 1949 deportations during which almost ten percent of the native population had been exiled. Then in mid-June, on the anniversary of the 1941 deportations, a hundred thousand marchers assembled in Riga. While Gorbachev tolerated such catharses for the health of the supra-national psyche, the jurors seemed unprepared to risk a miracle cure if this protest image were allowed to represent the Soviet Union within a global exposition. It is doubtful they realized the pertinence of such an international commemoration – the 1941 deportations included any Latvian with an arguably transnational perspective, even those whose only offence was membership of Esperanto and philately clubs,[8] those traditional hotbeds of political subversion – yet the jurors decided unanimously, on the spot, to annul the competition. The three pariahs retired to a nearby bar, where they happened to meet Dubrovskii, who explained to them the machinations of the architectural Establishment and opined that the jury expected the Latvians' acquiescence to this sudden reversal. According to Mailītis, Dubrovski hinted, 'It would be foolish for you not to work. They're simply waiting for you to disappear.' Such tacit support from the key official emboldened Mailītis to respond, 'Yes, we must work, but we'll also have to play around now. If this got on television, we could get away with building a doghouse.'

Actually Mailītis was well prepared to orchestrate controversy. In the course of researching Soviet participation in previous world's fairs, he met a General Filipov who had been responsible for the pavilion in Osaka. Filipov had boasted that when the Soviet delegation glimpsed the preliminary site plan for Expo70 before its official unveiling, they were perturbed that the American pavilion's location was more prominent than theirs. Imprecise threats to Expo organizers resulted in a switch, never publicized because of a Japanese media blackout. So, indeed, when Expo70 opened, the best location only enhanced the stature of a forty-metre, sickle-shaped roof atop the fair's tallest structure. Mailītis also heard that the Hamburg-based editors of *Der Spiegel*, ever interested in revelations from the East, were paying 1,000DM for verifiable scandal. He now knew of two. But before he could approach Filipov and Dubrovskii to be his pseudonymous co-authors of the exposé,[9] a second competition had been called by E. Rozhanov, chair of the USSR Architecture Committee.

This was to be an invitational competition, with submissions subsidized by the government. Perhaps to parry media attention, the Latvians were invited to participate – although, of course, there would be no disguising their identity this time. But that wasn't necessary: they resubmitted their first design, unchanged. In the interim, however, the jurors seemed to have had a radical change of heart. Perhaps, as Mailītis explained in an interview published on the eve of Expo92, Dubrovskii's threat to expose their backroom dealings at an impending Russian SSR Architects' Congress put the fear of *perestroika* in their hearts, or they simply resented Rozhanov's predetermination of the second competition results, which would yet again reward some Lenin Prize emeriti.[10] In either case, after the second round of balloting, the Latvian proposal received the same six of nine votes, and was announced the winner in February 1989.

In the Russian press, Dubrovskii hailed the design as an extension of 'the finest Soviet avant-garde tradition'[11] – namely, constructivism – but this was a stylistic affinity the designers did not particularly welcome. First of all, competing proposals had deployed suprematist and constructivist motifs so calculatedly that the Latvians wished to dissociate themselves from that modishness, and besides, by their own calculation the revivalist vogue for Soviet avant-garde visual vocabulary would have peaked in the West by the time of Expo92.[12] From a local vantage point, such quotations had already served their purpose within Latvian nonconformist art. Starting in the 1970s, the ideas of native son Gustav Klucis had been resurrected in such projects as a design for a kinetic installation based on his *Dynamic City* composition of 1919, or a television facility proposal that updated his pioneering multimedia agit-prop kiosks, the *Radio-Orators*.[13] If anything, the Expo92 proposal bore a certain resemblance to another unbuilt latter-day acknowledgement of Latvia's constructivist heritage. In 1966, a design for a commemorative structure specific to Riga's Strēlnieku laukums ([Red] Riflemen's Square) proposed filling that plaza with a trapezoidal mass of slanting stairs surrounding a concentration of shardlike forms erupting out of a central plinth – abstractions, possibly, of grouped bayonets or banners (Figure 11.3). Titled *16161*, this axiomatic structure anticipated the Expo92 proposal not only in morphology, oblique titling and obscure authorship, but also the distinct possibility that its fragmental form would constitute a heretical, dual commemoration, given that this memorial, ostensibly to Bolshevik defenders of the Revolution (Gustav Klucis among them), was to be built on the site of a

Figure 11.3 Sketch of a proposed monument to the Latvian Riflemen, titled *16161*. Author unattributed. c. 1966. From the journal *Māksla* no. 1 (1967), pp. 6–7

treasured medieval guild hall destroyed by Soviet bombs during the Second World War, a traumatic, enduring breach in Riga's urban fabric and Hanseatic identity.[14] So, although the Expo92 design did share elements of a formalist vocabulary with recent tributes to the avant-garde tradition, the pavilion for Seville connected in spirit with quite another indigenous tradition: architectural expressions of political dissent.

Not surprisingly, anti-colonial sentiment has informed Latvian art-making over the years, but certain manifestations have been surprisingly public, or have taken the form of personal interventions with public images. Foremost among the public examples, the national Freedom Monument (Brīvības piemineklis) has graced the centre of Riga since 1935, the timing of its debut ironic in that it presided over the twilight of Latvia's first period of independence (Figure 11.4a). Itself the product of a controversial string of annulled design competitions, the monument's orientation on the site became the object of public debate prior to its erection, as alluded to by this satirical newspaper illustration titled 'Easy Way Out', showing Milda, the Freedom Monument's crowning allegorical figure, mounted on a rotatable base (Figure 11.4b). Critics who advocated turning Milda's back to an increasingly menacing Soviet Union prevailed, so instead, she faced west – *the* West. Incredibly, this blatant insult was not destroyed after the Soviet takeover, reportedly due to the intercession of Vera Mukhina, dean of Socialist Realist sculpture and, as it happened, creator of the legendary sculptural ensemble *Worker and Collective Farm Woman* atop the Soviet pavilion at the 1937 Exposition Universelle in Paris. A Riga native, Mukhina attested to the monument's aesthetic worth, a brave act of advocacy, considering that her career had recently survived hostile rumours that the modelling of the drapery in her own masterpiece contained the profile of demonized Leon Trotsky.[15] So while the Freedom Monument was spared, it was also quarantined for

Mark Allen Svede

(a)   (b)

Figure 11.4(a) Freedom Monument, Riga. Sculptor Kārlis Zāle; architect Ernests Štālbergs. 1935. Photo credit: Indriķis Štūrmanis.; **(b)** Contemporaneous newspaper caricature, 'Easy Way Out,' by Kārlis Padegs. Clipping from the Jānis Siliņš Archives, formerly at the Latvian Studies Center, Western Michigan University. Original source unknown

fifty years by a buffer of heavy traffic and KGB plainclothesmen stationed in the adjacent park, ready to arrest anyone who dared approach Milda with the intention of paying homage. In March 1987, three months before the first organized demonstration at its base, the monument was swarmed by teenagers on a rampage through Riga, provoked by the sight of several performance artists lying in cage-like coffins as part of an annual arts festival.[16] Too young to have experienced the civil freedoms of the first Latvian Republic, the teenagers nonetheless understood the monument's symbolic significance.

A more immediate inspiration was the average Latvian's facility for compromising socialist monuments, either by supplying them with blasphemous meta-dialogues or by visually encroaching upon what Mikhail Yampolsky calls their 'sacral zone', a protective region of unapproachability enforced by the monuments' colossal scale.[17] A trio of prominent sculptures in Riga form the cast for one such blasphemy. First, the city's main statue of Lenin (Figure 11.5), with his back turned deliberately against the Freedom Monument and his upraised arm directed toward Moscow, beckons, as the joke goes, to the nearly one million non-Latvian immigrants who were imported to staff Soviet industry, eventually rendering Latvians a minority in the republic's seven largest cities. A short stroll away, the memorial to poet Jānis Rainis shows a dejected paragon of Latvian culture muttering to himself, 'But what shall we do with them, now that they're here?' Further on, a third sculpture reveals the grim answer: Bolshevik hero Pēteris Stučka, despite his political sympathies, gestures forcefully to the ground. The possibility that these three historical personages could have engaged in actual conversation – Stučka was an early associate of Lenin, and Rainis and Stučka were brothers-in-law – only enhances this intertextual bit of gallows humour directed at a menacing Other. Alas, the Expo92 pavilion's allusion to interment was nothing new.

For a time, by virtue of its location, this same statue of Lenin provided Rigans with another means of anti-authoritarian expression. While the native and immigrant communist faithful were laying flowers upon Lenin's pedestal, amateur photographers often congregated across the street, visually aligning Lenin's upraised hand with the crosses atop the domed Orthodox cathedral behind him. When officials learned of this practice, the crosses were removed and elements of a bookstore façade were extended onto the strategic point on the pavement, obliterating this opportunity for irreverent, camera-carrying pedestrians. Years later, however – concurrent with the Expo92 pavilion competition – people walking on the cathedral side of the street could once again align Lenin's hand with another anathematized symbol, the rehabilitated Latvian flag now flown above the Council of Ministers building.

But this was hardly Lenin's first salute to the emblem of the pre-Soviet bourgeois republic. Visible to much of the central city, and even more conspicuous within popular lore, the drapery behind the windows of the Intourist hotel 'Latvija' served for years as a key site of the nationalist Imaginary, but only the hotel drapery. The structure itself was widely considered to be a Soviet central-planner's deliberate attempt to mar the genteel skyline of Riga's Jugendstil quarter, just as the hotel was the first building in the city to exceed the height of the revered thirteenth-century Peter's Church – by one token metre. Compunding this affront and under-scoring the alien identity of Intourist, the hotel interior was off-limits to the average Rigan, maintaining the customary separation of foreign guests and Soviet citizenry. Though perhaps unfamiliar with its decor, the average Rigan was perfectly aware of the building's internal operations, evident from the popular Hotel Latvija quip: 'Sixty percent glass, thirty percent ferro-concrete and ten percent microphones.' But visible to even the most excluded Latvian, there were the curtains. Each guest room in this hotel had an expansive window, fitted out with maroon-coloured woollen curtains with a white lace panel in between. Every evening, the hotel façade was transformed into hundreds of handmade versions of the outlawed Latvian flag when visitors, often members of the diaspora forbidden to stay with family they left behind, performed the quotidian gesture of drawing curtains together, narrowing the white band of lace into roughly proper proportion with the maroon. It was appropriate that this cathexis of ordinary materials was effected, very democratically, by a simple ritual ensuring individual privacy. But best of all, these surrogate flags were hailed night after night by the gesticulating statue of Lenin across the street (see Figure 11.5).

Drapery's potential for subversive symbolism was further gauged in Riga even as the Expo92 plot unfolded. In 1990, on the occasion of the third annual 'Arsenāls' film festival, artists Sergejs Davidovs and Krišjānis Šics were selected to decorate the festival's main venue, which happened to be the de-crossed, deconsecrated Orthodox cathedral next to Lenin and across from Hotel Latvija, used for decades as a planetarium and exhib-ition space. Their proposal was to intertwine a vertical repeat-patterned fabric among the building's domes, forming a Claes Oldenburg-like soft-sculpture version of unspooling film. However, city officials were dismayed to discover that the most proximate celluloid model for the fabric's pattern was a porn movie's depersonalized shot of a woman's torso, a discovery made only after the fabric had been installed among the admittedly breast-like domes and, moreover, inflated to appear like a snake. In the same moment that Riga's most prominent architectural vestige of Mother Russia was so crudely feminized, the Church, like Eve, was depicted as being in collusion with the Serpent. The vagaries of *glasnost'* meant that Davidovs and Šics would go unpunished, while the manager of the fact-ory that had printed their custom 'snakeskin', as it were, was not so protected and lost his job.[18]

So, the Expo92 pavilion's emphasis on banners was truly topical, just as it undertook the contemporary critical work of problematizing notions

Figure 11.5 Lenin salutes the ersatz Latvian flags formed by the guest-room curtains of Hotel Latvija; Architects Arturs Reinfelds, Aija Grīna and Valters Maike. 1978. Photo credit: Indriķis Štūrmanis

of reception and even ownership as such matters pertain to any public work of art. The fact that the pavilion was bereft of a sacral zone – indeed, visitors were intended to tread upon its façade and, moreover, its flag – suggests affinities with yet another feature of local visual culture that demystified the colonial oppressor. In the recently completed Riga Motor Museum, visitors were delighted to find on display in the permanent collection, right alongside automobiles once used by Stalin and Khrushchev, the black Rolls Royce Silver Shadow that Leonid Brezhnev had drunkenly driven into a wall inside the Kremlin in 1980. The installation is among the most trenchant political examples of the assisted readymade. Banished to a shadowy corner, the limousine is crumpled against a grainy photomural of the accident scene, abutting the museum's fire extinguishers. A likeness of Leonid, slightly waxier than his original self, is in the driver's seat, belatedly and besottedly alarmed by the impact. In principle, the visitor can get close enough to smell the vodka. Government hardliners rued the day such damaging evidence was given to a seceding republic, but the mistake was understandable. Motor Museum administrators, as adept at doublespeak as anyone functioning within a totalitarian bureaucracy, had already pressured Moscow to finance construction of their facility by threatening to accept an American millionaire's offer to do so when, as their *coup de grâce*, they also managed to convince authorities that Brezhnev's 1965 Silver Shadow, which they described to American television audiences in 1988 as 'slightly altered by our former master,' would be dutifully restored before its display.[19]

Similarly, complicitous and duplicitous language protected the Expo92 pavilion proposal until it was built in Seville. The design had been publicized through lavishly illustrated articles, but accompanying texts were rather obscurantist. In one article, the façade was coyly described as a hill representing human endeavour. A restaurant on the lower level planned 'to offer delicacies from all regional cuisines of the USSR' – this, at a time when store shelves were empty and most Soviet restaurants, irrespective of locale, served the unpalatable fare shown in one Latvian photographic parody titled *McLenin*.[20] The computerized screen beneath the stepped façade was another reason for exaltation by the press, although such a system was almost assured of failure, given the state of Soviet technology. For Mailītis, whose colleagues were accustomed to simulating computer-generated images in graphic design work by drawing pixelated forms by hand because the real thing was unavailable, this potential for mechanical disaster was its most appealing reason for inclusion. The article's sly conclusion predicated the success of the Soviet design, 'as usual, on the foreign builders, [operating,] of course, at global levels of construction technology'.[21] If, as architect-theorist Paul Virilio has claimed, 'we are not dealing any more with the technology of construction, but with the construction of technology',[22] this pavilion was unique among exposition structures in its aggressive deconstruction of a technocratic vision dating from Paxton's Crystal Palace, a vision that Soviet central-planners and ideologues had long held sacrosanct.

So, four years and $16 million later, the pavilion was built at Expo92. Of course, by the time it debuted, the pavilion was identified solely with Russia, represented on the world stage with a dysfunctional mausoleum. The trope of a stage was more apt than the designers could have hoped. In a reversal of its good fortune at Osaka, Moscow found its pavilion relegated to a conspicuously lesser site.[23] Sidelined at the remote end of 4th Avenue, far from the Avenue of Europe and even removed from the precincts showcasing non-European industrialized nations, the pavilion's stepped façade appeared, from any distance, to be a mere continuation of the entertainment amphitheatre across the street. The metaphorical identification of Russia in relation to the world stage became that of spectator, rather than spectacle. And, as such, the pavilion didn't even afford the best seats, its inhabitants further removed and their sightlines interrupted by the amphitheatre's rooflet. On the bright side, this juxtaposition with the amphitheatre reinforced the pavilion façade's similarity to a glee-club's stadium flipcard section, although the computer system dependably malfunctioned the whole time and a pathetic row of privet saplings discouraged visitors from climbing the structure. [24] And so, the pavilion became increasingly felicitous as a metaphor for the Soviet past: irreparable and, despite official pretences of openness, still off-limits. Critic Ferruccio Calzavera, wholly unaware of the agitational nature of the design, was nonetheless agitated in his review of Expo92, published in the journal *L'Architettura*: 'Russia has not presented a pavilion, but a flight of steps that is furthermore impracticable due to the blue and red obstructions. Inside, one meets the past and the future. Sickening.'[25]

If Mailītis, Poga and Sparāns had staged a remarkable coup in Moscow, their subversion represented, in some ways, an even greater accomplishment within the resolutely depoliticized atmosphere of Seville. Exposition planners were so determined to avoid controversial content that they censored programming. One exhibition they cancelled outright was an installation scheduled for the Arts Pavilion that would include 'images of the recent dismantling of monuments in Eastern Europe.'[26] Perhaps such iconoclasm was less offensive as proof of an empire's perishability than it was an unnerving reminder of the teleological outcome awaiting most exposition architecture.[27] In any case, the censored artist, Dennis Adams, was not so committed to his concept that he refused the opportunity to make an alternative work for the Andalusian pavilion. As it happened, two other Spanish regional pavilions were the sites of Expo92's most politically charged symbolism – that is, aside from Russia's sickening stairway – but even these were laconic expressions. Antonio Tapiès's mural near the entrance to the Catalonia pavilion recalled graffiti from the grassroots struggle for Catalonian autonomy in the time of Franco, whose cultural policies against indigenous peoples were rather similar to the Soviets'.[28] And second, the exterior decoration of the Basque pavilion was an adaptation of its regional flag outlawed under the fascist regime. However, design liberties taken with the flag's pattern and colour placement may have reflected the apprehension of Expo officials, who reportedly feared terrorist action by the Basque separatist movement ETA[29] and thus altered what might have been too provocative a symbol.

Spanish officials never suspected that it would be the Latvians who would use a bomb to make their presence felt at Expo92. Deliberately uninvited to their pavilion's dedication, Mailītis and friends decided to reclaim what had been taken through geopolitical circumstances. During

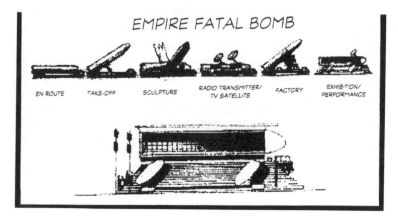

(a)

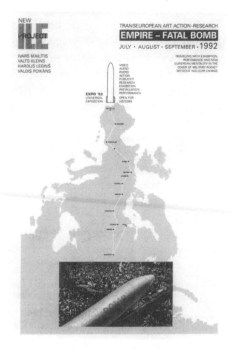

(b)

Figure 11.6(a) Conceptual sketch for a Latvian national pavilion at Expo92. Artist Ivars Mailītis, 1991–92. Author's archive; **(b)** Poster for the transcontinental performance, *Empire – Fatal Bomb*. Artist Ivars Mailītis, 1992. Author's archive

the preceding two years, while the Soviet and, then, Russian governments were exacting revenge by continually requesting design revisions and then using none of them, Mailītis first dreamt of creating a bona fide pavilion for Latvia (Figure 11.6a). Using the shell of a decommissioned Soviet nuclear missile, the design would incorporate a stage, television transmitter, exhibition space and – it was joked – even the Latvian Ministry of Culture, which had lost its offices due to post-Soviet reassignment of government property. Actually, the idea was pretty much a joke from the start, given the lack of government funding for any type of Expo92 participation. But Mailītis was sincere in his belief that Latvia needed to represent itself abroad, not for national glorification but to compile others' reactions toward a nation that had been invisible for so long.

Ultimately he settled for a transcontinental performance work titled *Empire – Fatal Bomb* (Figure 11.6b). In a newfound spirit of market capitalism, especially that of the military-industrial complex, Mailītis and three other artists founded the ersatz business firm *New Project – ile*, which sponsored a trans-European tour from Red Square to Seville.[30] Following the expected route of the once-feared Warsaw Pact warheads and the presently feared black-market smugglers of bomb-grade uranium, the men and their *project – ile* underscored the bankrupting of Soviet society by military expenditures bloated from paranoia and greed. These artists were hardly deluded about the efficacy of military means in an age when Latvia's defence budget was a fraction of what Rank Xerox or Pepsi could spend on corporate pavilions at a world's fair, or indeed, an age when control may be more effectively exerted through spreading a computer virus. Consequently, nobody seemed overly alarmed when Ivars Mailītis arrived at Expo92 on 1 September, wearing a ramshackle rocket that looked only a little less permanent than the average exposition pavilion and a lot more fun to be inside.

Notes

1. Bernard Tschumi, *Advertisements for Architecture*, 1975, reproduced in Bernard Tschumi, *Architecture and Disjunction* (Cambridge, MA: MIT Press, 1994), p. 64.
2. The competition overview is quoted by Jānis Lejnieks in 'Expo-92. Maskava – Sevilja (caur Rīgu?). Hronika ar atkapēm [Moscow – Seville (via Riga?). Chronicle with addenda]', *Māksla* [Art], no. 4 (1989), p. 8.

3. Calvin Tomkins, 'Onward and Upward with the Arts: E.A.T.' , *The New Yorker* (3 Oct. 1970), p. 133.

4. Information about the proposal taken from personal interviews with Mailītis and Poga, 11 and 14 June 1993, and from faxed correspondence from Mailītis on 3 September 1995.

5. Details of the competition are taken from the aforementioned interviews with Mailītis and Poga, and from a published interview between the three artists and Inga Šteimane: 'Piedalīšanās [Participation]', *Literatūra un māksla* [Literature and art], no. 14/2461 (17 April 1992), p. 5.

6. *People as Flags* appeared in the Neue Gesellschaft für Bildende Kunst exhibition 'RIGA: Lettische Avantgarde' at the Staatliche Kunsthalle Berlin, 24 July–24 August 1988.

7. Niels Peter Juel Larsen, 'Im Schatten des Gulag', *Zeit Magazin* (27 March 1992), pp. 28–9.

8. Andrejs Plakāns, *The Latvians. A Short History,* from the series Studies of Nationalities (Stanford, CA: The Hoover Press, 1995), p. 147.

9. In fact, he had already chosen their pen names: Bernson, Johnson and Karlson ('Piedalīšanās', p. 5).

10. Ibid.

11. Quoted in 'Piedalīšanās', p. 5.

12. 'Piedalīšanās', p. 5.

13. These unrealized designs were authored in the early 1970s by Jānis Borgs, Valdis Celms, and Māris and Anda Ārgaļi. Klucis, incidentally, had his own history of exposition debacles. As one of the designers of the USSR pavilion at the 1928 international exposition Pressa in Cologne, his photomontage displays were roundly disliked by the delegation of *apparatchiki* visiting the expo. Then, at a 1929 exhibition of Soviet art in Brussels, his displays of productionist porcelain and housewares were destroyed the night after the opening by vandals who broke into the exhibition space. Its wreckage, however, maintained constructivist-like form, to judge from a documentary photo of the damage. See Hubertus Gaßner and Roland Nachtigäller, *Gustav Klucis. Retrospektive* (Stuttgart: Gerd Hatje, 1991), p. 385.

14. A proposal sketch for *16161* was reproduced in Iuri Vasiliev, 'Revolūcijas varoņu tēla meklējumi [Quest for an image of the Revolution's heroes]', *Māksla* no. 1 (1967), pp. 6–7, the only unattributed design among those discussed in the article. The term 'axiomatic structure', denoting a built form of a type inhabiting the interstitial space between the categories *architecture* and *not-architecture* as mapped onto a Klein (or Piaget) group, is used by Rosalind Krauss in her theorization

of post-Minimalist sculptural practices, 'Sculpture in the Expanded Field', *October* 8 (Spring 1979), reprinted in Krauss, *The Originality of the Avant-Garde and Other Modernist Myths* (Cambridge, MA: MIT Press, 1985), pp. 284–7.

15. Matthew Cullerne Bown, *Art Under Stalin* (New York: Holmes & Meier, 1991), p. 130. Cullerne Bown's anecdote is apocryphal, as is the story of Mukhina's role in saving the Freedom Monument.
16. Titled *The Accident*, this performance was organized for Mākslas dienas (Art Days) by Oļegs Tillbergs and Sarmīte Māliņa.
17. See Mihkail Yampolsky, 'In the Shadow of Monuments. Notes on Iconoclasm and Time', in Nancy Condee, ed., John Kachur trans., *Soviet Hieroglyphics. Visual Culture in Late Twentieth-Century Russia* (Bloomington, IN: Indiana University Press, 1995), pp. 93–112.
18. The episode was described in conversations with Davidovs in 1994; details confirmed and elaborated in correspondence with former Arsenāls curator Liāna Bokša in November 1998.
19. Viktors Kulbergs, leader of Latvia's vintage auto enthusiasts and the organizing force behind the Riga Motor Museum, alludes to this deception in an interview with actor Roy Scheider in the 1988 Turner Broadcasting System television series *Portrait of the Soviet Union* (part 5: 'The Baltic Style'). Regarding the usefulness of doubletalk in a centrally planned society, there is a parallel anecdote about Chinese government approval of an architectural project for the 1990 Asian Games in post-Tiananmen Beijing, designed by an architect who never intended to build according to the official stylistic criteria. See Jianying Zha, *China Pop: How Soap Operas,Tabloids, and Bestsellers Are Transforming a Culture.* (New York: The New Press, 1995), pp. 74–6.
20. This 1992 photocollage of cafeteria gruel was created by Leonards Laganovskis, and is reproduced in the catalogue *Das Gedächtnis der Bilder. Baltische Photokunst heute*, ed. Barbara Straka (Kiel: Nieswand, 1993), n.p.
21. Lejnieks, 'Expo-92', p. 9.
22. As quoted in Tschumi, *Architecture and Disjunction,* p. 245.
23. Russia was excluded not only from the Avenue of Europe, around whose perimeter were grouped key EU members, but also the secondary tier of Central and Northern European nations encircling the axial Palm Avenue. Instead, Russia's neighbours included Venezuela, Sri Lanka, Monaco, Papua New Guinea, and, appropriately, those of its former satellites whose transition to a new world order was conspicuously less successful: Yugoslavia, Cuba and Romania. Also

nearby was the duplex-style structure shared by former Warsaw Pact colleagues Poland and Bulgaria, neither of which reportedly had the resources to build their own pavilion.

24. This vegetal barrier, by the way, recalled an example of landscaping in Riga from the Stalin period whereby the funerary monument to Latvia's interbellum president Jānis Čakste was sequestered from its grand boulevard in the city's main cemetery by a row of trees planted immediately after the Soviet annexation. Unlike Expo92's obstructing hedgerow, however, the cemetery's trees were mysteriously felled one night in the late 1980s by unknown, but presumably dissident, lumberjacks. I learned of this episode from sculpture specialist Ruta Čaupova.

25. '. . . la Russia che non presenta un padiglione, ma una gradonata per giunta impraticabile dagli ingombri blu e rossi. All'interno, si incontrano il passato e il futuro. Nausea.' Ferruccio Calzavera, 'Antiguida a Siviglia '92 [Anti-guide to Seville '92]', *L'Architettura*, 38 (October 1992), p. 707.

26. Judy Cantor, 'Carmen on a Motorcycle', *ARTnews* (February 1992), p. 36.

27. Regarding the ontology of the pavilion genre, see Sergio Polano, 'Expo '92 Seville: Much Ado About Architecture', *A + U*, no. 266 (Nov. 1992), p. 18; idem, 'The Chest and the Butterfly: Architectures for Exposition', *Expo '92 Seville: Architecture and Design* (Milan: Electa; and New York: Abbeville, 1992), pp. 46–50; and T. Sasaki, 'A Passage through the Dys-topia of Expo'70', *Japan Architect*, 45 (May/June 1970), pp. 143–50.

28. For example, both Catalan and Latvian were outlawed as regional administrative languages, and other assaults on these indigenous cultures and their institutions were unrelenting during the 1950s.

29. 'Expo's shaky start', *Design*, no. 520 (April 1992), p. 49.

30. Valts Kleins, Hardijs Lediņš and Valdis Poikāns were the other participants in *New Project – ile*.

Index

Note: Page numbers in **bold** type indicate material in captions to Figures; numbers in ***bold italic*** indicate additional textual reference on the page.

Index

Index

Index

Index

Index

Index

Index

Index

progress 8, 91, 191, 193
  allegorical sculptures of 71
  scientific-technological 154–5
  social 10, 156
Prohászka, Bishop Ottokár 75
proletariat/proletarian society 69, 81, 106, 130
propaganda 5, 10, 26, 52, 70, 78, 85–6, 90–1, 98, 128, 235
property rights 117
Prussia 52, 61
Prusskii klub 55
Przegląd Kulturalny (journal) 197
Przekrój (magazine) 189
Pskov 30
public art 2, 4, 8, 11, 65–84
'public privacy' 14, 119, 207–30
publicity
  'of the private' 184, 189, 210
  total 209
purges 23, 79, 124, 214

queues 15, 16
  communal 215, 217–18
'quiet life' 123, 124, 126, 127

radicalism 128, 130, 131, 136
Rainis, Jānis 239
Rákosi, Jenő 76, 80
rationalism 155, 182
reactionaries 68, 70
Reagan, Ronald 127
reconstruction 9–10, 23, 24, 25, 38, 49, 54, 55, 60, 67, 85–6, 88, 90–3, 190, 191, 192, 226
recreation 26, 35, 149, 150, 152
  disillusionment with collective 127
Recsek labour camp 82
Red Army 51, 68
Red Flag 78, 161
'Regional Studies' *(kraevedenie)* 51
Reinfelds, Arturs **241**
residence permits 218, 221
residents' committees 187
resistance 14, 56, 128, 131
  anti-communist 135
  favourable background for 59
  latent 57
  political 124, 126

tramping as 132–3
restaurants 87, 242
Révai, József 81
revisionism 75
Riga
  Freedom Monument 17, 237, 238, 239
  Jugendstil quarter 239
  main statue of Lenin 17
  Motor Museum 241
  Peter's Church 240
  Sports Maneže 233, 235
  Strēlnieku laukums (Red Riflemen's Square) 236
ritual(s) 6, 68, 160, 163, 165, 167
  mass 81
  military-style 148
  Pioneer 143, 148–9, 159
  political 11
  role of music 162
role models
  female 91, 100
  social 90
  typical 91
romanticism 129, 144
Rothermere, Harold Harmsworth, Lord 68
Rotundo, E. Anthony 144
Rozhanov, E. 236
Rubanenko, Boris 29
Rudnev, Lev 154
ruins 9, 24, 182

sacred topography 152
St Petersburg 13, 114, 208–12, 214–30
Sakharov, Andrei D. 16
Sarab'ianov, Dmitrii 167
schools
  boarding 146, 149
  maintaining 24
Schulhoff, Petr 135
sculpture 71, 162, 233, 239
'second homes' 107, 113
Second World War 23, 24, 25, 130, 237
  Hungary an aggressor state in 67
SED (Socialist Unity Party of Germany) 89, 90
Sevastopol 9, 5, 23–45
  Central, Northern and Shipside Regions 31

Index

Index